Heidegger and Poetry in the Digital Age

BLOOMSBURY STUDIES IN PHILOSOPHY AND POETRY

Series Editors: Rick Anthony Furtak, Colorado College, USA and James D. Reid, Metropolitan State University of Denver, USA

Editorial Board:

Daniel Brown, University of Southampton, UK
Kristen Case, University of Maine Farmington, USA
Hannah Vandegrift Eldridge, University of Wisconsin–Madison, USA
Cassandra Falke, University of Tromsø, Norway
Luke Fischer, University of Sydney, Australia
John Gibson, University of Louisville, USA
James Haile III, University of Rhode Island, USA
Kevin Hart, University of Virginia, USA
Eileen John, University of Warwick, UK
Troy Jollimore, California State University, USA
David Kleinberg-Levin, Northwestern University, USA
John Koethe, University of Wisconsin–Milwaukee, USA
John T. Lysaker, Emory University, USA
Karmen MacKendrick, Le Moyne College, USA
Rukmini Bhaya Nair, Indian Institute of Technology, India
Kamiyo Ogawa, Sophia University, Japan
Kaz Oishi, University of Tokyo, Japan
Yi-Ping Ong, Johns Hopkins University, USA
Anna Christina Soy Ribeiro, Texas Tech University, USA
Karen Simecek, University of Warwick, UK
Ruth Rebecca Tietjen, Tilburg University, Netherlands
Íngrid Vendrell Ferran, Philipps University Marburg, Germany

Bloomsbury Studies in Philosophy and Poetry explores ancient, modern, and contemporary texts in ways that are sensitive to philosophical themes and problems that can be fruitfully addressed through poetic modes of writing, and focused on questions of style, the relations between form and content, and the conduciveness of literary modes of expression to philosophical inquiry. With a keen interest in the intertwining of poetry and philosophy in all forms, the series will cover the philosophical register of poetry, the poetics of philosophical writing, and the literary strategies of philosophers.

The series provides a home for work on figures across geographical landscapes, with contributions that employ a wide range of methods across academic disciplines, and without regard for divisions within philosophy, between analytic and continental, for example, that have outworn their usefulness. Featuring single-authored works and edited collections, curated by an international editorial board, the series aims to redefine how we read and discuss philosophy and poetry today.

Titles in the series:

Everyday Poetics, by Brett Bourbon
Thought and Poetry, by John Koethe
A Poetic Philosophy of Language, by Philip Mills
Maurice Blanchot on Poetry and Narrative, by Kevin Hart
A Philosophy of Lyric Voice, by Karen Simecek

Forthcoming titles:

Philosophical Fragments and the Poetry of Thinking, by Luke Fischer
Skepticism and Impersonality in Modern Poetry, by Joshua Adams

Heidegger and Poetry in the Digital Age

New Aesthetics and Technologies

Rachel Coventry

BLOOMSBURY ACADEMIC
LONDON • NEW YORK • OXFORD • NEW DELHI • SYDNEY

BLOOMSBURY ACADEMIC

Bloomsbury Publishing Plc, 50 Bedford Square, London, WC1B 3DP, UK
Bloomsbury Publishing Inc, 1385 Broadway, New York, NY 10018, USA
Bloomsbury Publishing Ireland, 29 Earlsfort Terrace, Dublin 2, D02 AY28, Ireland

BLOOMSBURY, BLOOMSBURY ACADEMIC and the Diana logo
are trademarks of Bloomsbury Publishing Plc

First published in Great Britain 2024
This paperback edition published 2025

Copyright © Rachel Coventry, 2024

Rachel Coventry has asserted her right under the Copyright, Designs and
Patents Act, 1988, to be identified as Author of this work.

For legal purposes the Acknowledgements on p. x constitute
an extension of this copyright page.

Series design by Ben Anslow
Cover image: Abstract painting
(© Dinodia Photos / Alamy Stock Photo)

All rights reserved. No part of this publication may be: i) reproduced or
transmitted in any form, electronic or mechanical, including photocopying,
recording or by means of any information storage or retrieval system without
prior permission in writing from the publishers; or ii) used or reproduced
in any way for the training, development or operation of artificial intelligence (AI)
technologies, including generative AI technologies. The rights holders expressly
reserve this publication from the text and data mining exception as per
Article 4(3) of the Digital Single Market Directive (EU) 2019/790.

Bloomsbury Publishing Inc does not have any control over, or responsibility for,
any third-party websites referred to or in this book. All internet addresses given
in this book were correct at the time of going to press. The author and publisher
regret any inconvenience caused if addresses have changed or sites have
ceased to exist, but can accept no responsibility for any such changes.

A catalogue record for this book is available from the British Library.

A catalog record for this book is available from the Library of Congress.

ISBN: HB: 978-1-3503-4780-9
PB: 978-1-3503-4784-7
ePDF: 978-1-3503-4781-6
eBook: 978-1-4411-2382-4

Series: Bloomsbury Studies in Philosophy and Poetry

Typeset by Deanta Global Publishing Services, Chennai, India

For product safety related questions contact productsafety@bloomsbury.com.

To find out more about our authors and books visit www.bloomsbury.com
and sign up for our newsletters.

In memory of Kathleen Coventry
(1939–2019)

Contents

Acknowledgements x

Introduction 1

1 Truth 11

2 Language 45

3 Metaphor 65

4 Technology 93

5 Eco-poetry 123

6 Towards an ontology of digital poetry 143

7 Post-internet poetry and the essence of technology 179

8 Conclusion 207

Notes 213
Bibliography 215
Index 221

Acknowledgements

I am deeply indebted to Professor Felix O'Murchadha, who supervised the research on which this book is based and provided unfaltering support and guidance. I would also like to thank the Department of Philosophy at the University of Galway, especially Professor Markus Wörner, Professor Pascal O'Gormon, Dr Tom Duddy, Dr Tsarina Doyle and Professor Paul Crowther. My doctorate was funded by the Galway Doctoral Scholarship.

I would like, also, to thank those with whom I spent long hours discussing the ideas expressed in this book, especially Dr Aengus Daly, David Beirne, Fintan Coughlan, Dr Leo Keohan, Kevin Higgins, Dr Patrick O'Connor, Dr Lorna Shaughnessy, Susan Millar DuMars and Dr Michael Farry.

I would like to thank Jade Grogan and Suzie Nash at Bloomsbury and the two anonymous reviewers whose generous comments allowed me to rethink aspects of the book.

Finally, I would like to thank my mother, Kathleen Coventry, who provided with me the time and space to write this book.

Introduction

This thesis concerns contemporary poetry or poetry in the age of technology. To speak of technology now means to speak of digital devices and processes. If Heidegger's account of technology is still relevant, then it must be able to account for the digital. This book will argue that Heidegger's view of technology is indeed appropriate to digital technologies. This view is of particular interest to those interested in poetry and poetics because Heidegger defines technology, in part, by its tendency to prevent the authentic showing of poetic language, which for Heidegger is truth. Technology is the greatest danger simply because it prevents the unconcealment of truth.

As life becomes increasingly dominated by digital technologies, it becomes more and more difficult to ignore Heidegger's warning. For this reason, Heidegger's view of technology implies bleak consequences for contemporary poetry; in fact, it questions the very possibility of great poetry in this age. Heidegger exalts poetry. Poetry is granted the position of the highest art form in his work because provides the basis for all other art forms. The later writings, especially, concern the nature or essence of poetry. However, Heidegger is not simply interested in poetry for its own sake but rather in what the nature of poetry tells us about reality. Poetry is language at its most authentic, and as, for Heidegger, it is language that makes reality manifest, then the poetic is the most authentic expression of reality. In short, Heidegger views instances of great poetry as truth. However, the ability of poetry to authentically manifest in this way is not guaranteed, but rather, it is dependent on how reality *is* in a given historical epoch. Heidegger understands history as a series of periods or epochs, each dominated by a particular understanding of being or what it means to exist. While being is always made manifest through language, language itself has different possibilities; for example, it has the potential to be authentic or inauthentic. The question for us, after Heidegger, is whether we retain the possibility of great poetry in the technological age. If we do, it is precisely by thinking technology in its truth, and not simply thinking technologically.

This book will claim that Heidegger's pessimistic view of technology and his account of poetry allows us to interrogate and understand contemporary poetry in a new and powerful way. If Heidegger's characterization of technology is apt, then the claim that it obfuscates the nature of poetry should be evident in contemporary poetry. However, as we are already under the sway of technology, as it is already prior to us, uncovering this 'evidence' is no simple matter. Despite this, there seems to be signs of a crisis in contemporary poetry.

While the idea of a crisis in poetry may be one with a long history, arguably, there is something different about the current sense of crisis, with many contemporary practitioners agreeing that something is amiss. In the last few years, for example, the Poetry Foundation announced that its president and board chairman would step down following intense criticism of the Foundation's recent statement (Poetry Foundation 2020) on Black Lives Matter. Moreover, many commentators such as Robin Robertson (2018) and the novelist Rose Tremain claim that contemporary poetry is in a 'rotten state' (Parmar 2018). While the notion of a crisis within poetry is complex and multifaceted, this thesis will argue that Heidegger's account of poetry can shed light on this situation. Heidegger's account of poetry is rooted in concepts of truth, language, metaphor and technology. We can understand all these in terms of ontology. Authentic or *essential* poetry requires that reality is graspable in an essential way, and Heidegger maintains that technology makes the nature of poetry puzzling. In this way, Heidegger's ontological account, rather than poetry criticism, brings us to the heart of what ails contemporary poetry.

While this book argues that Heidegger's accounts of poetry and technology provide a powerful way to understand contemporary poetry, conversely, it claims that some contemporary poetry illustrates Heidegger's warning about poetry in an age of technology. Such an analysis flows from Heidegger's poetic notion of truth as *Aletheia* or unconcealment. Heidegger moves from correspondence theory theories of truth towards the notion of truth as actuality. This move has garnered much critical analysis. I will engage with the critique formulated by

Ernst Tugendhat (1994) because it is representative of the criticisms against Heidegger in this respect. Central to Tugendhat's critique is the idea that a theory of truth must be able to distinguish between truth and falsity. Without this, it fails to meet the most basic requirement for such a theory. He contends that Heidegger's account fails in this respect. I will argue that Tugendhat's interpretation of Heidegger's notion of truth replaces it with a conception of truth that is more akin to a strong formulation of a correspondence theory. While there is undoubtedly an ambiguity in Heidegger's use of the word 'truth', this ambiguity is reflected in many philosophical accounts; we view this ambiguity as a general philosophical problem with truth, which is made explicit, though not resolved, in Heidegger's account. Heidegger's account moves away from correspondence theory by pointing out there is no way to separate the uncovering of truth from what is uncovered. In this way, Heidegger's account seems at risk of sliding towards relativism. However, this is prevented with recourse to art. For Heidegger, great art becomes the paradigm of truth because it gives us the thing and the manner in which it appears, allowing us to grasp the concealment essential to unconcealment. The work gives both the uncovering and the uncovered. As the audience (or preservers) of the work, we recognize the truth of great art, and this is not a matter of subjective opinion.

This book also engages with ongoing debates in Heidegger studies concerning how to characterize technology, especially how to fit digital technologies into a Heideggerian account. Although in Chapter 4, we see how commentators are divided on this question, some commentators, such as Ihde (2010) think that the current technological age can be further subdivided into different ontological epochs. This book argues that the digital is a continuation and intensification of what Heidegger calls 'new' technology. I will defend the claim that new technology is associated with science, especially physics, that the difference between old and new technology is ontological, and that the differences between various digital technologies are ultimately superficial. In this way, the work done by theorists such as Borgmann and Dreyfus on now, mostly outdated, pre-Web 2.0 technologies are still relevant to this discussion because Heidegger's ontologically broad use of the term 'technology' does not distinguish between technology as a mode of unconcealment and the devices or process that we usually associate with the term. It is pertinent here that digital technologies, be they pre- or post-Web 2.0, are fundamentally enframing.

Similarly, we can argue that any difference between digital and pre-digital technologies, such as television, are differences of degree rather than kind and that the digital is simply an intensification of the process of enframing because it speeds up the enframing of humanity itself. Of course, Heidegger saw the enframing of humanity as an integral part of technology. This thesis argues that the digital can be seen as the realm where the enframing of humanity is realized more effectively.

Drawing again from the work of Borgmann and Dreyfus, and Spinosa, I will examine what it means to confront technology and whether such a confrontation is possible, with a view to considering what role digital poetry could play in such a confrontation, given the further erosion of subjectivity in the digital. Borgmann advises us to look away from the technological and towards focal practices. However, this refocusing away from technology is, arguably, not possible from a Heideggerian perspective because technology as a mode of unconcealment is already prior to us, and it affects how all things are disclosed and not just technological things. Dreyfus and Spinosa suggest that we affirm technology by becoming disclosers of technology, but this option does not fully recognize the increasing power that digital technology has to enframe humanity. Heidegger tells us that we must affirm and negate technology, that is, say 'yes' and 'no' to it. I will argue that Dreyfus and Spinosa's account fails because it does not acknowledge what Heidegger means by affirming technology. To affirm a technological device, it must 'thing' or open the fourfold. Dreyfus and Spinosa's metaphorical reading of the fourfold, especially concerning the divinities, obstructs our ability to allow the fourfold. Wrathall, on the other hand, suggests a more literal interpretation of the fourfold. However, as we shall see in Chapter 3, for Heidegger, the literal/figurative divide is central to the metaphysics he is attempting to overcome, and thus, neither reading is ideal. Suppose a digital poem is to function as a way of developing a free relation to digital technology. In that case, it must 'thing' in the sense of opening the fourfold, and we cannot simply understand this thinging as either figurative or literal. If a digital poem can thing in this sense, then it provides us with a way to affirm digital technology, and if it does not, then we must ask what is it about digital technology that prevents this world opening. In attempting to answer this question, we investigate how the earth function in poetry in various poetic modalities.

I will also agree with Thiele's (1997) reading of Heidegger on boredom, especially his contention that profound boredom, as the fundamental attunement of the technological age, involves a refusal of anxiety. The three types of boredom described by Heidegger, 'becoming bored by', 'being bored with' and profound boredom, or 'it is boring for one', are continuous with one another and can all be understood in terms of the things. For Heidegger, technology is the greatest danger because it prevents the unconcealment of truth. In this way, Sam Riviere's post-internet poetry illustrates Thiele's reading of profound boredom as a refusal of anxiety.

Chapter 1 interrogates Heidegger's notion of truth, especially in terms of how it contrasts with other philosophical notions of truth, especially correspondence theory. While Heidegger accepts that correspondence theory is both dominant and inevitable, we trace Heidegger's path away from propositional accounts of truth towards a notion of truth as unconcealment. Heidegger's work, in this respect, flows from a critique of metalogical accounts of truth, which view truth as validity. From the start, Heidegger understands truth not as a feature of logico-scientific proposition but rather as the actuality of a given state of affairs. He calls this the 'primary being of truth' or 'disclosedness'. For Heidegger, logical accounts of truth rely on an ontology of being as presence. While we understand being in this way, we are left with philosophical questions about how to explain the relationship between an object and the perceiving subject. With recourse to Husserlian intentionality, Heidegger begins from a different starting point. He starts with things themselves. Heidegger's account of truth is *primordial* in that it begins with our individual and naïve perception of this particular object. This starting point is generally ignored or forgotten by philosophers in the Western tradition, but it is the realm of poetry. Heidegger places the ontological significance on this starting point. In Heidegger's account, art becomes, rather than science becomes, the paradigm of truth because art allows us to access this primary being of truth.

In the second chapter, I consider Heidegger's account of language. To begin, I will contextualize Heidegger's unique contribution in terms of the linguistic turn in twentieth-century philosophy. Heidegger entreats us to accompany him on a journey towards language while acknowledging that we can only take this journey from within language itself. As in the analysis of truth, Heidegger contends that language is not in a passive relationship with the world. Instead, language *shows* the world. Again, this showing contains what is shown and the showing itself. Traditional accounts of language tend to miss how language shows the world and focus on what is shown. This tendency is not accidental, but rather it is an inherent feature of language. Language conceals itself in order to disclose or unconceal reality. In this way, Heidegger rejects the idea that language passively reflects a pre-existing world. In addition, language use varies in its ability to disclose reality; not all language is true. However, Heidegger does not argue that reality, itself, is a linguistic construct. Prior to the showing of language, there is an 'indication that it will let itself be shown' (Heidegger 1959: 123). However, this prior self-showing is relational or dialogical in some sense and can be understood as a demand. Both the self-showing of reality and language have the ability to show, and this is because, in the first instance, reality is saturated with the categorial. So while there may be 'something' prior to language, we cannot understand this as a pre-existing reality to which our language refers because '[a]ll perception and conception is already contained' (Heidegger 1959: 123) within the saying of language. Great poetry, especially the poetry of Hölderlin, overcomes language's tendency to conceal itself and brings language into the open. The most authentic or essential language is poetic language in that it gives us both what is unconcealed and the manner in which it is unconcealed.

Such a view of language implies a radically different way of understanding metaphor. Chapter 3 examines Heidegger's notion of metaphor. Within contemporary poetics, metaphors are still generally understood as figurative tropes, be they scientific models or poetic. As Heidegger's account of language does not privilege any part of language, it cannot accommodate a distinction between literal and figurative language. Obviously, the philosophical implications of this are significant. However, even if, along with Heidegger, we reject the literal/figurative distinction, it can sometimes make sense to talk of metaphor. Heidegger contends that we can analyse bad poetry in terms of metaphor. A less-than-great poem stays within the received metaphysical framework, whereas a great poem always transcends it. Heidegger claims that a poem, or other text, understood in terms of metaphor, cannot be an authentic example of language's showing. There is much controversy within the literature about how to understand Heidegger's recasting of metaphor as metaphysics while making sense of the seeming metaphorical saturation of his work. Despite this, Heidegger's notion of metaphor clearly has significant consequences for an analysis of poetry. However, a great deal of contemporary poetry criticism still locates metaphor within the figurative and can, therefore, be considered *aesthetic*. This chapter closes with a comparison between Heidegger's account and aesthetic accounts with respect to some examples of contemporary poetry.

In Chapter 4, we turn to Heidegger's account of technology. Heidegger uses the term 'technology' in an ontologically broad way which covers technological devices and processes, as well as a mode of unconcealment. Technology is, for Heidegger, the current epoch, and in this way, it is an ontohistorical process. However, technology is unique in that, unlike previous epochs, the coming into presence or becoming intelligible of something associated with technology is not poetic in the sense of *poiēsis*. Instead, it challenges (*Herausfordern*). For this reason, Heidegger's account of technology is essentially pessimistic. Heidegger demarcates between old and new technology. While both are associated with Cartesian subjectivism, new technology is understood in terms of its link with science, especially physics – new technology challenges in the sense that it reveals both the subject and the object as standing reserve. The meaning-rich associations of things in the old technology are lost in a techno-scientific mode of concealment. The movement from old technology to new technology is a move from truth to the validity or correctness associated with science, a move that has drastic consequences for art. This book concerns the possibility of responding to these consequences. We argue, first, that Heidegger's account accommodates the advent of digital technologies; second, that the enframent of the subject, which Heidegger holds as inevitable, is achieved in the digital age. Given this, the question becomes, can this enframed subject still respond to the dangers of technology? Different theorists have suggested various possible responses. Nevertheless, it is clear that despite the recasting of the subject as standing reserve, Heidegger maintains that we can confront technology and develop a 'free relation' to it, but to do so, we cannot simply avoid the technological; we must approach it head-on.

He offers two interrelated ways in which we can achieve this. The first is by using meditative thinking leading to *Gelassenheit*, or 'releasement', with respect to technological devices. The second is the poetic. In fact, the poetic is a saving power already contained within the technological, understood here as the digital. To harness this poetic solution, we must become clear that technology is indeed a mode of unconcealment; we need 'essential reflection' (Heidegger 1978: 337) on this fact. The essence of technology must be captured by art in order for its sway over us to be challenged. The chapter ends with an account of the middle voice and how it allows us a way of thinking about this confrontation.

In a technological age, all things, even natural things, become technological in the sense that they are standing reserve, awaiting exploitation. For example, Heidegger is adamant that the dammed-up Rhine is not the river of Hölderlin's poem. Such an account has serious implications for eco-poetry. Eco-poetry is a movement within contemporary poetry which attempts to address the climate crisis and environmental issues more generally. Chapter 5 will consider how technology affects our understanding of eco-poetry. Heidegger's account of technology, the idea that the natural world has become a resource standing by to be exploited, is one with obvious appeal to ecologists. While many philosophical accounts of environmentalism begin with Heidegger's critique of technology, theorists such as Botha (2003) point out that Heidegger's work cannot be invoked as a basis for ecological activism because technology is prior to us, and thus, no course of action can overcome it. However, as poetry can influence metaphysics, it arguably has a role in changing how the world is for us. From such a perspective, eco-poetry can be understood as an attempt to recover environmental things from their status as commodified resources. However, most contemporary poetics cannot account for the metaphysical status of great poetry and, therefore, cannot account for poetry's role in this respect. From the perspective argued here, the value of eco-poetry derives not from its ability to promote environmental awareness, which may lead to action, but rather from great poetry's ability to challenge technology at the level of metaphysics. However, eco-poetry often attempts to affirm the natural world in terms of its prior significance. This significance cannot be reclaimed in the digital age. Therefore, any account of eco-poetry which fails to acknowledge technology's influence on the environment is ultimately impotent. Let us consider Jane Hirshfield's 2020 'Ledger' as a case in point. Hirshfield's work deals with the same ordinary, everyday things that concerned the later Heidegger. Her poems are viewed as an attempt to make things, such as a ream of printer paper 'thing' in this Heideggerian sense of the fourfold, but this attempt is complicated by technology and, arguably, this is not fully acknowledged in the poems. Accordingly, we will see that the things chosen by Hirshfield are no longer essential and are ultimately enframed.

If the digital challenges poetry's ability to disclose environmental truth, what can be said of poetry that employs digital technology in its composition. Chapter 6 employs Heideggerian themes to move towards an account of digital poetry. This chapter's central question is whether digital poetry can confront technology and lead to a free relation to it, or is it simply an expression of how the digital drives out poetic truth. In any epoch, the artwork is the exemplary thing. In it, we find the 'sheltering agent', (Heidegger 1971: 41) or earth from which the world of the work struggles. The question becomes, how do digital technologies operate as earth, or can a world opening be won from the concealment of a digital earth? As language is, first and foremost, the earth of poetry, much of the discussion becomes centred on how language is disclosed in digital poetry. This disclosure is also understood in terms of the other elements of earth, such as paper and books and, ultimately, digital technologies. The analysis here is confined to a number of earth elements, that is, the screen, software and the computer programming languages that underpin them, and case studies are used to illustrate.

In particular, we consider Geoffrey Squire's texts for screens, and the Apostrophe Engine, a hyperlink poem utilizing software. We note, for example, that we cannot simply employ new technologies without considering the ontological consequences of doing so, that is, without asking what it would mean to overcome the concealing tendency of these formats. At the very least, technologies employed in digital poetry challenge the poet to overcome the concealing tendency of these technologies. While arguably the poems we have considered have had varying degrees of success in this respect, a success would certainly represent a confrontation with digital technology.

In Chapter 7, we consider post-internet poetry, in particular, the collection *Kim Kardashian's Marriage* by Sam Riviere, which is viewed here as an attempt to confront the digital. I will argue that Heidegger's account of technology provides a new way to understand this collection, which is not available to contemporary poetics. Following the analysis in the previous chapter, we will see how the things described in Riviere's collection cannot be understood as metaphors but as resources awaiting manipulation. Moreover, the subject of these poems is also enframed. The question is can this eroded subject think technology in its truth. Another way to understand the relationship between digitized subjects and objects is in terms of deep or profound boredom, a fundamental mood which discloses reality. I will argue that the post-internet poetry of Sam Riviere illuminates this deep boredom while ultimately remaining trapped within it. In the digital age, profound boredom is the fundamental attunement, and Riviere's collection will be viewed as an expression of this. While the poems can be described as boring, they are boring in this deep, disclosive sense of boredom. In this way, the things described in the collection are not just boring; they are also somehow engaging enough to keep our attention. However, this attention is ultimately bored. As the poems are composed of fragments of Google searches, an analysis of this collection allows us to see how Google reveals things as standing reserve or in the mood of profound boredom. In this way, Google becomes understood as inherently enframing, which is to say, it is the essence of technology. Digital devices are continuous with and intrinsically tied up with how things are in the digital. In Riviere's poems, we see how things are now unconcealed. Using the example of sunglasses, a motive within the collection, we see how digital things can no longer stand in for other things metaphorically; they can no longer unconceal essence. They merely presence as standing reserve. If this is required for art to be great, then this collection does not deliver it. Yet, it perhaps prepares a way for a confrontation with technology.

1

Truth

1.1 Science as the paradigm of truth

Since the rise of science in the seventeenth century, we have increasingly looked to science to know the truth about the world. We tend to see science as the final arbitrator in debates. Our best scientific theories give us the most accurate description of the objects and laws that make up our world. Consider the sun; it is true that the sun is a star, an almost perfect spherical ball of hot plasma with an internal convective motion that generates a magnetic field via a dynamo process. It is 150 million kilometres away from the earth. We accept these facts, and there is no reasonable way to dispute them. If I were to claim that the sun is a god or that it moves around the earth, I would be simply wrong with respect to the body of current scientific knowledge.

Since Descartes, one of philosophy's most important tasks has been to provide philosophical 'underpinnings' for the sciences. Today, this task falls to philosophers of science, and the philosophy of science has, for the last 150 years, dominated the philosophical landscape. While the relationship between philosophy and science is long and complex, it can be argued that this dominance has waned somewhat since the second half of the twentieth century. From some historical viewpoints, such as Logical Positivism, all philosophy becomes methodology, concerned only with sharpening the tools scientist use to dissect the world. In the twentieth century, the philosophy of science was dominated by the realist/anti-realist debate. While it is a caricature to characterize the philosophy of science in terms of one debate, arguably, scientific realism can be seen as the dominant view within the philosophy of science. Of course, there are myriad realist and anti-realist positions referring to both the physical and the social sciences. Scientific realism can take many forms depending on the science in question and how realism is understood. To understand the issues at hand, we have to simplify. Papineau (1996: 2) defines scientific realism as any body of knowledge that involves the conjunction of two theses.

1. An independence thesis that states judgements about the world answer for their truth to a world that is independent of our awareness of it.
2. A knowledge thesis stating that, by and large, we can know which of these statements are true.

Realism, thus understood, is traditionally open to various criticisms. Papineau classifies these anti-realist objections in terms of which thesis is rejected. Idealists reject the independence thesis, whereas sceptics argue that we cannot know whether our statements about the world are true or not and so reject the knowledge thesis. Both these positions turn on a notion of truth, which holds that the propositions of science are either true or false or that they at least have the capacity to be true or false, whether we can know this or not. Even the truth of the proposition 'the world is independent of our knowledge of it' is a proposition that is true or false with respect to some reality. A typical scientific realist, therefore, maintains that the object, which is the sun is independent of our knowledge and that we can know that the aforementioned theoretical statements are true.

The problem for both realists and anti-realists is a philosophical one. We do not perceive the world directly. Sense data from the sun comes to us via our fallible perceptual apparatus, and as every first-year philosophy student knows, we could be dreaming or hallucinating. Even though we feel the sun's heat on our skin, we cannot say for sure that this heat is the result of the sun. Since Descartes, Western philosophy has had to contend with a gap between my statements about the sun and the sun itself or in itself. This gap between subject and object has stubbornly remained a feature of philosophy and is reformulated by Kant. While there are comprehensive, workable theories about the sun, the ongoing debate between the realists and the anti-realists tells us that we have not conclusively answered one key question is there actually a sun 'out there'. We cannot say the proposition 'the world is independent of our theories' is unambiguously true. However, most scientists do not worry too much about these philosophical questions. They carry on assuming the independent existence of the objects and laws in their theories.

Even if we, along with the scientists, set this problem aside, there is another problem. The scientist's job is to get to the truth about the sun. People say many things about the sun. For example, the sun is a god, or the sun moves around the earth; the sun coming out is a sign that everything is OK. So how does the scientist sift through all these things to get to the truth of the matter? Scientists are trained in scientific method, which provides them with a way to separate the wheat from the chaff. Scientific methodology leads us to evidence, and this evidence is the basis of truth.

There is a lot to be said about scientific methodology; its main virtue is that it results in objectivity. It provides a line of demarcation between scientific knowledge and other less rigorous forms of knowledge. At first glance, objectivity involves the idea that scientists must eliminate subjective biases or personal commitments from their investigations so they can discover real objective truths. Beyond this, methodology is generally deductive or inductive; it often involves experiments or other *ceteris paribus* conditions where some factors are held back so that a single effect or group of effects can be measured in isolation. These special observations result in a collection of facts confirming or denying our theories about the sun.

1.2 The logical prejudice

The idea that truth is a feature of these evidential propositions is traced back to the logical accounts of truth that dominated early twentieth-century philosophy. However, it must be noted that logic itself does not deal with questions concerning the nature of truth. These questions come under the rubric of 'metalogic' or the 'philosophy of logic'. Within these disciplines, truth is often construed as the application of the predicate 'true' to propositions.[1] In such accounts, questions of truth often become questions of 'truth statements'. Throughout his doctoral dissertation and habilitation, Heidegger had already begun to question these logical accounts of truth. Indeed, in his habilitation, he claims that philosophy's task must be to reach for a 'breakthrough into the true actuality and actual truth' (Dahlstrom 2001: 7). From the outset, Heidegger questions the notion that truth is a feature of propositions; this idea is what Daniel Dahlstrom describes as the 'logical prejudice'.

The logical prejudice is a consequence of a tendency to view truth in terms of indicative assertions. A thought can only be 'true' to the extent that it can be expressed as propositions, assertions or judgements. The predicates 'true' and 'false' can only be attributed once this propositional structure is in place. Such an account of truth seems so obvious as to be self-evident. It is connected to the symmetry of true and false, and it can be connected with the world via correspondence. A true proposition reflects a conviction about a state of affairs, it is a proposition that has been confirmed, or that can, in principle, be confirmed. In this way, the indicative proposition becomes the primary unit of scientific knowledge. The notion of truth that flows from this is so widely accepted by philosophers and scientists that the question becomes on what grounds can Heidegger even begin to question it. There is an overwhelming philosophical consensus that predates Heidegger and continues after him, which overwhelmingly agrees truth should be understood in these terms. Despite this, Heidegger tries to understand what he calls 'the primary being of truth' (Heidegger 1926).

Dahlstrom claims that we can understand this primary being of truth with recourse to the two Marburg Lectures of 1925–6 (Heidegger 1926) and *Being and Time* (Heidegger 1962). In the 1925 lectures, Heidegger engages with Husserl's contribution in order to point out the importance of using phenomenology to illuminate fundamental ontology. In the 1926 lecture series on logic, he gives a critical overview of the state of contemporary logic and the philosophical accounts of truth that underpin them. He attempts to demonstrate how truth is linked to time and to show how the logical prejudice ignores time and thus leads to a forgetfulness of being.

Dahlstrom points out that Heidegger's critique of logic fails to mention Russell, Whitehead, Frege or the early Wittgenstein. It would seem that any overview of twentieth-century logic which fails to mention these critical figures in the history of logic is lacking. However, Dahlstrom argues that Heidegger's critique holds for all these philosophers' accounts of truth because they all take the logical prejudice for granted. Despite the differences in their respective logical-philosophical positions, all these philosophers treat truth as the ability to apply the predicate 'true'. For example, Frege (1977) engages in a debate about 'truth bearers' or what it is that corresponds to 'P' in the sentence 'P is true'. As Dahlstrom points out, both sides of the debate rely on the notion of truth being carried or borne by 'truth bearers' and thus depend on the logical prejudice. There are also logico-philosophical accounts that come close to Heidegger's position, but they do not fully shake off the logical prejudice:

> even if a pragmatic theory of truth renounces the idea of timeless truths and deems any criteria for determining what is true a matter of perspective, historical contexts, interests, and so forth, this pragmatic construal of the truth remains derivative of something more basic Heidegger's eyes. What he variously calls 'the primary being of truth' or 'disclosedness'. (Dahlstrom 2001: 28)

Heidegger's critical engagement with logic focuses on Hermann Lotze. Lotze was an important figure then, but he is now less well-known. Despite this, Heidegger regards Lotze as the central figure in modern logic because he formulates the concept of validity on which much of modern logic relies.

Because the notion of validity requires that truth is a feature of propositions, it grounds the logical prejudice as self-evident. As validity becomes the central concept for a generation of logicians, it is Lotze that, historically, gives the logical prejudice its ontological underpinning. Indeed, it is not just Heidegger who recognizes Lotze's considerable influence. Lotze's students include Frege and Carl Stumpf, who supervised Husserl's doctorate. Husserl acknowledges Lotze's influence in the *Logical Investigations* and, as we shall see, Heidegger holds that it is Lotze's influence that prevents Husserl from seeing the consequences of the categorial intuition. Before Heidegger's Marburg Lectures, Bruno Bauch writes, '[t]hrough Lotze the concept of validity has been conceived as the fundamental concept not only of philosophy but of all science and knowledge' (Dahlstrom 2001: 36).

Lotze attempts to defeat scepticism with recourse to Plato's doctrine of ideas. He points to Plato's claim that mental phenomena, such as the impression of a colour, can be fundamentally distinguished in terms of what is received and what is represented. He maintains that through the process of naming, we transform what is received into a representation. By naming a received impression of a colour, it becomes an idea. Our ideas are not fluid or unconstrained; rather, they are fixed and, according to Lotze, 'eternally valid, true claims'. In Lotze's interpretation of Plato, truth becomes merely a designation of an idea.

Once the difference between the received sense data and the idea is established, Lotze attempts to describe the nature of an idea. He remarks that an idea is 'something' and not 'nothing'. He notes that we can distinguish between one idea and another, which means they have some sort of reality, but how does he characterize this reality? He does not want to say that the idea is the actual thing, so he claims that ideas should be understood in terms of their 'affirmedness' (*Bejahtheit*). An idea is not a thing; it is the 'affirmedness' of some other actual state of affairs, but as Dahlstrom points out that the word 'affirmedness' is misleading, and Lotze changes it to 'validity' to convey the notion that the idea is 'actually true' (Dahlstrom 2001: 36).

Lotze distinguishes four forms of actuality or validity and maintains that these are not reducible to one another. These are: '(1) the being of things, (2) the happening of events, (3) the obtaining of relations, and (4) the validity of sentences (truths)' (Dahlstrom 2001: 41). While there are many difficulties with this classification, what is of particular interest to Heidegger is that Lotze restricts the being or 'the real' to things that are material. In this way, Lotze claims that the actuality of being can only be correctly applied to things.[2] This has huge consequences for Lotze's reading of Plato. As Dahlstrom puts it: 'Lotze is of the opinion that when Plato speaks of the eternity of the ideas and their independence from things and minds, he is not thinking of the actuality of a thing that also continues to exist in the absence of human consciousness', (Dahlstrom 2001: 42). Lotze claims that 'Plato wanted to teach nothing else but . . . the validity of truths'. In fact, the very fact that Plato uses the notion of 'ideas' derives from the fact that there is no Greek word for valid. Once Platonic ideas are no longer considered as beings, then Plato's ontology fits neatly into Lotze's.

It is beyond the scope of this book to engage fully with Lotze's reading of Plato. Still, it is important to note, along with Heidegger, that Lotze's classification of actualities entails an ontological difference. If the proposition is the locus of truth and the truth of the proposition is equated with its validity. Then, for Lotze, validity entails independence and constancy of content. Therefore, the actuality of the true sentence is fundamentally different from the actuality of the thing. This is the case even if the actuality is an instance of that truth. The actuality of the truth is not equal to the state of affairs it relates to. Knowing a truth (an actual event) is fundamentally different from the truth as it is given in the sentence, and this difference is an ontological difference.

Heidegger makes three further criticisms of Lotze's classification that flow from these ontological differences. The first is that it says nothing positive about truth as such. Lotze's account does not determine the truth. Lotze ascribes truth as a form of actuality, but he does not explain this. The concept of validity does not explain truth; it only says what is true. The second criticism relates to an ambiguity in the German term '*Wahrsein*' Dahlstrom suggests that we can understand this ambiguity in English by considering the difference between the terms 'being true' and 'true being'. Heidegger suggests that Lotze's account of truth and validity conflates these two meanings. In the sense of 'being true', *Wahrheit* can be used to say that a sentence is true. In the second sense, it says what it is for something to be true. By conflating these two senses, Lotze's account confuses saying what is true with what is the nature of truth. Heidegger claims this is the 'seductive ambiguity to which modern logic, the logic of validity, has thoroughly fallen prey' (2001: 44). Though Dahlstrom suggests that this criticism is targeted more at Lotze's followers than at Lotze himself, Lotze himself claims that seeing truth as validity is a 'fundamental concept resting thoroughly on itself alone' (Dahlstrom 2001: 45). The difference between Lotze and Heidegger comes to rest on this point.

Does the concept of truth as validity require further ontological elaboration beyond Lotze's assertion that it is 'affirmedness'? For Lotze, this seems to be fundamental; for Heidegger, it has not even touched on the essence of truth or 'truth being'.

In his last criticism of Lotze's notion of truth and his classification of actualities, Heidegger points to Lotze's claim that the forms of actuality are indefinable. While Heidegger acknowledges that we cannot define truth or validity in the same way we do objects, he says that this does not mean that we cannot say anything substantive about the nature of truth. What is at stake here is the understanding of being supporting Lotze's system. Heidegger claims that Lotze's actualities are based on an ontology of presence and indeed that Lotze's entire account is based on a Greek ontology of being as presence.

1.3 Intentionality

Equating truth with valid propositions is entwined with the idea that perception is driven by representation. Our truth scientific theories are representations, and in this respect, they reflect how perception works by forming internal representations of external things. Heidegger develops an alternative account of truth as validity or judgement and the idea that perception is representational. This account is indebted to and dependent on Husserl's intentionality. We will begin with a simple overview of Husserl's notion of intentionality and the related concept of categorial intuition and then consider Heidegger's particular interpretation of these. Heidegger's controversial claim is that Husserl fails to see the full and radical implications of intentionality and the categorial intuition.

For both Husserl (1964) and Heidegger, intentionality is the fundamental structure of lived experience. At base, it is the idea that every lived or 'psychic comportment' is directed towards something. Thus, remembering is a remembering of something, expecting is the expectation of something and perception is perception of something. In this way, the basic ontological structure becomes an intentional relationship rather than the discrete

Cartesian subject. Such an approach seems to have the advantage of bridging the Cartesian gap between 'inner' psychic events (in the subject) and real things (the objects). Even in cases where perceptions are hallucinatory or simply mistaken, they are still structurally intentional. Heidegger contends that in these cases, the deceptive content is what the perception is directed at. Thus, Heidegger claims that perception is not considered intentional because it involves a relationship between something physical and something psychic, though this may be the paradigm example. In this way, intentionality is not beset with the metaphysical dogmas that its critics accuse it of. Intentionality cannot be understood in Cartesian philosophy, where inner consciousness is contrasted with the 'outer' world. It is, instead, an entirely new starting point where all perceptions are inherently intentional. This is the case whether the perceptions are real, hallucinatory or deceptive. It is the structure of directedness that is important rather than the status of what the perception is directed towards. Thus, intentional accounts of perception cannot be fitted into a model of perception based on representation and judgements. I do not judge some aspect of reality; Heidegger uses the example of a chair against my mental representation of the chair in question. I perceive the chair itself, meaning there is no gap to cross between subject and object. 'What makes us blind to intentionality is the presumption that what we have here is a theory of the relation between physical and psychic, whereas what is really exhibited is simply a structure of the psychic itself' (Heidegger 1992: 35). This structure is fundamental regardless of whether we work within the philosophical frameworks of idealism or realism. Accepting this basic structure of intentionality means that we have 'avoided the danger of lapsing into construction and into a theory which goes beyond what is before us' (Heidegger 1992: 35).

If intentionality cannot be understood in terms of 'inner' and 'outer' or in terms of 'subject' and 'object', how are we to understand the 'object' perceived or the *perceived as such*? In the case of a chair, Heidegger asks, 'what can I say about the chair?' He is concerned with natural, everyday perceptions. In his example of a chair, he says, 'I would say that it stands in Room 24 next to the desk, and it is probably used by lecturers who prefer to sit while they lecture. It is not just any chair but a very particular one' (Heidegger 1992: 35). In these natural perceptions of everyday objects, we encounter 'environmental things'. If I think about the chair further, I can say more about it, for example, that it is made of wood or I can lift it and drop it. These statements are not just applicable to the particular chair but could be applied to any wooden chair. Now the perceived thing becomes a 'natural thing' (Heidegger 1992: 39). The chair is both an environmental thing and a natural thing.

There can be further investigations into the nature of the chair. For example, I can say that the chair has materiality or extension or matter and form. In these cases, I am no longer talking about this particular environmental chair or any 'natural' wooden chair; I am now talking about 'thingness'. Science and epistemology are primarily concerned with thingness and natural things, but intentionality starts with the naïve perception of environmental things. It regards this naïve perception as its starting point. 'What we want is precisely naïveté' (Heidegger 1992: 39). The naïve perception of the chair is the starting point to all subsequent investigation, yet philosophers generally forget this starting point.

Heidegger considers three cases of intentional perception, perceiving a thing, empty intending and perception of a picture. We will briefly consider all three. Perceiving a thing is, according to Heidegger, 'an exemplary case' (Heidegger 1992: 37) of intentional perception. 'By intentionality we do not mean an objective relation which occasionally and subsequently takes place between a physical thing and a psychic process, but as the structure of a comportment as comporting to' (Heidegger 1992: 37). When I look at a chair, I just see that chair. The perceived thing is understood just as I understand it. To say, as a philosopher might, that this chair has materiality or extension is not to say something fundamental about the chair; rather, to say something that results from subsequent research. To say something fundamental about the chair is to say something like 'this chair is uncomfortable'. Philosophical analysis does not bring us closer to the fundamental nature of the chair; rather, it brings us further away. In fact, once I begin to talk about the chair in terms of materiality or extension, I am no longer talking about this chair per se, but now I am talking about 'thingness'. Intentionality is concerned with the naïve perception of a particular chair.[3]

The fundamental structure of intentionality is the perceiving rather than the perceived. Intentionality is about how the perceived thing is perceived. To elucidate this, Heidegger draws an important distinction between perception and representation. 'The expression *the perceived as such* now refers [not to the perceived entity in itself but] *to this entity in the way and manner of its being perceived*' (Heidegger 1992: 40). Being perceived belongs to intentionality. It is the perceivedness that is emphasized. Heidegger asks, what can we say about this perceivedness? First of all, it has bodily presence. The perceived entity is bodily there or intuitively fulfilled. When I look at the chair, it is given to me bodily. Heidegger claims that '*[b]odily presence is a superlative mode of the self-givenness of an entity*' (Heidegger 1992: 41).

The next case of perception discussed is envisioning or 'empty intending' – for example, when I recall the chair later in conversation. In this case, the conversation is left intuitively unfulfilled. In fact, Heidegger suggests that intuitive representations are rare, and this empty intending accounts for much of our general talk. However, when I tell my friend about the uncomfortable chair in my apartment, I do not refer to a representation or an image of the chair; I still mean the chair. This conversation about the chair may be unfulfilled, but when I tell my friend that my chair is uncomfortable, I do not refer to an image of it.

The third type of intentional perception is the *perception of a picture*. This clearly demonstrates the difference between perception and representation. Heidegger maintains that perceiving a picture has an entirely different structure from normal perception or envisioning. This is because what is bodily given is the format of the picture, be it a photograph, painting or a postcard. The perception of a picture is different from perceiving a thing and empty intending. The perception of a picture has a different structure to general perception. This is why, according to Heidegger, it does not make sense to view picturing as the paradigm of perception. The picture thing is different from other things in that it represents something else. Our normal perception of things does not work like this. These 'modes of representation' are structurally interrelated in terms of their levels of fulfilment. For example, envisioning is unfulfilled, but it has the possibility of fulfilment,[4] whereas direct perception is fulfilled.

Heidegger distinguishes *intentio* and *intendum*. The *intentio* is the way something is intended, and the *intendum* is the entity in the 'how if its being perceived'. How does this distinction differ from the representation models of perception? Heidegger points out that these terms indicate a 'particular interpretation of directing-itself toward' (Heidegger 1992: 45). Its purpose is to show that intentionality is only fully determined when *intentio* and *intentum* are brought together. However, this analysis still does not explain how the 'being intended' of an entity is related to that entity. To understand this, we need to understand categorical intuition.

1.4 Categorial intuition

This deceptively simple notion is central to Heidegger's philosophy and his account of truth. Heidegger takes the concept from Husserl but amends it and argues, against Husserl, that phenomenology is necessarily ontology. The categorial intuition shows, for Heidegger, that the being of an entity appears in the entity without being identifiable with it. Two interrelated ideas are central to the concept. The first is that even our most simple perceptions are category-laden (or categorial), and second, the Husserlian insight that all perception is expressed.

The word 'intuition' here means 'simple apprehension of what is itself bodily found' (Heidegger 1992: 47). The 'categorial' refers to the idea that categories are given in apprehension. Categorial intuition is simply the idea that categories are seen in all perceptions, even the most simple. Complex perceptions are not 'built up' from simple ones combined by the use of 'inner' categories that organize raw perceptual data into meaningful objects. For example, I can perceive a book and a laptop on my desk. The 'and' and the 'on' are not added by me, but they are inherent in the perception itself. If we accept this first idea, then it leads to the second idea that all our comportments are expressed. This does not mean that they are formally expressed or verbalized but that they are 'expressed in a definitive articulation by an understanding that I have of them' (Heidegger 1992: 47). Perceptions are not Humean raw data fed into the machine of a mind. Rather we 'live' in our perceptions; that is, we have an understanding of things that is already inherent in our perceptions of them.

The three cases of intentional perception represent a sequence of interrelated levels of fulfilment. The emptily intended is fulfilled in the envisioned, and the envisioned is fulfilled in direct perception. It is important to note that no matter how fully something is envisioned, it cannot match fulfilled perception and even then, the bodily given only shows itself in one adumbration. 'Fulfilment means having the entity present in its intuitive content so that what is at first only emptily presumed in it demonstrates itself as grounded in the matters' (Heidegger 1992: 49). Fulfilment is an act of identification. 'The intended identifies itself in the intuited; selfsameness is experienced [*erfahren*]' (Heidegger 1992: 49). This identification is not, however, experienced as selfsameness 'Identification is for its part not already an apprehension of identity but solely as the identical' (Heidegger 1992: 49). In direct perception insight is gained or added to the envisioned. The envisioned is not *validated*. This insight shows the groundedness of what it is that is given in perception. This is Heidegger's account of evidence (*Evidenz*). 'The emptily presumed is compared to the matter itself so that in fulfilment, I obtain insight into the groundedness of the matter itself. More precisely, I obtain insight into the groundedness in the matter of what was before only presumed' (Heidegger 1992: 49).

This account of evidence as identifying fulfilment demonstrates the full extent of Heidegger's departure from logical versions of truth and the accounts of evidence on which they rely. From a Heideggerian perspective, evidence can no longer be seen as a correspondence between a mental representation and an object. At the time Heidegger was writing, and still today, evidence is viewed as a special type of perception which differs in some way from general perception. Evidence is generally connected to judgement.

> It is something like a sign which wells up at times in the soul and announces that the psychic process with which it is associated is true. As everyone knows, this transcendent reality cannot itself become immanent. So there must be a way in which it can be announced on the inside. (Heidegger 1992: 50)

Heidegger denies there is something different or special about the perception of evidence. Furthermore, he claims, this faulty premise is central to many philosophical accounts of truth. There is no way to justify the claim that in these evidential perceptions, we *really* see the truth and know this for sure. In short, for Heidegger, there isn't a special class of perceptions that provide evidence for propositions. In logico-scientific conceptions, evidence is linked to judgement. In a similar vein, judgements are special cases of perception where the perceiver knows that what is perceived is true in a way that is not the case in general perception. For Heidegger, it is clear that the perception of evidence is like all fulfilled perception; that is, it is identifying fulfilment. He claims that evidence is 'comprehensible only if we regard the intentionally in it' (Heidegger 1992: 50).

Evidence is regional in that it picks out a particular state of affairs. 'All evidence is in its sense geared to a corresponding region of subject matter' (Heidegger 1992: 50). There are different types of evidence, and each of these is unique to its own subject area and cannot be applied to other subject areas; for example, mathematical evidence is only relevant in mathematics. In this way, Heidegger critiques the notion that mathematics is the paradigm of evidential rigour, and therefore he attaches no virtue to the mathematization of the sciences or the idea of a hierarchy of methods with mathematics at the top. Heidegger suggests that the intentional structure of evidence is the same across all perceptions and, indeed, all comportments or acts. There is 'evidence of willing and wishing, of loving and hoping' (Heidegger 1992: 51).

This discussion of evidence in science has widespread ramifications. For example, in the later work, Heidegger tells us that his own philosophical writings on Hölderlin are not to be subject to the requirement of being proven true. 'We do not need to prove anything here. All proof is always only a subsequent undertaking on the basis of presuppositions. Anything at all can be proved, depending only on what presuppositions are made' (Heidegger 1971: 220).

Heidegger proposes a threefold demonstration of truth.

1. Truth is '*being identical of presumed and intuited*'. (Heidegger 1971: 220). This concept holds truth as something that is '*experienced but

not apprehended', (Heidegger 1971: 220), only the subject matter itself is apprehended, not the identity. Thus 'I do not thematically study the truth of this perception itself, but rather I live *in* the truth' (Heidegger 1971: 220). This is the concept of truth that accounts for 'being true'; it is the truth of the *intendum*.

2. The second concept of truth is correlated to the *intentio* or the act of apprehending itself. It is the being identical that comes into view in this second concept. Heidegger is clarifying what he sees as the central ambiguity of Lotze's notion of truth and all logical accounts that embody the logical prejudice and collapse the concept of truth into the first concept. Both these concepts are required to understand truth.

3. In the third concept of truth, Heidegger equates truth with being or 'the intuited entity itself' (Heidegger 1992: 53). The truth is the state of affairs or 'the very object that it is' (Heidegger 1992: 53). This third concept of truth is central to Heidegger's notion of truth, and it overcomes the ontological difference that Heidegger claims is inherent in Lotzean accounts.

For Heidegger, the first two concepts entail the third. They illuminate the link between truth and being, which has been obscured since the time of the Greeks. What comes into focus is the being of the true state of affairs. The phrase 'the desk is solid' cannot be understood in terms of just the first or the second concept but requires all three concepts to be fully comprehended.

1.5 Being and time, truth and Tugendhat's critique

Heidegger develops his account of truth and the critique of propositional theories in section 44 of *Being and Time*. This section will examine this development and Tugendhat's strong critique of Heidegger's account. As we have seen, Heidegger offers an alternative to notions of truth based on validity and representation. Perhaps the dominant philosophical account of truth in this respect is correspondence theory. Correspondence theory, stated simply, maintains that a proposition is true when it corresponds to an actual state of affairs in the world. A proposition is either true or false with respect to some entity or state of affairs. In opposition, Heidegger's account of truth is concerned with uncovering. A proposition does not merely passively correspond to some state of affairs but actively points it out. In *Being and Time*, Heidegger claims that Dasein uncovers a world and then maintains or preserves what it uncovers. For the most part, Heidegger is unconcerned with distinguishing the true from the false. This Heideggerian account is subject to strong criticism from Tugendhat. Tugendhat maintains that for a concept of truth to be meaningful and responsible, it must aim to distinguish between truth and falsity.

There are two main parts of Tugenghat's argument against Heidegger. First, he argues that Heidegger is actually committed to what I will call a strong formulation of truth, namely that whatever is uncovered by Dasein *is* true in the sense of not being false. Second, given this, there is an ambiguity in how Heidegger uses the word 'uncovered'. On the one hand, Heidegger is committed to identifying truth with uncovering, but on the other hand, in some passages, He maintains that falsity is a kind of covering. If we hold with the first claim, then we have difficulty with instances of error or falsity. If it is possible to uncover a state of affairs that is false, then the truth can be false. However, as Tugendhat himself points out, Heidegger's talk of truth requires some interpretation (Tugendhat 1994: 228). I will argue that Tugendhat's interpretation of Heidegger's notion of truth replaces it with a conception of truth that is more akin to a strong formulation of a correspondence theory. While it is clear that there is an ambiguity in Heidegger's use of the word 'truth'. This ambiguity is reflected in many philosophical accounts, and we can view it as a general philosophical problem with truth that is made explicit, though not resolved, in Heidegger's account.

1.5.1 Authentic and inauthentic truth

While Heidegger's project in *Being and Time*, is, of course, to understand the nature of Being, truth is central to this investigation. He begins section 44 of the first division with a discussion of Parmenides and the notion that thinking and Being are the same. If thinking and Being are the same, then truth becomes the way in which thinking and Being are shown to be the same. Truth is that which manifests or makes possible this sameness of being and thought. Either Being and thought are the same, and what is thought makes manifest what is, or they are different, and thought remains in its own domain, in which case the question of truth does not arise (although the question of meaning does).

The first division of *Being and Time* concerns the meaning of Being with Being itself, rather than the being of specific entities. Heidegger attempts to understand this question by enumerating the *existentiale* or the structures of Dasein's Being in the world. Section 44 is the final section of the first division. It is also the first section to deal systematically with truth. Section 44 is also notable in that it summarizes the rest of the first division. Heidegger starts *Being and Time* with the question of Being and comes, in section 44, to truth.

While Heidegger's account does not turn on the true/false distinction, he does distinguish between

a. Truth as uncovering. Thus, Dasein is in truth because Dasein is uncovering.

b. Truth as uncoveredness in the sense of a state of affairs that is uncovered.

This distinction matches the *intenio* and *intendum* distinction from the *History of the Concept of Time* described earlier. Heidegger claims that truth is constituted by a 'state of mind, understanding and discourse' (Heidegger 1962: 263). Disclosing is fundamental to Dasein and because of this, 'the most primordial phenomena of truth is attained' (Heidegger 1962: 263). To put it crudely, Dasein discloses a world and does so with understanding. This is the nature of Dasein; we only encounter our own Dasein along with the world it discloses. We disclose, and we understand what is disclosed and what is disclosed is, for Heidegger, truth. We are never in pre-understanding. Correspondence theories of truth are derivative. Heidegger claims, 'Dasein is *in the truth*' (Heidegger 1962: 263). However, truth here is a variable state; there are different ways of being in truth. Dasein can be either authentic or inauthentic. 'The most primordial, and indeed the most authentic, disclosedness in which Dasein, as a potentiality-for-Being, is the *truth of existence*' (Heidegger 1962: 264), this means that at its most authentic, Dasein is aware of the inevitability of its death. Dasein can also be, and is mostly, inauthentic or fallen. In this case, Dasein still discloses, but it does so in a mode where truth has been disguised and closed off by idle talk, curiosity and ambiguity. There is still the understanding that is essential to disclosure and, therefore, truth, but this disclosure is fallen. As Heidegger puts it, 'Being towards the entities has not been extinguished, but it has been uprooted' (Heidegger 1962: 264). In such a case, the disguised entities show themselves in the mode of *semblance* where the entity is not disclosed authentically by my own Dasein but by the 'they' in idle talk.

In these cases, Heidegger maintains that Dasein is in untruth. So when Dasein is fallen, it is both in truth and untruth. While this seems to be a contradiction, it is vital to note that 'untruth' in this context should not be understood as falsity. Untruth is not the opposite of truth; it is, in fact, a variety of truth once truth is understood in terms of a continuum between authentic and inauthenticity. Heidegger maintains, '[i]n its full existential-ontological meaning, the proposition that "Dasein is in the truth" states equiprimordially that Dasein is in untruth' (Heidegger 1962: 265). The concept of being fallen is to be understood ontologically. In fallenness, Dasein uncovers in an inauthentic way, and that Being which is uncovered is inauthentic in its uncoveredness. Heidegger describes a situation where Dasein is mostly fallen, and truth in the authentic sense has to be 'wrested' from the objects. For the most part, Dasein encounters things in the mode of semblance, or as the 'they' see them. Seeing an entity in truth becomes a struggle against how it has been communicated to us in idle talk. Truth is not a flat correspondence between Dasein and some aspect of reality; we have to work for it. Heidegger says, 'It is therefore essential that Dasein should explicitly appropriate what has already been uncovered, defend it *against* semblance and disguise, and assure itself of its uncoveredness again and again' (Heidegger 1962: 265).

1.5.2 Propositions and correspondence

Many philosophers, including Heidegger, have compared the account of truth as uncoveredness or unconcealment with correspondence theories. It is important to note that it is not Heidegger's intention to provide an alternative to correspondence theory. Indeed, despite the many philosophical critiques that can be made against correspondence theory, Heidegger takes it for granted (Heidegger 1962: 265). He claims that seeing truth as correspondence is so accepted that it is seen as self-evident. Despite this, different philosophers understand the relationship between truth as unconcealment and truth as correspondence in radically different ways. Some philosophers, including Heidegger himself, view truth as unconcealment as a departure from treating truth merely as a correspondence. While other philosophers, such as Wrathall, view truth as unconcealment as a basis for correspondence theory, in that it provides correspondence with its conditions of possibility, by such a reading, Heidegger's account of truth includes correspondence. Others, including Tugendhat, see truth as unconcealedness as insufficient as it cannot adequately distinguish between truth and falsity.

As we have seen, if we view truth as a correspondence between a proposition and some state of affairs, then several well-known philosophical problems arise. For example, we can ask how our subjective perceptual apparatus connects with objective phenomena? The issue of how to link subjects and objects is a stubborn one, with different philosophers expressing it in different ways. Heidegger is unconcerned with attempting to reconcile this gulf; rather, the question of propositional truth is interesting to him because it is the 'traditional conception of truth' (Heidegger 1962: 257). Heidegger neither defends nor criticizes the focus on proposition and correspondence; rather, he wants to explain why we conceive of truth in this way. Although he does maintain that the gap inherent in correspondence can never be closed (Heidegger 1962: 259).

Heidegger lays bare the 'ontological foundations' (Heidegger 1962: 275).of a propositional account of truth so that 'the *primordial* phenomena of truth become visible'. This 'laying bare' will, according to Heidegger, allow us to see how this traditional conception of truth derives from Dasein's structure as Being in the world. It is important to see this because our focus on propositional accounts of truth has confused us; we are bewitched by the world's objects and, thus, blind to our own uncovering of them.

Heidegger claims that 'the roots of the truth of assertions reach back to the disclosedness of the understanding'. Truth as agreement or correspondence is derived from a more fundamental understanding of truth as unconcealment. An assertion is about something; it 'communicates entities in the how of their uncoveredness' (Heidegger 1962: 266). The uncoveredness is then preserved in the assertion. The assertion or proposition then becomes something which is itself objectively present, and it can be taken up and spoken again. There is still a relationship between the uncovered entity and the assertion. This relationship can be many things, including correspondence, although, unlike generally correspondence theories, assertions always explicitly disclose the entity in the 'how' of its uncoveredness. So while it seems as if Heidegger gives us an account of correspondence, this account is not identical to general philosophical formulations of correspondence theory.

For this reason, it is arguable whether Heidegger's account can be seen unambiguously as the conditions of possibility for correspondence theories, but it may entail them. Another reason why Heidegger's account differs significantly from traditional correspondence theories is that it is possible for the nature of the relationship between the uncovering and the uncovered to change. The assertion becomes 'exempted from having to uncover [the entity] again' (Heidegger 1962: 266). Again we see a more complex account of truth. The entity is present, and so is the assertion. As it is spoken, again and again, it does not necessarily continue to uncover the entity, although it does maintain some relationship to it. The story of the relationship between the proposition and the entity is fluid and changing. While traditional accounts of correspondence can, perhaps, capture one moment of this story, we cannot reduce Heidegger's account to this one moment. The story becomes even more complex when we consider the hearsay of *Das Man* or the 'they'. To a large extent, an entity's uncoveredness is appropriated, not by my own uncovering, but rather by the hearsay of the 'they'. When this happens, '[t]hat which has been expressed as such takes over Being-towards those entities which have been uncovered in the assertion' (Heidegger 1962: 266). We see the entity expressed in the assertion as 'they' see it. Once this process is underway, the question becomes how is the uncoveredness preserved.

Dasein is uncovering or disclosing, but this uncoveredness becomes a property that is present-at-hand or objectively present. This property is split because Dasein understands itself in terms of entities within the world. Thus Dasein 'sees' the entity but not the fact that it is what allows the entity to appear. Thus truth, in its most primordial sense, is an *exitentiale* of Dasein.

1.5.3 Tugendhat's critique

Tugendhat's critique can be better understood if we break it into two parts. In the first part, he attempts to demonstrate how Heidegger has committed himself to a strong account of truth, which sees truth as a self-showing of the thing as it is in itself. This argument is complex and has a number of moving parts. Tugendhat begins by noting that initially, Heidegger's account of truth based on categorial intuition merely 'reproduces' Husserl's account. Husserl shows us that a single object can have different modes of givenness. We can speak of an object as it is given and as it is 'in itself', but both of these simply represent different modes of givenness; in short, the 'in its self' of an object is not transcendent. Thus, when Husserl speaks of the thing as it is 'in itself', he is talking about a mode of manifestation. When Heidegger speaks of the thing in itself in section 44, he does not refer to Husserl, but Tugendhat claims it is reasonable to conclude he means it in this Husserlian sense. If this is the case, it becomes difficult to differentiate Heidegger's position from Husserl's. Tugendhat locates the difference in Heidegger's successive reformulations of what a true assertion is in section 44. These are as follows.

1. Initially, Heidegger claims, 'the assertion is true when it so indicates or discloses the state of affairs as it is in itself' (Tugendhat 1994: 230). This, Tugendhat contends, is identical to Husserl's claim. Tugendhat holds that the 'so-as' in this formulation is necessary because it 'describes the correspondence of the state of affairs just as it is

disclosed by the assertion with precisely this state of affairs "as it is in itself"' (Tugendhat 1994: 230).

2. Later Heidegger restates the claim without the 'so-as', which makes it 'an assertion is true when it discloses the state of affairs as it is in itself'. In this formulation, the 'so-as' is missing but still implied, so the claim is still identical to Husserl's.

3. In the third formulation, Heidegger drops the 'as it is in itself' and states, '[the true assertion] uncovers the state of affairs'. This strong formulation means that truth must be understood in terms of disclosdeness. This formulation moves beyond Husserl and commits Heidegger to the notion that truth is disclosedness.

Once Tugendhat establishes that Heidegger is committed to this strong account of truth, his critique then revolves around the ambiguity in Heidegger's use of the word 'uncover'. Tugendhat identifies two ways in which the word is used. The first is a general pointing out which can refer to pointing out in both correct and incorrect cases. However, Heidegger also uses 'uncover' in a second sense where a false assertion is not an uncovering but a covering over. Thus Tugendhat points to both a broad and a narrow sense of 'uncover' in Heidegger's account of truth. He points out that for Heidegger, 'The covering up of the false assertions does not exclude a certain uncovering' (Tugendhat 1994: 232). Thus the false can uncover, and if truth is uncovering, the false can be true. This ambiguity requires that Heidegger explains in what sense does a false assertion uncover and in was sense it covers up. Heidegger does not give us an explanation of this in section 44.

1.5.4 A response to Tugendhat

The difficulty Tugendhat has with Heidegger's concept of truth could, on the face of it, be solved if Heidegger had split his notion of truth into two separate concepts. This spit would be identical to the distinction he already draws between (a) and (b), earlier, truth as uncovering and truth as uncovered. By employing this distinction, we could attempt to draw a line between the uncovering of Dasein and the uncoveredness of the state of affairs. The uncoveredness could be either true or false and need not be completely tied up with the uncovering. To understand this imagine a situation where I wake and see the stars above my head, but unbeknownst to me, the sky I am looking at is not a sky but a screen that has been put there to deceive me. If we break Heidegger's account of truth apart, I could say that my uncovering is truth, perhaps in the sense that it is true for me, but the uncoveredness is false. We can imagine an account of truth where uncoveredness is 'truth 2' and uncovering is 'truth 1'.

If this were the case, then Tugendhat's critique would lose its force because we could still attempt to distinguish truth from falsity in some way. However, Heidegger's account of truth would also lose its distinctiveness and perhaps begin to collapse back into a sort of correspondence account. We cannot separate 'truth 1' and 'truth 2'. We can only say, along with Heidegger, that both these elements are contained in truth; we cannot separate them in a meaningful way. Thus, if I wake up under a screen that I think is the sky, but I am deceived, either I stay in my deception, and this is 'the truth' for me, or I investigate further and discover the deception, and then the truth is I was deceived, but now I know that something else is true. This is similar to the situation we find ourselves in any way, for example, in the history of science. We believe we know the truth, but on further investigation, we discover that we were wrong and amend our account of some entity or another. We cannot separate the uncovering from the uncoveredness. This becomes apparent in Heidegger's discussion of Newton's laws. He maintains that without Dasein, there is no truth: '"[t]here is" truth only in so far as Dasein is' (Heidegger 1962: 369). Truth is an *existentiale* of Dasein; it is fundamental to the structure of Dasein. Before there was Dasein, there was no truth, and after Dasein is gone, there will be no truth. There can be neither uncovering nor uncoveredness without Dasein. Concerning Newton, Heidegger maintains that his laws were not true before he discovered them, but it does not follow that they were false. They were neither true nor false. The entities described in Newton's laws may have been uncovered, but in Newton's laws, they become true through him. The laws make the entities described in the laws accessible to Dasein.

The problem Tugendhat points to in Heidegger's philosophy merely reflects a problem with most philosophical accounts of truth. That Heidegger's account of truth cannot deliver a correspondence with a state of affairs as it is in itself is hardly a criticism against him. His account starts from a rejection that this is the way to approach truth. For Tugendhat, such a response will not suffice; he maintains that while traditional correspondence theory 'may not accomplish much, . . . [i]t does at least furnish the minimal condition that must be met if it is to feature at all as a concept of truth' (Tugendhat 1994: 229). Tugendhat holds this to be self-evident, but the history of philosophy has shown that meeting this minimal condition has been a difficult, if not impossible, task.

It is also worth noting that if we cannot successfully distinguish between 'truth 1' and 'truth 2', then a Heideggerian account of correspondence cannot be considered isomorphic with a more usual understanding of correspondence. When Heidegger claims the true proposition 'uncovers the state of affairs', he does not commit himself to a strong formulation of a correspondence theory. For this to be the case, he would also need to be committed to a metaphysics of objects and subjects. Heidegger's conception of a world is not a collection of objects, but rather it is the 'openness of Being' (Heidegger 1962: 267). Dasein's is constituted by this disclosedness. The 'state of affairs' is Dasein's disclosure of its world and nothing more.

If, as Heidegger claims, we cannot bridge the gap between the two elements of correspondence theory, then Tugendgat's critique cannot proceed because it presupposes that an account of truth can, at least in principle, unite these two elements. Otherwise, there is no way of distinguishing our knowing from what is known; such an account of truth is required to make Tugendhat's critique work. It is, in fact, a strength of Heidegger's account that it realizes both the impossibility of this situation and of our insistence that we can overcome it. This insistence is not merely a philosophical position among others but rather a feature of how we make sense of the world. The state of affairs that a proposition attempts to correspond to is Dasein's disclosing its world. Despite this, Tugendgat's critique brings to the fore another important issue. Heidegger's account of truth seems to slip into relativism. If the truth disclosed to me is racist, can we use Heidegger's philosophy to justify it? Do we not have a responsibility to continue seeking a rational truth? Do

Heidegger's political alliances not make this painfully clear? In some ways, the disagreement between Heidegger and Tugendhat turns on this point. Even if we can never meet Tugendhat's minimum condition for truth, it is incumbent on us to try. Heidegger begins with the impossibility of meeting this condition, but he does not advocate relativism with respect to truth. Heidegger's account of truth demands more of us. His insistence that truth needs to be 'wrested' from the entities implies that it is our responsibility to seek the truth, to rescue it from the inauthentic truth of *Das Man*. Moreover, truth is not timeless or transcendental in a Platonic sense but has to be sought continually anew. Many years after *Being and Time*, in a discussion of poetry from the 1955–6 lecture series, Heidegger writes, 'A constantly renewed that is more original appropriation is needed in order for mortals to have a true beholding of something' (Heidegger 1996: 46). In this way, we are brought to the relationship between truth and art.

1.6 Art and truth

The account that views truth as a property of propositions which correspond faithfully to a worldly state of affairs is based on an ontology of subjects and objects. As we have seen, such an ontological framework leads to ontological disconnection. While this causes many problems for post-Cartesian philosophy, it also does important philosophical work because it demarcates the objective from the subjective. This ontological gap allows us to claim that our statements refer to a world that is independent of us. As Tugendhat points out, it gives us the possibility of an objective truth that we can employ to settle debates. The facts about the sun that it is a star and an almost perfect spherical ball of hot plasma with internal convective motion and that it generates a magnetic field via a dynamo process are not subjective. They are true of the sun. Do Heidegger's criticisms really challenge these facts? As we have seen, Heidegger maintains that our perceptions are laden with categories and that they are expressed. He also states that scientific evidence is not a special form of perception. Thus, for Heidegger, the proposition 'the sun is an almost perfect spherical ball of hot plasma' is not a privileged statement.

It is an intentional statement that expresses a perception of the sun. As I write it, it is unfulfilled for me. It has little to do with my perception of the sun. By the very fact of its objectivity, it is not grounded in my experience. These statements about the sun do not acknowledge that it is something I experience. However, these scientific perceptions are not a correspondence; they are an expression of something that could have been expressed in another way.

According to Heidegger, the scientist does not come to the sun as a blank sensory receptor but instead brings something unfulfilled that is fulfilled in the scientific perception. Truth, in this sense, is the 'being identical of presumed and intuited' (Heidegger 1992: 51). Science is no longer a paradigm of truth; in fact, it fails to capture this 'primary being of truth' (Dahlstrom 1994: 21). If we follow Heidegger, we cannot accept an ontology of truth based on Lotzean affirmedness but rather as an identity of the presumed and the intuited. While not dismissing the importance of scientific research, Heidegger comes to see truth in terms of art. In the 1930s he further developed his account of truth in terms of the Greek word for unconcealment or 'Aletheia'. In 'The Origin of The Work of Art' (Heidegger 1978), Heidegger investigates the nature of the essence of art. In this way, his critical focus is centred not on logic and science but on *aesthetic* accounts of art, which he contents bring metaphysics to the realm of art.

1.6.1 Aesthetics

Heidegger's work on art can be considered anti-aesthetic. Heidegger claims that the term 'aesthetics' is not merely a label for the philosophy of art but rather represents the application of enlightenment thinking to the realm of art. In particular, aesthetic accounts remove the truth-disclosing properties that the Greeks associated with art and relegate them to the realm of mere 'experience'. The job of art becomes merely to provide a pleasurable experience. In this way, as Young points out, art understood as aesthetics is decontextualized from our everyday concerns. 'We attend to the object of perception in and for itself, abstract, that is, from every relation it may have to our intellectual and practical interests' (Young 2001: 9). It becomes 'disinterested' in the Kantian sense. Crucially, Heidegger maintains that such an identification of art with experience is, for Heidegger, catastrophic for our understanding of art. At the end of 'The Origin', we are told, '[y]et perhaps experience is the element in which art dies' (Young 2001: 9).

1.6.2 Art as thing

To facilitate a rethinking of what art is, Heidegger begins by interrogating our implicit understanding. In the first instance, a work of art is a thing; it's a piece of sculpture or a painting. As Heidegger is seeking the essence of art, it seems that this physical thing, the work itself, is a good place to start. However, when we consider the work as a thing, we unwittingly fall into existing philosophical conceptions of what things are. Heidegger considers three philosophical conceptions of 'thingness': the thing as a bearer of traits, as a gestalt, or as matter and form. He maintains that form and matter is the dominant concept, and thus, we will focus on this for the time being. Despite the obvious associations with art, Heidegger links the Aristotelian notion of things as formed matter to a historical tendency to view objects in terms of equipment. For this reason, he claims that in order to understand the thingly character of the artwork, we must first begin with the equipmental character of equipment.

For Heidegger, the equipmental character of equipment, or its essence, is usefulness. We only encounter the character of equipment in its use. In order to illustrate this equipmental character of equipment, Heidegger suggests an example of a pair of shoes. To bring these to mind, he suggests we consider van Gogh's painting of a pair of work shoes. In an account of the painting, which some commentators such as Young (2001), suggest is 'largely irrelevant' (Young 2001: 22) to the overall thrust of the essay, Heidegger shows how the painting discloses to us the shoes and what they tell us about the life of the peasant woman who wears them as she toils in the field is also disclosed. However, Shapiro famously challenges Heidegger's account of a peasant woman's life by pointing to the fact that the shoes belonged to van Gogh. But for Heidegger, the poetic description of the peasant woman serves to illustrate the idea that equipment, shoes in this case, become entirely lost in their use. In the language of *Being and Time*, the shoes are ready-to-hand as the woman works, yet it is precisely the shoes that enable her work. Equipment links the worker to their world, but in this process, the tools slip entirely from the worker's attention. The tool only comes back into view when it breaks or wears away. When this happens, the tool becomes 'mere stuff'.

In both of these cases, while the shoes are in use or when they are broken, the worker is not aware of the *being* of the shoes. It is only the account of van Gogh's painting that brings the shoes into awareness. 'The artwork lets us know what the shoes are in truth' (Heidegger 1978: 162). In this way, Heidegger firmly links art with truth. He claims that 'the essence of art would then be this: The truth of beings setting itself to work' (Heidegger 1978: 162). The essay's conceit is to reverse its strategy; the thingly character of a work does not reveal something about the work; it is art that reveals something about the truth of things. Art discloses truth; this is its essence. We cannot understand the work in this way when we see it as formed matter. In fact, Heidegger maintains that we cannot understand the artwork at all if we focus on its thingly character.

> As soon as we look for such a thingly substructure in the work, we have unwittingly taken the work as equipment, to which we then also ascribe a superstructure supposed to contain its artistic quality. But the work is not a piece of equipment that is fitted out in addition with an aesthetic value that adheres to it. (Heidegger 1978: 165–6)

Heidegger is calling into question the basic presuppositions of aesthetic theory. He claims that we cannot understand how art discloses truth in terms of the metaphysics of subjects and objects. In fact, from this metaphysical viewpoint, art's truth-disclosing function is blocked. Given this, we need a different notion of truth, one more akin to the pre-Socratic understandings of art. To this end, Heidegger develops a distinction between 'world' and 'earth' and introduces them with the example of a Greek temple. The temple, standing majestically on the rocky cliff, allows those who built it, appreciated it and worshipped in it to apprehend the landscape in which it is set.

> Standing there, the building holds its ground against the storm raging above it and so make the storm manifest in its violence. The lustre and the gleam of the stone, though itself apparently glowing only by the grace of

the sun, yet first brings to radiance the light of day, the breadth of the sky, the darkness of the night. The temple's firm grounding makes visible the invisible space of air. (Heidegger 1996: 169)

The temple has the ability to bring a 'world' into view, and concurrently, it makes the 'earth' apparent. According to Heidegger, the notions of world and earth are offered as an alternative to seeing the work as a thing with aesthetic qualities, which is the basis of aesthetics. World and earth cannot be fully untangled from each other because the earth is that from which the world emerges: 'Earth is that whence the arising brings back and shelters everything that arises' (Heidegger 1996: 169). Great artworks open up a world, but this world opening is not simply a brute fact; it is the locus of a struggle or strife. Art unconceals a world, but all unconcealment is accompanied by a tendency towards concealment, which in 'The Origin', Heidegger understand as earth. This tendency of concealment similarly relies on world openings. Truth is that which is unconcealed from a tendency to conceal. As we can see, this represents a dramatically different view of truth to correspondence theory.

1.6.3 Truth, the role of the artist and the role of preservers

In the final section of the essay, Heidegger discusses the role of the artist. He maintains that the work is self-sufficient in the sense that once created it no longer requires its connection to the artist. It is not the reputation of the artist that makes a work great. However, the work's character as work depends on the fact of its creation by an artist and this can only be understood with respect to the creative process. There can be no question of discovering what the origin of the work of art is without reference to this. To this end, Heidegger again contrasts art with equipment. Equipment, like art, is constructed and it is useful to ask what the difference is between making art and making equipment. This difference is not immediately obvious for, both endeavours require craftsmanship, for example. Thus, while Heidegger points out the similarities in process between the making of equipment and the making of art, the process of making art is ultimately very different:

> [T]o create is to let something emerge as a thing that had been brought forth. The work's becoming a work is a way in which truth becomes and happens. It all rests in the essence of truth. But what is truth, that it has to happen in such a thing as something created. (Heidegger 1978: 180)

In Heidegger's picture the artist opens an area of the earth and this opening instigates a strife that is truth. Heidegger defines truth as untruth in the sense that it comes from the not-yet-revealed, or the un-uncovered, or concealment. Heidegger uses this reference to 'double constraint' to indicate that concealedness involves a double restraint or refusal. Truth occurs at the opposition of the lighting and double concealing. These two elements move apart in primal strife. The artist 'wins' the open area. This open area is strife. The being unconcealed in truth is not simply revealed, but it reveals itself, withholds itself and withdraws itself. Strife moves lighting and concealing apart. In between them is the open region that the artist wins. The openness of the open region is truth. It is '*this* openness, only if and as long as it establishes itself within its open region. Hence there must always be some being in this open region' (Heidegger 1978: 181). The artist does not create the truth; she facilitates the winning of an open region. This open region must coincide with a being and the work is this being. Thus creation is not creation in the sense of building something but rather it is a 'bringing forth'.

The idea of 'strife' and of the 'open' in this respect is related to the idea of '*Spielraum*'. Heidegger explains this notion in *Being and Time* in section 70 (Heidegger 1962: 418). It is a part of the 'existential-analytical inquiry as to the temporal conditions of the spatiality that is characteristic of Dasein' (Heidegger 1962: 418). *Spielraum* is translated variously as 'leeway', 'free space', and 'freeplay'. The sense of play is also clearly at work in the term. Dasein does not occupy space, in the sense that it is understood by physics; Dasein is not an object located at particular coordinates of longitude and latitude. 'Dasein takes in space; this is to be understood literally. . . . In existing it has already made room for its own leeway [*Spielraum*]' (Heidegger 1962: 420). This leeway is the room Dasein makes for itself and this space or 'region' is tied up, inexorably, with Dasein's concerns or involvements. Our scientific and philosophical notions of space, all flow from the 'ecstatical temporality of the spatiality that is characteristic of Dasein' (Heidegger 1962: 420). In particular, the idea that we can conceive of space as separate to time depends on *Spielraum*, as the room that Dasein makes for itself. In terms of the work, the idea of *Spielraum* is important because it is linked, as Heidegger goes on to say in 'The Origin of the Work of Art', to the idea that 'in some manner, the essence of unconcealment belongs to being itself . . ., then it is being, which in virtue of its essence, allows the freeplay of openness (the clearing of the "there")' (Heidegger 2002: 36). The work generates the space in which it has meaning.

Heidegger maintains that createdness consists in two essential determinations. The first is that 'Truth establishes itself in the work' (Heidegger 2002: 36). Here we can see how radical Heidegger's position is. Traditionally, we view the artist as fully responsible for the creation of the work. We see the work as a reflection of the artist's view, as an expression of the artist's attitudes or feelings about the world. This may be the case from the artist's perspective, but this does not make the work great. Heidegger claims that in great art truth is established. But what sort of a truth is this? If it is obviously not a subjective created truth, then its status of truth must come from a source other than artist. Does the audience convey truth on to the work? Does the audience recognize the truth in a work? Is this what makes the work great? The answer to all these questions is no. They result from the faulty way of looking at things described earlier. Truth is not simply added to the work by either the artist or the viewer. The truth is a world opening up in continuing strife. It is the shared world of both the artist and the audience. The work wins the unity of the world and earth. The world and the earth won are the world and earth of a given historical community. 'As a world opens itself, it submits to the decisions of a historical humanity the questions of victory and defeat, blessing and curse, mastery and slavery. The dawning world brings out what is as yet undecided and measureless, and thus discloses the hidden necessity of measure and decisiveness' (Heidegger 1978: 181).

While the artist may no longer be seen as the sole author of a work's significance, the status of the work is raised far above its general position in aesthetic theory. Contextualists, for example, claim that the social and historical context of a work supplies its meaning. Heidegger rejects this and claims that the art creates the context within which it has meaning. The work creates the space in which certain themes become relevant and others become irrelevant. It is not simply that a work instigates a new fashion where old concerns or themes fall out of favour. Art creates a world that decides what is literally seen and understood by a community. The strife that is created by the work is strife between world and earth. This strife opens up a region and while, as we have seen, this is no simple case of a clear region of two opponents (both world and earth define each other and contain each other). We can argue that in the case of new world emerging some beings are revealed as world, some beings are swallowed up in to earth.

The second essential determination of createdness is concerned with production. In the case of both art and equipment something is produced. Indeed, this is true of everything, as Heidegger points out, but in the case of art, createdness stands out. The createdness of a work is a living feature. It does not withdraw into usefulness but remains a part of its being. This createdness does not point us to the artist. It is not the signature that makes a work great. In fact, the more successful the work is the more 'cleanly it seems to cut ties to human beings' (Heidegger 1978: 183). Heidegger acknowledges that the work needs a creator but he highlights the role of the 'preserver'. The work is preserved by those who are party to the displacement it instigates. 'To submit to this displacement means to transform our accustomed ties to world and to earth and henceforth to restrain all usual doing and prizing, knowing and looking, in order to stay within the truth that is happening in the work' (Heidegger 1978: 183).

The notion of preservation in 'The Origin', is complex. It does not mean that the work relies on an interplay between the artist and its audience for its status as a work. Such an idea fails to acknowledge that the work functions as a 'displacement' and it is this displacement that the preservers preserve. 'To submit to this displacement means to transform our accustomed ties to world and earth and henceforth to restrain all the usual doing and prizing, knowing and looking, in order to stay within the truth that is happening in the work' (Heidegger 1978: 191). Heidegger's notion of preservation goes beyond the idea that the work needs to be witnessed to include the idea that the truth that happens in the work relies on this preservation. A work 'always remains tied to the preservers' (Heidegger 1978: 192), even when 'it is still only waiting for them'. The truth of the work, its ability to reconfigure world and earth for a historical people, relies on its preservers.

The fact of the works createdness is not fully realized until the work is viewed and it is only realized in great works. Thus, we have the counterintuitive idea that the artist is not fully responsible for the work's status as a created work. This idea is less counterintuitive, though, when we remember that Heidegger is not talking about creation in the sense of making the work, he is talking about the notion that the works createdness stays alive in the work. Equipment is created, but its createdness is swallowed up by usefulness; not only does its createdness slip from our view but its being disappears entirely. A less-than-great artwork can similarly disappear from our view; certainly its createdness is not an issue for us. The fact that something is created is only apparent to us when we are in some sense surprised by it.

1.7 Conclusion

Heidegger critiques the idea truth is a feature of logico-scientific proposition and instead sees it as the actuality of a given state of affairs or 'disclosedness'. For Heidegger, logical or scientific accounts of truth are based on an ontology of being as presence. While we understand truth in this way, we are left with philosophical questions about how to explain the relationship between an object and the perceiving subject. With recourse to Husserlian intentionality, Heidegger begins from a different starting point. He starts with the things themselves. Heidegger's account of truth is *primordial* in that it begins with our individual and naïve perception of this particular object. In this way, Heidegger appears to shift the philosophical emphasis from linguistic propositions to the actuality of states of affairs. It is art, rather than scientific propositions, that reveals this actuality, and therefore great art becomes the locus of truth for Heidegger. As this thesis is concerned with poetry, we must ask how we are to understand the role of language, especially poetic language, in this picture, given this turn from propositions to actuality. In the next chapter, we turn our attention to Heidegger's account of language.

2
Language

2.1 Language and philosophy

Our investigation of truth as unconcealment already tells us something about language. For Heidegger, logico-scientific propositions are not vehicles for truth. While, on the face of it, this seems to be a claim about language and its ability to reveal the truth, Heidegger is clear there are no special propositions that can serve as evidence. However, this does not mean that all language is equal in terms of truth. Heidegger views art as the realm of truth, and as we saw for Heidegger, poetry is the highest form of art precisely because it is language based. So while Heidegger de-emphasizes the idea that the scientific proposition can be true in the sense of correspondence, he elevates poetic language in terms of its ability to disclose truth. Poetry does not objectify or attempt to decontextualize its subject matter; therefore, it gives both what is revealed in the poem and the manner in which this revelation happens.

How we understand language is how we understand poetry. Traditionally, to understand language, we look to linguistics or philosophy. Linguistics is the scientific study of language, which views language as a system of conventional symbols used in speaking and writing, investigating the correlations between symbols and sounds. Given its scientific grounding, we can view it as one possible philosophical position among several. Philosophy itself has long been concerned with language. In fact, during the twentieth century, it became the key focus of philosophers in the Anglo-American tradition. These philosophers came to characterize long-standing philosophical problems as problems of language. As we will see, Heidegger's account of language lies outside this linguistic turn in analytic philosophy. For his part, Heidegger attempts to rethink language and free it from its metaphysical limitations. From a Heideggerian perspective, an understanding of language is needed to account for poetry, but the converse is also true: an understanding of language requires poetry; it is our long-held metaphysical biases that blind us to this point.

The linguistic turn in analytic philosophy is, in part, a response to the dominance of science within philosophy since the rise of science in the seventeenth century. As we saw in the previous chapter, philosophy became the handmaiden of science. Its main task was simply to buttress scientific methodology or provide 'underpinnings'. Scientific method is based on a mechanical model of nature where mathematical models can capture universal physical laws. As we saw, human experience was displaced as the starting point for gaining knowledge about the world. Instead, scientific knowledge becomes a question of isolating statements or logically precise propositions that are cleansed of the ambiguity of natural languages. This thinking reached its apex during the twentieth century when a group of philosophers known as the Vienna Circle attempted to create an ideal language to support science but also rid philosophy of its enduring problems, which were, by then, characterized as problems of language use or misuse. For example, Russell's Logical Atomism contains both a methodology and a metaphysical framework. The world is viewed as composed of simple discrete entities or atoms that are somehow combined to form complex states of affairs. It was thought that by linking each of these atoms to a single word, a logically ideal language could be developed. Such a language would dissolve the problems of metaphysics, traditionally construed. These problems were seen as a result of messy natural languages laden with metaphors and other ambiguities; these linguistic ambiguities led philosophy into error. Famously, the logical atomist and logical positivist projects ended in failure for a number of reasons, not least of which was the inability to rid language of its metaphorical content (Soames 2010).

In the face of this failure, twentieth-century philosophy turns back to an analysis of 'natural' languages. We can clearly trace this movement in terms of Wittgenstein's two seminal works, the *Tractatus Logico-Philosophicus* and *The*

Philosophical Investigations. The desire to map the world with an unambiguous point-to-point language in the *Tractatus* gives way, in the *Investigations*, to the idea that meanings are to be understood in terms of the particular language game in which they are used.

2.2 Central themes of Heidegger's philosophy of language

While Heidegger is writing outside this historico-philosophical story, his later work also moves increasingly towards language. After *Being and Time*, there is a shift in Heidegger's thinking that is known as the Turn, or *die Kehre*. This turn is often characterized as a 'turn around', which happened sometime between 1930 and 1933. There is much debate among Heideggerian scholars as to when the turn actually happens and what it means. What is clear, however, is that by the time Heidegger is writing 'The Origin of the Work of Art' (1935–6), he is doing something quite different from *Being and Time*. This turn in Heidegger's thinking is associated with language in two main ways. First of all, Heidegger's philosophy becomes profoundly concerned with language and second, his own use of language changes. The writing of the later Heidegger is famously difficult. His use of language is poetic and complex; 'elliptical' is a word often used to describe Heidegger's language in this period. As we have seen in the first chapter, Heidegger holds that art is truth, and poetry is paradigmatic of art as it is language based. It is little wonder, then, that Heidegger's style should tend towards the poetic.

Heidegger discusses language in several texts. In the essay, 'The Way to Language' (Heidegger 1959), Heidegger employs a novel approach. To understand language, he tells us, we must take a journey towards it. The culmination of this journey is an experience with language itself. Heidegger intends the essay as a series of signposts towards this experience. The journey begins by acknowledging the difficulties inherent in understanding language. Philosophers and other language theorists generally recognize these difficulties, yet, according to Heidegger, they are often sidestepped quickly in a rush to explain language with recourse to something else. In these efforts, language becomes something ready-to-hand, a tool like the other tools available for human use. Heidegger takes a step back to linger with the fundamental problems of trying to account for language. These difficulties should not be dismissed easily. It is Heidegger's intention to acknowledge them fully; in fact, he wonders if they can be surmounted. Of course, the most pressing difficulty is the banal fact that to understand language, we must use language; our attempts to understand language always take place within language. Heidegger tells us we need to face this fact head-on, rather than simply rushing past it to give another account of language, which sidesteps this. We need to meet these difficulties squarely and then find a way to experience language in terms of them. Of course, the idea of a journey towards language is metaphorical. Still, as we will see in the next chapter, Heidegger does not accept his journey towards language is metaphorical. Leaving this to one side, for the time being, Heidegger asks us how can we find a way towards language if we are already located within it?

We already possess and use language. However, he is at pains to point out that the ability to use language is not simply one human ability among others. It is this ability, according to Heidegger, that makes us human. It is the 'foundation of the human being' (Heidegger 1959). We do not begin at a distance from language; rather, we are always already *within* language. Heidegger asks, 'But are we at that point?' (Heidegger 1959). Are we too caught up in language? Is it possible to understand the nature of language from where we are, already immersed in language?

Heidegger wants to understand language, not as something ready-to-hand but rather language *as* language. The essay uses a number of what Heidegger calls 'guidelines' to bring us to such an understanding. The initial formulation of the guideline is 'to speak about speech *qua* speech'. Heidegger points out that words relating to speech occur three times within this guideline.

Each time they mean something different, but they are also the Same (*das Selbe*). The motif of sameness is a recurring theme in the middle and later periods of Heidegger's writing (White 1980). It is generally capitalized, in English translations, to capture Heidegger's distinctive, sometimes counterintuitive, usage. For example, Heidegger claims that metalinguistics and rocket technology are the Same and that technology and science are the Same (White 1980). Clearly, he is not using either or both terms in an ordinary, everyday sense. In this particular context, Sameness, Heidegger contends, is the 'distinctive property of language' (White 1980). We can understand it in terms of 'oneness'. In this way, the guideline points us to a 'web of relations' that we are an extricable part of. We cannot simply acknowledge the web and carry on regardless. We have to 'loosen' it. Heidegger says:

> Perhaps there is a bond running through the web which, in a way remains strange, unbinds and delivers language into its own. The point is to experience the unbinding bond within the web of language. (Heidegger 1959: 113)

Heidegger is talking about the possibility of a new understanding of language, which he claims, perhaps unfairly, has been missed by all other language theorists. And this understanding seems inherently metaphorical.

2.3 Language as showing

Heidegger characterizes language first as speaking or as articulated sound, though as Nowell Smith (2013) emphasizes, Heidegger's account also includes all non-verbal articulations. His starting point is the human body and the organs of speech. Though this may seem like a departure from many philosophies of language, the deep connection between language and speech organs is made clear in words and phrases such as 'mother tongue' or 'lingo'. Heidegger notes that Aristotle also begins with this point. He quotes his own translation from a passage from 'On Interpretation':

> Now, what (takes place) in the making of vocal sounds is a show of what there is in the soul in the way of passions, and what is written is a show of the vocal sounds. And just as writing is not the same among all (men), so also the vocal sounds are not the same. On the other hand, those things of which these (sounds and writings) are a show in the first place, are among all (men) the same passions of the soul, and the matters of which these

(the passions) give likening representations are also the same. (Heidegger 1959: 113)

It is here, in this passage, that we are brought to Heidegger's key idea that language is showing. Heidegger's translation links *semia* (that which shows), *symbola* (that which holds to each other), and *homoiomata* (that which likens) in terms of showing. Language is essentially concerned with showing in the sense of *Aletheia*. 'In various ways, disclosing or disguising, Showing makes something come to light, lets what has come to light be perceived, and lets the perception be examined' (Heidegger 1959: 113). It is Heidegger's contention that the link between the showing and what it is that is shown is recognized but not fully developed by the Greeks and then lost altogether in subsequent philosophy of language. Instead, theories of language become centred on explaining the relationship between sign and signifier, which is still the basis of modern semiotics. This shift towards the notion of language as showing radically changes how language is understood and has far-reaching ontological implications.

2.4 Showing as Saying

Though Heidegger begins with the act of speaking, he quickly distinguishes it from Saying. As we have seen, speaking is a vocalization, and thus, it is a human activity, but we cannot understand language simply in terms of this. Rather, Heidegger notices that we can only talk about these characteristics insofar as they make an appearance because something has been said. Saying, unlike speaking, means to show. Thus, we can only consider vocalization because it is something shown to us by language. While vocalizing may seem like the first element of an account of language, it comes after language's showing. This showing is always related to what is not shown.

[T]o speak *to* one another means: to say something, show something to one another, and to entrust one another mutually to what is shown. To speak *with* one another means: to tell of something jointly, to show to one another what that which is claimed in the speaking says in the speaking, and what it, of itself, brings to light. What is unspoken is not merely something that lacks voice, it is what remains unsaid, what is not yet shown, what has not yet reached appearance. That which must remain wholly unspoken is held back in the unsaid, abides in concealment as unshowable, is mystery. That which is spoken to us speaks as dictum in the sense of something imparted, something whose speaking does not even require to be sounded. (Heidegger 1959: 113)

Again, we see Heidegger's ontology of concealment and unconcealment. In different ways, the spoken comes from the unspoken; what is shown comes from unconcealment. This alethic showing unifies the various aspects of language. It is the 'peculiar characteristic' by which we must first understand language. Echoing the passage in *Being and Time* where Heidegger discusses idle talk, curiosity and ambiguity, language is related to truth and the different modes of being in truth. Even in idle talk, there is still the understanding that is essential to disclosure and, therefore truth, but this disclosure is fallen. As Heidegger puts it, '[b]eing towards the entities has not been extinguished, but it has been uprooted' (Heidegger 1962: 211). In such a case, the disguised entities show themselves in the mode of *semblance* where the entity is not disclosed authentically by my own Dasein, but it is disclosed by the 'they' in idle talk.

Heidegger claims the fact that Saying comes from the unspoken is what leads to the mistaken belief that language is somehow separate from its speakers and their concerns. This mistake leads to the objectification of language. Heidegger is emphatic: the spoken is what allows speakers to attend to their concerns. In this way, we cannot separate language from its purpose, which is to say.

2.5 Design

For Heidegger, it is a structural feature of language that we continually fail to grasp its nature. When considering language, we fall into error. We don't just miss the point; we have an inbuilt tendency to miss the point, and to understand this is an essential part of getting to grips with language. Language conceals itself and thwarts our efforts to bring it to light. For Heidegger to miss the point means to fail to 'see directly the unifying unity of the being of language" (Heidegger 1959: 121). This 'unifying unity' links the different elements identified in the signpost described earlier. There is no name for this 'unifying unity' because we continually miss it. 'The traditional names for what we have in mind under the rubric "language" indicate this unity always only in terms of one or another of the aspects which the being of language has to offer' (Heidegger 1959: 121). Heidegger, however, calls this unity 'design', linking it to the idea of the 'sign' in design, in the Latin word, *secare*, to cut. He maintains, '[t]o design is to cut a trace'. This is not our usual understanding of the word 'sign'; rather, it is derived from his account of its etymology. According to Heidegger, we make a sign when we cut a furrow in the soil to 'open it to seed and growth' (Heidegger 1959: 121). In obviously metaphorical terms, Heidegger tells us we can understand language as design, where design is that which opens up a furrow. 'The design is the drawing of the being of language, the structure of a show in which are joined the speakers and their speaking' (Heidegger 1959: 121). The nature of language is, then, associated with its ability to cut its own furrow into whatever soil the speaker is concerned about.

2.6 Language as showing

The essential being of language is Saying as showing (Heidegger 1959: 123). This means the design of language is to be thought of in terms Saying as showing but not in terms of signs in the traditional sense. Language, in its essence, is not a system of signs. Saying as showing is prior to the signs we usually associate with language. It is this prior showing that we are concerned with here. As Heidegger puts it, 'all signs arise from a showing within whose realm and for whose purpose they can be signs' (Heidegger 1959: 123). So to see language as a system of signs is to overlook that this showing must happen first. Building a system of signs can only happen once language is already established as that which shows.

It is important to note that this does not mean that showing is an 'exclusively, or even decisively, the property of human activity' (Heidegger 1959: 123). This is a complex idea, but we can understand it this way: language is Saying as showing, but not all showing is saying. What shows itself is always a self-shown appearance. 'Self-showing appearance is the mark of the presence and absence of everything that is present, of every kind and rank' (Heidegger 1959: 123). Even when Saying brings showing, there is something that precedes this showing. This is the indication that it will let itself be shown (Heidegger 1959: 123). How are we to understand this 'indication that it will let itself be shown'? In the first instance, we could see it simply as a disclaimer against the idea that the world is a linguistic construct. Saying is not a uniquely human activity; it also encompasses the self-showing saying of things in the world. These things are saturated in the categorial. In some sense, they Say. Again, we must remember that we are working within Heidegger's unique ontology. We are always in some relation with entities in the world. Sometimes this relation is expressed in terms of the saying of our language, but not always. Sometimes entities demand from us in another way. They show *themselves*. Like language, this self-showing is always relational or dialogical in some sense.

2.7 Speaking and listening

Heidegger tells us that we only speak by way of language. While this seems trivial, it is intended to show us that language is always prior to speaking, and because of this, speaking is, first and foremost, a listening to language. Again, we are pointed to a complex ontological picture. When we speak, we are, first and foremost, listening to the language. This listening is prior to all other listening. Before any particular linguistic act, we first hear the language speaking. Because language is showing, it defines the parameters of what can be spoken; it shows what can be spoken. In this way, it shows us the world. There is never access to the world without the categorial speaking of language. 'Language speaks in that it, as showing, reaching into all regions of presences, summons from them whatever is present to appear and to fade' (Heidegger 1959: 123). When we listen to language, 'we let it say its Saying to us' (Heidegger 1959: 123). 'All perception and conception is already contained' (Heidegger 1959: 123) in this Saying of language. The full implications of Heidegger's account become clear. His position goes far beyond the idea that when we speak, we are merely drawing on a pool of accepted linguistic practices. Language is not simply a collection of words and associated grammatical rules. It is also the categorial saturation of all perception and conception. It is this that allows Heidegger to maintain that language itself, shows.

In this way, Heidegger maintains that showing comes before perception. As a group of language users, we belong within a language, and for this reason, we hear the Saying of the language. 'Saying grants the hearing, and thus the speaking, of language solely to those who belong within it' (Heidegger 1959: 123). This is the essence of language. How are we to understand the relationship between our Saying and the Saying of language, or rather how are we to understand what separates them? Somewhat enigmatically, Heidegger asks of the Saying of language:

> Is it separated from our speaking, something to which we must first build a bridge? Or is Saying the stream of stillness which in forming them joins its own two banks-the Saying and our Saying after it? (Heidegger 1959: 124–5)

Heidegger's point here is that while language 'remains unmistakably bound up with human speaking' (Heidegger 1959: 125), it is not exhausted by this. Heidegger presents us with an ontology of language, which contains two linked elements: our speaking, the language and some sort of bond between them. Again, this smacks of the metaphorical, but Heidegger draws our attention to this connecting bond. This move elegantly accounts for the fact that though language is only manifest in speaking, it is also undoubtedly prior to speaking. In some ways, it seems to have more control over us than we have over it. This is obvious when we concede that our ability to express anything is limited by its parameters. 'Language needs human speaking, and yet it is not merely of the making or at the command of our speech activity' (Heidegger 1959: 125). Given this, Heidegger asks again on what does the being of language rest?

2.8 Owning

The contention that language is Saying as showing does not, however, provide us with the necessary experience with language. We still are not on the way to language, though we are told that: 'the way to speaking is present within language itself' (Heidegger 1959: 126). We are still looking for something concealed from us, something which accounts for the difficulty philosophers have when they attempt to conceptualize language. This feature 'conceals itself in the way in which Saying allows those who listen to it to reach language'. This concealment is associated with our relationship to language, and this relationship is one of belonging to language. To understand language's nature, we must understand how we belong to it. '*The moving force in Showing of Saying is Owning*' (Heidegger 1959: 126). Owning, Heidegger tells us, is what brings everything that is present and absent into their own, 'from where they show themselves' (Heidegger 1959: 126). We can understand Showing in terms of appropriation. Appropriation 'yields the opening of the clearing in which present beings can persist and from which absent beings can depart, while keeping their persistence in the withdrawal' (Heidegger 1959: 127). Again, we are brought before Heidegger's ontology of concealment and unconcealment. What is appropriated is Shown by Saying. Appropriation is 'the giving yield whose giving reach alone is what gives us such things as a "there is," a "there is of which even Being itself stands in need to come into its own as presence"' (Heidegger 1959: 127).

There is something paradoxical about this view of appropriation as a giving. What does this appropriation give us? It gives us a 'there is' or the '*es gibt*'. The appropriation that motivates Showing supplies the 'there is' by which everything else is given to us; it clears an opening. Language clears the opening in which beings are. This is how we are to understand language. 'Appropriation assembles the design of Saying and unfolds it into the structure of manifold Showing. It is the most inconspicuous of inconspicuous phenomena' (Heidegger 1959: 128), so inconspicuous that we continually miss it. Language clears the opening in which beings appear, but it conceals this function so that we cannot apprehend its role in this respect. However, as Heidegger points out, some verses in Goethe's poetry seem to capture the idea by using the word 'own' in a meaning that is close to 'showing itself'. In this way, it is the poet rather than the philosopher who catches the truth of language. The great poet can see beyond the concealment of language. In fact, Heidegger's philosophical awareness depends on the poet's ability to see beyond the philosopher's tendency to miss the point.

'Appropriation grants to mortals their abode within their nature so that they may be capable of being those who speak' (Heidegger 1959: 128). Appropriation is what allows us to be human; it is what lets us speak. 'Because showing of Saying is appropriating, therefore the ability to listen to Saying-our belonging to it- also lies in Appropriation' (Heidegger 1959: 129). We have seen that Saying is showing and that this is an appropriation. We have also seen how speaking is a listening to the language to which we belong. It follows then that listening is also an appropriation. This idea changes our understanding of our relationship to language. When we speak, we are always answering language. Appropriation is linked intimately to human nature. It allows us to appropriate what we encountered in Saying. 'Appropriation, needing and using man's appropriation, allows Saying to reach speech' (Heidegger 1959: 129).

The structure of Saying is appropriative, and so is human nature: appropriation uses man's appropriation to let Saying be spoken. Heidegger says, 'The way to language belongs to Saying determined by Appropriation. Within this way, which belongs to the reality of language, the peculiar property of language is concealed. The way is appropriating' (Heidegger 1959: 129).

2.9 Way making

The Swabian dialect contains the word 'wëgen', a verb meaning to clear a way or a path as one clears a way through the snow. To get to the nature of language, we do not travel along a pre-existing path; we must clear a way as we go. As we accompany Heidegger on his way to language, we have followed the path he has cleared before us. He says, 'way-making ... means to bring the way ... forth first of all and thus to *be* the way. "Appropriation appropriates man to its own usage." This is how language works; it makes pathways appropriate to the their usage. Showing as appropriation thus transpires, and Appropriation is the waymaking for Saying to come into language' (Heidegger 1959: 120). The way is made by Showing as appropriation. In a typical move, Heidegger led us to believe that there could be a progression of our thinking that would lead us to a destination. Now everything has changed. The path is being cleared as we walk along it.

'Language, thus delivered into its own freedom, can be concerned solely with itself' (Heidegger 1959: 131). The bond that binds the elements of language is concerned with freedom. What sort of thing does this make language? Does it make it something that is concerned only with itself? No,

> language does not insist upon itself alone in the sense of a purely self-seeking, all oblivious self-admiration. As Saying, the nature of language is appropriating showing which disregards precisely itself, in order to free that which is shown, to authentic appearance. (Heidegger 1959: 131)

Language disregards itself so that it can free what it shows. Language is free, but this freedom is the freedom to show what is shown. To do this, it must disregard itself. This is why it is difficult for language to show itself or to be understood.

> Language, which speaks by saying, is concerned that our speaking, in listening to the unspoken, corresponds to what is said. Thus silence, too, which is often regarded as the source of speaking, is itself already a corresponding. Silence corresponds to the soundless tolling of the stillness of appropriating-showing Saying. As Showing, Saying, which consists in the appropriation, is the most proper mode of Appropriating. Appropriating is by way of saying. Accordingly, language always speaks according to the mode in which the appropriation as such reveals or withdraws. (Heidegger 1959: 131)

2.10 Language and poetry

Given this account of language, how are we to understand poetry and its relation to language? Heidegger confers language with a rich and active role in human affairs; it distinguishes humans from animals. Humankind is defined by its ability to attest to his own existence, and it is only language that makes this possible. Heidegger's engagement with poetry, specifically the poetry of Hölderlin, dates from around the same time as 'The Origin'. In a lecture series delivered in Rome and concerning poetry, which was subsequently published in translation as 'Hölderlin and the Essence of Poetry', Heidegger emphasizes the importance of language telling us it is also 'the most dangerous of goods' (Heidegger 2000: 55) in that it 'first creates the possibility of danger' (Heidegger 2000: 55). Heidegger's account of language is incomplete without reference to poetry. Language is the most dangerous good because 'it is only by virtue of language that man is exposed to something manifest' (Heidegger 2000: 55). Language manifests beings and preserves them, and this happens most authentically 'in the linguistic work' (Heidegger 2000: 55). In this way, poetry has a particular role in this making manifest of beings. Such a view is obviously contrary to aesthetic accounts of poetry, which presuppose an account of language where language, including poetry, refers to a pre-existing reality. In aesthetic accounts, poetic language is distinguished from everyday language in terms of its aesthetic qualities, such as beauty, or by its use of tropes such as metaphor. Heidegger's accounts of language suggest a complex relationship between language and poetry. As we have already seen, it is a feature of Heidegger's account that language does not manifest beings in a uniform way. Language can be authentic or inauthentic, essential or inessential.

As we saw in the previous chapter, Heidegger distinguishes between hearsay, idle talk, curiosity and ambiguity in *Being in Time*. These categories demonstrate different ways that language is related to truth or the different modes of being in truth. In later work, Heidegger's focus turns to poetry. Great poetry, especially the poetry of Hölderlin, is considered the most essential use of language. Therefore, it is possible to roughly sketch a hierarchy of language use, where Hölderlin's poetry occupies the very highest position, as it is an essential use of language. In fact, Heidegger uses a sequence of fragments from Hölderlin to show the relationship between poetry, language and truth. Great poetry unconceals essential truth; thus, Heidegger's philosophical explanation relies upon and must begin with poetry in order to gain access to this truth.

Hölderlin is the highest source of truth for 'mortals', but Hölderlin is himself listening to something higher. Quoting one fragment, Heidegger claims that 'the first fruits are not for mortals . . . they belong to the Gods' (Heidegger 2000: 55). This first fruit of language is the most pure or essential unconcealment of being;[1] it is beyond human. We can, perhaps, understand it in terms of the categorial saturation of reality or in terms of the unspoken from which the spoken emerges. What is clear is that it is difficult to describe this pure unconcealment without recourse to metaphorical language. We can say, however, that it is related to the manner in which things are unconcealed and, thus, to Being. Below this, in our hierarchy, there is Hölderlin.

Hölderlin is the poet's poet because his poetry concerns poetry itself. For this reason, it is the most essential language use available to 'we moderns'. Poetry concerning poetry deals with the unconcealment of Being rather than just of particular beings; it concerns the unconcealment of language itself. We are told that '[w]hat supports and dominates beings as a whole must come into the open' (Heidegger 2000: 58). The more essential the language, the more it resists the inherent tendency to conceal the unconcealment itself. 'The poet names the gods and names all things with respect to what they are' (Heidegger 2000: 59). It is clear that this account is far removed from any view of language that links words to a pre-existing, pre-known reality or pre-manifested reality. It is the essential word of the poet that 'first nominates the beings as what they are' (Heidegger 2000: 59). Things become known as beings; it is in this naming that they become manifest. Language is inherently creative, but creative, in this context, goes far beyond what we usually mean by the term; it is the 'how reality is manifested' that is created. '[T]he essence of things can never be calculated and derived from what is present at hand, they must be freely created, posited, and bestowed. Such a free bestowal is a founding' (Heidegger 2000: 59). Poetry founds the manifestness of beings, but in this, it does not simply conjure up beings; instead, it responds to the pure unconcealment that Hölderlin calls the first fruit.

Below the level of great poetry are progressively less essential uses of language; at these levels, the manner of language's unconcealment is also increasingly concealed, though the subject matter is generally shown in some relation to truth. Finally, at the bottom of the scale, we find the realm of the common and deception, where the things themselves are concealed or shown in the mode of hearsay. Somewhere in the middle of this scale is the sort of language used in this book. This language serves as an adequate vehicle of meaning. It communicates in such a way that the ideas presented are allowed to come forward. It is the very withdrawal of language that facilitates this coming forward. Because of this, this language is not essential because it does not bring language itself into the open, but neither is it completely inessential to the point that it deceives or brings 'non-beings' into the open.

However, it is not always clear to us whether a given piece of language is essential or not. At every level of the hierarchy, there is the possibility of being deceived. 'The pure and the common are both equally something said. The word as word never offers any immediate guarantee as to whether it is an essential word or a deception' (Heidegger 2000: 55). However, because the most essential use of language is poetic, we read the nature of language from poetry and not the other way around. Despite this, we must acknowledge that even poetic language contains within it the tendency to deceive that is inherent to the structure of language. As in the account of truth in the previous chapter, there is no sure or final way to arbitrate between truth and falsity. Language can both reveal and reveal in the mode of deception, but there is nothing accessible to us 'beyond' language that allows us to check or measure in the sense of a correspondence with an already manifest reality.

Heidegger relates language to metaphysics, and he wants to show how great poetry uses language without falling into the objectifying tendencies that he claims are inherent within metaphysics. Heidegger's interest in poetry is primarily philosophical; that is, he is concerned with how poetry discloses something essential about human reality rather than poetry criticism per se. As we have seen, the turn in Heidegger's thought is a turn towards language, especially poetic language. Commentators differ about how to characterize the turn. Some, such as Richardson (1967) see it as demarcating two entirely different projects, while others, such as Sheehan (2014), see a continuation and development between the earlier and later works. Notwithstanding these different approaches, it is clear, in the later work, Heidegger abandons the methodological approach of *Being and Time* with its focus on formal indication and moves towards poetry. While a methodological comparison between the early and later Heidegger is beyond what we can accomplish here, it is worth noting that as Dan Dahlstrom points out, 'the obvious similarities between Heidegger's characterisation of philosophical concepts as "formal indications" and the nature of certain artistic compositions. Much as in a script or a score-in contrast to a sketch-something is expressed or formulated but in such a way that what it is can only be realised by being performed' (Dahlstrom 1994: 790). Babette Babich notes, 'in his closing reflections in *Introduction to Metaphysics* where he tells us that *Being and Time* is no book but rather a task to be fulfilled' (Babich 2003: 163). Babich sees this as evidence of continuity between the early and later Heidegger.

The formal indications of *Being and Time* represent a methodological attempt to overcome the objectifying tendencies of science, where 'science' is broadly construed as a body of knowledge which explains some aspects of reality in terms of theoretical assertions. Dahlstrom maintains, '[s]uch assertions are central to the way that a science entertains and investigates its objects. It does not matter whether the science be mathematics or theology, physics or psychology, or whether it be theoretical or practical' (Dahlstrom 1994: 778). Formal indications differ from the theoretical assertions of traditional sciences in two main ways. First, they are *provisional* in that they point towards an understanding that has to be carried out by the reader herself. 'Thus, *Sein und Zeit* is not the depiction of some fact (*Sachverhalt*), but rather an indication of a way of approaching what "to be" means' (Dahlstrom 1994: 782). Second, they 'invert the normal perspective and way of posing questions, namely, away from particular beings toward the generally unspoken and unexamined horizon within which they are respectively encountered and have the manner of being that they do' (Dahlstrom 1994: 786). In this way, formal indications are concerned with what is formally indicated *and* the manner in which it comes to be and, in this way, they resist the objectifying tendency of scientific language particularly and language generally. '[W]hat is "formally indicated or signalled" is not given as something already complete and understandable through comparison, contrast, and classification; instead, what is "formally indicated" is understandable only insofar as the philosopher performs or carries out some activity himself' (Dahlstrom 1994: 784).

One way to understand the difference between the methodology of formal indications in *Being and Time* and the use of poetic language in the later work is to see the later works as a direct performance rather than as a 'score' to be performed by the reader. If we accept this, the difference between the earlier and the later works is that the earlier works provide a score, whereas the later works are a performance. As we have seen, in the later works, we actually accompany Heidegger on a path towards our destination, which is language. To understand language, we must have an experience with it, and Heidegger guides us towards this experience by providing a sequence of 'guidewords'. If this journey is successful, we reach the destination, along with Heidegger. Working backwards, the shift from formal indications to poetic language can be viewed as a metaphor, allowing us to see what is unique about poetry as an art form. The poem allows the reader or listener to inhabit the poem's subject matter directly. A poem is not a description of an experience or something ready-to-hand, but rather it is the experience. We could argue that what is unique is, in fact, poetry's immediacy. I, the reader or listener, am brought along on an experience. Though it is not my experience, the poem allows me direct access to the experience of the poet.

The role of the reader in this account is crucial. As we saw in Chapter 1, great art is preserved. We can say that great poetry is a founding that is preserved. But because being and the essence of things can never be calculated and derived from what is present at hand, they must be freely created, posited and bestowed. Such a free bestowal is a founding. A significant consequence of this is that Heidegger's account is not set in stone. As we will see in the last three chapters, poetry's founding ability is subject to the metaphysical tendencies of the time. In our time, this is the influence of technology. Heidegger shows that the manner in which language and truth are related plays a role in determining metaphysics. For example, in the *Contributions*, we are told, 'all essential titles have become impossible on account of the exhaustion of every basic word and the destruction of the genuine relation to words' (Heidegger 2012: 5).

2.11 Conclusion

For now, we can note that for the later Heidegger, language, especially poetic language, is granted a significance it is denied in other accounts, which tend to view language as a system of signs and signifiers. At the heart of Heidegger's account is the idea that freedom is the basis of language. Language disregards itself to free what is shown. In this disregard of itself, language can show in many ways. It has the freedom to be inauthentic or inessential. Thus, language can actually function as it is held to within conventional accounts of language, given the metaphysical positions that underpin them. If we understand language as something in correspondence with a pre-manifest reality, then language can be inauthentically understood in this way. This notion chimes with Heidegger's critique of scientific evidence in the previous chapter. Heidegger maintains that there can be no privileged perception to which our scientific propositions refer; that is, there is no substantial difference between the proposition being tested and the proposition it is tested against. However, science proceeds precisely by holding that there is a difference. In the same way, philosophers of language can maintain that language refers to a pre-manifest reality and, given the freedom of language, language can be that which does exactly this. However, if we are to take Heidegger seriously, then we must accept that this prior reality only becomes manifest through language. In this way, metaphysics 'decides' how language is understood, and language decides how metaphysics is understood. If we understand language, as a collection of signs that relate to a pre-existing reality, then poetry is not linked to the essence of language and it becomes at best trivial and at worst a distortion of language. Another way to examine this territory is to consider the metaphorical, which is what we will do in the next chapter.

3

Metaphor

3.1 Introduction: Philosophy and metaphor

As we saw in the previous chapter, For Heidegger, an understanding of language presupposes an understanding of poetry because great poetry is the most authentic use of language; thus, it is the most exemplary language use. We contrasted this with aesthetic view, which tends to view poetry as a sort of deviation from everyday language. From this perspective, poetry is language that is made more beautiful by the use of metaphor and other tropes. The critical force of Heidegger's account of language is most clearly demonstrated in his understanding of metaphor. Rather than viewing metaphor as a decorative flourish to everyday language, Heidegger sees it as the line that demarcates the literal and the figurative and, therefore, the very engine of metaphysics. In this way, Heidegger's account stands in stark opposition to some contemporaneous accounts of metaphor, which viewed metaphor as dispensable. Indeed, in the early twentieth century, the logical atomists attempted to create a pure, literal language by ridding natural languages of metaphor. However, the failure of this project has meant that analytic philosophy has had little choice but to make peace with metaphor. Max Black's seminal 1969 article 'Metaphor' is one expression of this peace. Black replaces the dominant substitution and comparison views with an interactive view.

The substitution and comparison views are consistent with the positivist view that privileges literal language. The substitution view holds that a metaphorical expression is a substitute for some literal term. The meaning of the expression can be grasped by switching back the figurative term for the literal one. As Black points out, the substitution view regards the metaphor as a sort of puzzle, which is solved once the literal meaning is grasped (Black 1955: 280). From the substitution view, the metaphor is used for one of two reasons. The first is stylistic, and the second catachresis, where a metaphorical term is introduced to make up for a gap in language.

The comparison view, generally traced back to Aristotle, can be seen as a special case of the substitution view (Black 1955: 283). It also holds that a literal term is swapped for a metaphorical one, but this view attempts to explain how the two terms are related. In this way, it provides a sort of rule for understanding metaphor. The two terms are linked to each other in that they are similar or analogous to each other. When we read 'Richard is a lion', we take it to mean that Richard is a lion (in that he is brave). The bracketed words are implied but not stated by the metaphor, so the comparison view can be seen as providing a sort of rule to solve the metaphorical puzzle. In both these views, the metaphor is essentially dispensable because a literal translation can always be found except, perhaps, in cases of catachresis. Black's interactive view holds that metaphors are not 'props for feeble minds', they cannot be paraphrased away, and in the case of strong metaphors, they are indispensable. Black concedes something to the mystery of metaphor. He holds that we cannot say in advance what the effect of the metaphor will be; we cannot predict or control the interaction of the two domains. However, the literal/figurative distinction that underlies metaphor is still accepted. So, while metaphor enjoys a philosophical revival, it stays located squarely in the realm of the figurative. For example, philosophers of science may accept that scientific models are metaphoric, but they tend to confine this metaphoricity to the realm of discovery. Metaphorical models begin as imaginary devices but advance towards ontological commitment once tested. Outside the realm of science, we can think of this in terms of 'dead' and 'live' metaphors. Once a metaphor 'dies', it becomes somehow literal, thus maintaining the literal/figurative distinction, albeit in a more ambiguous way. However, if live metaphors can die and become literal, and metaphoric models can advance towards ontological commitment, the literal/figurative distinction becomes problematic. The severity of this problem varies according to the theorist considered. We are left with a situation where, even in analytic philosophy, the conceptual foundations of metaphor are continually challenged, yet the concept of metaphor remains meaningful.

The link between metaphor and poetry is obvious, and their fortunes have been linked throughout the history of Western philosophy. They have fallen in and out of favour together. When the philosophical wind turns against poetry, it also tends to turn against metaphor. While Heidegger's writing on language is extensive, his entire output on metaphor amounts to little more than a few paragraphs. However, these paragraphs are the focus of considerable attention because what is a stake is the literal/figurative distinction, which is a central tenant of most accounts of language. Heidegger's casual dismissal of metaphor as metaphysics is a strong critique of the division between literal and figurative language. If Heidegger's critique holds, poetry loses much of the metaphysical baggage it has picked up along the way. If there are no grounds to privilege literal language, then we cannot dismiss poetry as merely a decorative use of language.

What is more, Heidegger's dismissal of metaphor is not a complete abandonment of the term. He acknowledges that even if we argue against the literal/figurative distinction, it can still make sense to talk of metaphor. It is his contention that we can analyse bad poetry in terms of metaphor. A bad poet stays within the metaphysical framework, and a great poet transcends it. Heidegger acknowledges that for the most part, poetry is trapped within a metaphysical prison, which prevents the Saying of truth. Thus, there is a criterion for poetry implicit in Heidegger's account of metaphor.

3.2 Heidegger's dismissal of metaphor

Heidegger's most comprehensive treatment of metaphor is found in lecture 8 of the 1955–6 lecture series, translated into English as the Principle of Reason (Heidegger 1996). This account is embedded in a discussion about how Leibniz's Principle of Reason demands grounds or reasons for states of affairs. Heidegger restates the principle in terms of why questions and explanations. A 'why' poses a question, and a 'because' delivers a reason or a ground. If the principle of reason is foundational, then this 'why/because' structure shows us something fundamental about the nature of human cognition. Despite the philosophical import of this discussion, Heidegger immediately points to a poetic example from Angelus Silesius, which seems to contradict this cognitive architecture. The very fact that Heidegger sees a line of poetry as a counter-example to Leibniz's Principle of Reason already smacks of the metaphorical. The discussion advances until Heidegger comes to the point that 'thinking is a listening that brings something into view' (Heidegger 1996: 47). Although this is by no means the first metaphor in the text, it is this one that Heidegger comments on in terms of its metaphorical status.

> Yet we are quick on the draw in explaining that thinking can be called a hearing and seeing only in a figurative sense. No doubt. What one listens to and brings into view in thinking cannot be heard with our ears nor seen with our eyes. It is not perceivable by our sense organs. If we take thinking to be a sort of hearing and seeing, then sensible hearing and seeing is taken up and over into the realm of nonsensible perception, that is, of thinking. In Greek such transposing is called μεταφέρειν. The language of the scholar's names such a carrying over 'metaphor.' So, thinking may be called a hearing and a listening, a viewing and a bringing into view only in a metaphorical, figurative sense. Who says, 'may' here? Those who assert that hearing with the ears and seeing with the eyes is genuine hearing and seeing. (Heidegger 1996: 47)

Heidegger's denial of metaphor is disarmingly simple. To consider the phrase 'thinking as a hearing' as a metaphor is to ignore that hearing is not simply a function of the ear. 'Of course, we hear through the ear, but not with the ear' (Heidegger 1996: 47). As Heidegger points out, even a deaf person can hear. It is not our ears that hear 'the titmouse or the lark' (Heidegger 1996: 47). Similarly, it is not the eyes that see 'Apollo in the statue of a young man' (Heidegger 1996: 48). This seemingly innocuous little passage amounts to a powerful attempt to overturn one of the central tenets of Western philosophy. Heidegger's discussion of the 'thinking metaphor' attempts to illustrate the artificiality of any literal/figurative distinction.

The 'thinking metaphor' demonstrates the artificiality of splitting language into sensuous or nonsensuous realms. However, it is not this structural feature of metaphor that Heidegger concentrates on initially. Metaphor is also characterized in terms of the similarity or 'likeness' between the two realms joined in the metaphor. 'There was a thought familiar to the old Greek thinkers, a thought that one all too crudely portrays thus: like is only known through like. What is meant is that what speaks to us only becomes perceivable through our response' (Heidegger 1996: 48). Thus, we can isolate two features of metaphor that are salient to Heidegger's account. First, a metaphor involves a transposing between two categories of language and second, it involves some sort of structural similarity. This structural similarity becomes known through our response to it. Heidegger quotes a segment of poetry that Goethe credits to an 'old mystic writer' in his Theory of Colours (Goethe 1840: xxxix).

> If the eye were not sunny,
> how could we perceive the light? (translation from open access source)

Heidegger is hinting towards another understanding of metaphor that is obfuscated for us by the need to prioritize one part of language over another. 'It seems', we are told, 'that up till today we have not yet sufficiently pondered what the sunliness of the eye consists of' (Heidegger 1996: 48). But given the seeming metaphorical saturation of Heidegger's own text and his complete rejection of the sensible/nonsensible distinction, we see that Heidegger intends to make up for this deficit. Heidegger's rejection of metaphor is a rejection of the distinction between the sensible and the nonsensible, but also the way in which we understand or characterize metaphors. In the usual understanding, it is precisely instances of metaphor that demarcate the boundaries between the sensible and the nonsensible or the literal and the figurative. It is the very act of categorizing a statement as a metaphor that allows us to decide what is figurative and, therefore, what is literal. This notion, and thus the importance of being able to classify some statements as metaphorical, is central to metaphysics.

> The idea of 'transposing' and of metaphor is based upon the distinguishing, if not the complete separation, of the sensible and the nonsensible as two realms that subsist on their own. The setting up of this partition between the

sensible and the nonsensible, between the physical and nonphysical is the basic trait of what is called metaphysics and which normatively determines Western thinking. Metaphysics loses the rank of the normative mode of thinking when one gains the insight that the above-mentioned partitioning of the sensible and the nonsensible is insufficient. (Heidegger 1996: 48)

According to Heidegger, without the sensible/nonsensible distinction, the statement 'thinking is a listening' is just as true as the statement 'thinking is the activity of using your mind to consider something', which is how thinking is defined in the *Cambridge Dictionary*.

The fear, for many philosophers, is that without some way of distinguishing between these statements, we cannot defend rationality from poetry or nonsense. Heidegger is telling us that there is nothing qualitatively different between listening and thinking. If we see listening as a sensible mode that allows us to hear and then view thinking as a separate faculty, which does not have direct access to the sensible world, we are simply wrong. We do not hear with our ears or see with our eyes. '*We* hear, not the ear' (Heidegger 1996: 47). But for Heidegger, his discussion of 'thinking metaphor' is enough to challenge an entire history of metaphysics, but of course, the question of thinking is seriously contested within this tradition. While it may be reasonable to claim that thinking is a hearing, what can we say about more obviously poetic incidences of metaphor? Language is 'the flower of the mouth' (Heidegger 1959: 99), Heidegger tells us, quoting Hölderlin's *Germania* in the *Nature of Language*. Again, Heidegger claims we cannot write this off as a metaphor; to do so, he tells us, would be to stay bogged down in metaphysics. If language, especially poetic language, speaks being, then there can be no important distinction between literal and figurative language. Heidegger claims that the phrase 'language is the flower of the mouth' is superior, in terms of truth disclosure, to a scientific definition because the scientific definition objectifies language; rendering it as something present-at-hand, whereas Hölderlin's poetic utterance speaks the being of language as it is prior to any attempts to objectify it. Theoretical or scientific propositions relating to language have already removed us from our direct or initial experience of the topic under consideration. In the first instance, language is not an object to a subject; it is not something ready-to-hand. To say something true about language, that is, to speak its being, means we must get beyond the distinctions of metaphysics. Metaphysics conceals language, but as we saw in the previous chapter, this concealment is also a feature of language itself. But Hölderlin's poetic phrase allows us to approach something about the being or the essence of language: poetry can approach the unconcealment of language.

Without the distinctions of metaphysics, we perhaps, lose the sense of the metaphorical term, in this case, 'flower'. Hölderlin's poetic clause may be true in an alethic sense, but to see this clause as equal or even superior to the statements of science might erode the sense of what a flower is. In this way, a flower becomes anything that blooms. However, language tends to operate like this anyway, both in poetry and in everyday language. For example, it makes perfect sense to say of a pregnant woman, 'she is blooming'.

3.3 Metaphor and poetic greatness

When Hölderlin calls language the flower of the mouth, he uses the term 'flower' in a non-metaphoric way. If we agree with Heidegger that there is no transposing, can we still recognize the phrase as a metaphor? Even in the face of a complete dissolution of the sensible/nonsensible divide, we still recognize 'flower of the mouth' as an incidence of metaphor. Heidegger gives us one way to make sense of this situation. In the work of Hölderlin, the idea that language is the flower of the mouth is not metaphoric because there is no linguistic boundary for him to cross. The phrase 'words, like flowers' is not metaphorical but, rather, Heidegger tells us, 'the word is given back into the keeping of the source of its being' (Heidegger 1982: 100). When we read such a phrase, we are called upon to hear it authentically. The phrase speaks the being of language. What is required to understand it is the 'gentle force of the singular and innocent capacity to hear'.

Furthermore, as Gottfried Benn suggests, the phrase is not a 'creative transformation' that 'is not a primary statement' (Heidegger 1982: 100). However, we can still recognize the distinction between primary and secondary statements in the works of lesser poets. While it is inappropriate to talk about metaphor in relation to Hölderlin's poetry, it is a valid tool in the analysis of lesser poetry. A lesser poet does not speak being; that is, she does not use essential language but instead remains within the linguistic framework imposed on her. Thus, Heidegger proposes a two-tier metaphor account where good poetry transcends the arbitrary divisions of language, and bad poetry is trapped within them.

In this way, the question of poetic greatness becomes an ontological one. A great poet is not constrained by, or does not recognize, received metaphysical categories that would prevent the speaking of Being. As we have seen, when Hölderlin describes language as a flower, he is unconcealing something of the essence of language. Such a poetic phrase cannot be fully grasped from within metaphysics because, as we have seen, metaphysics makes the nature of language difficult to grasp at best and at worst as something ready-to-hand. However, lesser poets work within this metaphysical framework, and it is appropriate to recognize instances of metaphors within their work because this work operates within the parameters set by metaphysics.

We must note here that when we use the terms 'greatness' and 'less than great', we mean it solely in terms of Heidegger's metaphysical reading. When we say that a poem is less than great in this sense, it is not to be understood as a pejorative judgement. A poem that 'fails' to be great here is one that operates within metaphysics without challenging it. This specialized notion of greatness in no way means that works that do not achieve greatness, in this ontological sense, are without value. As we will see in Chapter 5, great art is constitutive of the culture in which it is valued. An account of such works does not exhaust what we generally refer to when we speak of art. In fact such works represent a small subset of what we commonly term art. However, this subset is what Heidegger refers to when he speaks of great art.

3.4 Heidegger's metaphoricity

As we have seen, even if we agree with Heidegger that language cannot be divided into categories of primary and secondary meaning, we still recognize incidences of metaphor. Indeed, much of the secondary literature revolves around how the question of how to categorize Heidegger's own 'metaphors' given his rejection of the concept. There is an apparent tension between the fact that much of Heidegger's work, especially the later work, is so seemingly metaphorical and his almost desultory dismissal of the concept. Derrida, for example, suggests that 'the metaphoric power of the Heideggerian text is richer, more determinant than his thesis on metaphor' (Nowell Smith 2013: 103). What can we say about Heidegger's metaphors now that the concept has been so thoroughly rejected as metaphysical? Derrida continues to speak about the 'metaphoricity' of Heidegger's work, and other theorists, such as Greisch (1987), Ricoeur (1977) and Casenave (1982), have attempted to maintain a non-metaphysical concept of metaphor. These attempts all share an assumption that Heidegger's text is, in fact, metaphorical. But for Heidegger, the problem is not the use of metaphors in a poem or a philosophical text but rather their characterization as metaphors. It is this characterization that prevents us from hearing the text's saying. Heidegger is particularly concerned with our theoretical treatment of metaphors. However, the fact that most theorists insist on continuing to discuss the metaphoricity of Heidegger's work is either because they still need a label for the instances of the trope or because they reject the notion that Heidegger has discovered a language that 'speaks being' in a way that is beyond the scope of metaphysical language. Stellardi, for example, claims, 'Heidegger's text is overrun by metaphor. It does not control it: Expelled, metaphor comes back, uninvited, all the time, which would explain the occasional reaction, at times almost violent, of the author and master' (Nowell Smith 2013: 105). It is perhaps the case that Heidegger fails to overcome metaphysics, but this does not mean that the attempt is wrong-headed, only that it is difficult or perhaps impossible. But despite all this, it still makes sense to speak of metaphors even if we accept Heidegger's critique of metaphysics and his insistence that we understand metaphor (and metaphysics) in terms of a sensible/nonsensible divide rather than in terms of the more accepted literal/figurative divide. In the next section, we shall ask how this insistence on the sensible impacts Heidegger's account of metaphor.

3.5 Sensible/nonsensible versus literal/figurative

The analysis of metaphor involves the transposing of something between two realms that are, in principle, separable. Heidegger says,

> The idea of 'transposing' and of metaphor is based upon the distinguishing, if not the complete separation, of the sensible and the nonsensible, between the physical and nonphysical is a basic trait of what is called metaphysics. (Heidegger 1996: 48)

Heidegger is clear; the distinction here is between the physical and the nonphysical. However, one possible line of argument against Heidegger's account of metaphor rests on his insistence on the sensible/nonsensible divide rather than the more usual literal/figurative divide. These distinctions are not the same, and it is worth investigating the effects of their difference on Heidegger's account. If it is the case that the sensible/nonsensible distinction can be viewed as a particularly rigid version of the literal/figurative divides, we can ask what effect this has on Heidegger's account of metaphor, especially in the face of contemporary accounts. As we have seen, metaphors for theorists such as Black are not simply decorative flourishes that can be paraphrased away. In this way, Black's account opened the door for a revival of interest in metaphor in modern philosophy, especially within the philosophy of science. He was one of the first theorists to acknowledge the metaphorical nature of scientific models (Black 2019). Since then, theorists such as Stahl (1987) and Jones (1982) in the case of physics, and Mirowski (1989) and McCloskey (1985) in the case of economics have all pointed to the metaphorical nature of science. However, these accounts are all still based on a literal/figurative distinction. Even when theorists such as McCloskey situate all science within the realm of the figurative. What becomes clear is that the literal/figurative divide cannot be understood strictly in terms of the sensible, as Heidegger insists. For theorists like Black, the metaphoric element of science is confined to the logic of discovery; metaphorical models advance towards ontological commitment when they are tested. Once a model is successfully brought before the bar of experience, it is no longer a figurative creation; it becomes a part of our understanding of reality: it becomes literal. However, it is, perhaps, more problematic to say the nonsensuous becomes sensuous. In this way, the sensuous/nonsensous is a particularly strong characterization of the literal/figurative divide, and few analytic philosophers would now hope or want to maintain such a distinction.

Furthermore, even if we fully accept the impossibility of demarcating between the sensuous and the nonsensuous, we can still recognize metaphors in terms of novelty. A distinction between conventional and non-conventional language use is enough to provide us with a divide over which the metaphor transposes. If we accept this, Heidegger's critique of metaphor becomes little more than the demand that great poetry uses original language. In fact, it is difficult to imagine a situation where we cannot recognize a metaphor as an instance of novel language. Nowell Smith (Nowell Smith 2013: 106) suggests Heidegger himself uses the term 'literal' in this way. In *The Letter on Humanism*, he suggests that 'bringing to language' within the phrase, 'thinking in its saying merely brings the unspoken word of being to language' (Nowell Smith 2013: 106), should be taken literally. Nowell Smith maintains that rather than seeing this as a slip into the metaphysics that Heidegger is trying to avoid, we should see this use of 'literal' as referring to 'a system of conventional signs' rather than 'a movement from originary openness to speech'. If we view the literal/figurative distinction in terms of conventional/unconventional language, as Nowell Smith claims Heidegger does in this instance, does his critique of metaphor still work?

If we say a metaphor is simply a transposing between two linguistic categories, we will have all we need to recognize an instance of metaphor. Heidegger's strong contention that these categories are essentially metaphysical, perhaps, makes a claim beyond what is necessary. While, it may be the case that Heidegger's categories explain some metaphors, there remains the possibility of transposing between other linguistic categories. However, as we saw in the account of evidence in Chapter 1, Heidegger denies that any segment of language can be privileged or considered more or less rational.

What is at stake is the openness of language and thinking. Heidegger is certainly against a rigidity of thought. Staying within some sort of literal/figurative framework means that thinking becomes stifled, preventing it from really getting to the matter under consideration. Poetry understood in terms of more or less rational segments of language will never be anything more than banal because it is prevented from its Saying. In this way, a metaphysical reading of a great poem can prevent its truth disclosure. A metaphysical reading of a great poem prevents its saying from being heard. As we know from Chapter 1, art happens in the relationship between the work and its preservers. It is impossible, therefore, from a Heideggerian perspective to understand the greatness of any work of art in isolation from its preservers. Greatness is found in the relationship between the work and its preservers. This greatness can be lost in a number of ways. A poet can write from within the received metaphysics, and such work does not have any potential to be great, but greatness is also something that an audience must be capable of preserving. As we have seen, the problem with a metaphysical reading is that it considers the figurative as less than rational. In this way, the saying of the poem is blocked. The poem may or may not have the potential to unconceal truth, but if it has this potential, this potential is thwarted by a metaphysical reading, which analyses the poem in terms of metaphor. Even the potential of a great text can be destroyed in the reading or interpretation. Nowell Smith points out that,

> Anaximander's saying, Theophrastus complains, has transgressed the boundary between the conceptual boundaries of two mutually incommensurate realms, . . . However, Heidegger counters, the boundary that Anaximander has transgressed was set up by Theophrastus himself: the saying itself admits of no such boundary, and thus 'no possibility of boundary transgression, no possibility of the illegitimate transfer of representation from one area to another.' (Nowell Smith 2013, 110)

In this passage, the responsibility for the distinction is put squarely on the reader. The saying itself may have the potential to 'speak being' perfectly well. If I say *X* is a metaphor, what I mean is that *X* expresses something in a strange way, but it is I who confers this strangeness onto the text and thus, I decide what is strange. This brings us back to the passage in *The Principle of Reason* where Heidegger asks, 'Who says, "may" here? Those who assert that hearing with the ears and seeing with the eyes is genuine hearing and seeing'

(Heidegger 1996: 47). The 'claim thinking is hearing' is entirely legible and only becomes metaphoric with recourse to a linguistic convention. While the traditional philosophical problem associated with metaphors would appear to be that they blur a line between sense and nonsense, what is really at stake is convention and the 'who' that defends it.

3.6 Metaphor in science and philosophy

Given Heidegger's account, we can understand the difference between great and less-than-great poetry in terms of metaphor. Great poems, such as those of Hölderlin's, cannot be understood in terms of metaphor. Whereas it is appropriate to comprehend lesser works in this way. The separation of language that is necessary to the concept of metaphor is retained in the majority of poetry. Such a view of poetic metaphor seems to map onto a Kuhnian account of science. Thomas Kuhn's (1970) contribution to the philosophy of science was to disrupt the positivist idea that science progressed by the accrual of new pieces of knowledge, which were added to an existing store. Ultimately, this progression was thought to bring science closer to the truth. However, Kuhn recognized that rather than this linear progression, the history of scientific development consists of stable periods of what he termed 'normal science', (1970: 10) punctuated with periods of 'extraordinary' or 'revolutionary' science. Kuhn characterizes normal science in terms of problem-solving, whereas periods of revolutionary science involve an entire restructuring of the scientific field in question. As a result, a question or a problem that was relevant in one period may no longer be relevant in another. A revolution marks a qualitative break in the theoretical understanding of a specific body of scientific knowledge. Revolutions can be brought about by a failure in the problem-solving activity of normal science, leading to a questioning of the entire theoretical paradigm. Kuhn highlights how a given scientific community relies on shared theoretical constructs and practices and how these can undergo transformations.

Like the great poet, the revolutionary scientist disregards the conventions of normal science and uses a metaphoric process to redescribe the scientific field in question. Once this revolution is accomplished, the paradigm changes entirely and research questions that were appropriate in the previous paradigm lose their relevance. Does this Kuhnian picture of scientific revolution with its relativistic worries mirror Heidegger's account of poetic metaphor? If not, what does Heidegger's account of metaphor offer us beyond this? As we saw earlier, metaphorical models only move towards ontological commitment after testing. In periods of Kuhnian revolutionary science, this is reversed. Now the ontological commitment comes first, and this is where relativism seeps into the picture. If our successful models are reflections of a pre-existing reality, then it becomes difficult to explain what happens in periods of revolutionary science. In Heidegger's account, no linguistic entity, be it a scientific model or a poem, reflects a pre-existing reality. As we saw in the previous chapter, language plays an active role in the disclosure of reality.

Language makes reality manifest. Great poetry uses language to make being manifest, but this manifesting is not merely a construction of the poet but a response to something beyond her that will become manifest. As we saw earlier, in *The Way to Language*, Heidegger says showing of language is not 'exclusively, or even decisively, the property of human activity' (Heidegger 1971: 123). Showing is also a 'self-showing appearance' (Heidegger 1971: 123). This self-showing appearance acts as a limit to metaphoric redescription. Speaking being is constrained by being itself. We preserve great poetry because we recognize its truth. This explains why we readily understand some poetic metaphors, even when they do violence to our linguistic conventions. However, the potential for this metaphoric redescription is not limitless.

Episodes of revolutionary science are extraordinary events: revolutions punctuate long periods of normal science, but this is not the case with poetry. Great poetry must consistently challenge the received metaphysics. There need be no period of normal poetry from which great poetry emerges. Linguistic conventions do not need to settle before they are upset. The poet's relationship to language seems to require a constant renewal, 'that is more original appropriation is needed in order for mortals to have a true beholding of something' (Heidegger 1996: 46). However, as we have seen, even cases of potentially great poetry can be misread; the greatness can also be lost with the reader. For Heidegger, the poem aims to break through banal images that act as placeholders for chunks of conventional semantic meaning. When we view the poem in terms of metaphors, we prevent this breaking through. We tame the poet's thinking when we consider the poem in terms of metaphor.

Related to this is the philosophical idea that the problem of metaphor is a problem of subjectivity. This problem can be understood by asking how a subjective metaphor can acquire objectivity, given its subjective basis or how a metaphor can create new yet appropriate meaning. Heidegger's account has been employed in this respect. For example, As Cazeaux points out, Ricoeur and Hausman draw upon Kantian ontology in different ways to solve the puzzle of new meaning. A Kantian solution relies on the schema with all its inherent difficulties. Cazeaux attempts to buttress the Kantian schema with recourse to Heidegger's account of time. 'The basic move which Heidegger makes to salvage Kant's notion of a schema is to emphasize the significance of time in the Critique' (Cazeaux 1995: 352). In this way, the transcendental object necessary for the unity of consciousness is considered a 'temporal action' that constitutes objectivity. While we can perhaps question Heidegger's dismissal of metaphor in terms of its grounding in a sensuous/nonsensuous distinction, its basis in terms of the alethic truth is harder to question. As we have seen, Cazeaux uses Heidegger's account to plug a hole in Kant's account. The question of how new meaning is created through metaphor can be understood within a framework of concealment and unconcealment. Metaphoric redescription involves both unconcealment and concealment, whether in the realm of science or art. The metaphor can create new meaning because it conceals prior meanings.

What is important for our purposes here is that language, for Heidegger, is to be understood in the way-making movement of appropriation rather than in terms of signified and signifier. Language is Saying as showing it 'yields the opening of the clearing in which present beings can persist and from which absent beings can depart while keeping their persistence in the withdrawal' (Heidegger 1971: 127). Way making cuts a path through the earth of concealment. There is no privileging of any category of language simply because there is no way to cut up language like this. The mystery often associated with metaphor results from the imposition of a metaphysics of presence on language.

3.7 Metaphor and contemporary poetry

Despite Heidegger's substantial influence, contemporary poetry criticism is still dominated by what we will, along with Heidegger, characterize as an aesthetic approach. This dominance of this approach becomes clear in terms of metaphor, which is still understood as figurative, almost without exception. In the rest of this book, I will argue that Heidegger's rich accounts of poetry and language make sense of contemporary poetic movements in ways that aesthetic accounts cannot. For our purposes, it will be sufficient to say that an aesthetic view of poetry criticism is any view which includes the idea that metaphors are a figurative trope. In this section, I will give a recent example of criticism that demonstrates this aesthetic view. Despite the dominance of aesthetics, in this respect, contemporary poetry can be characterized in terms of its novel and perhaps extreme use of metaphorical language. With recourse to several examples, I will sketch an account of metaphor within contemporary poetry. It is worth noting, however, that while Heidegger's account of poetic metaphor implies a criterion for poetry, I do not claim that we can use this to assess contemporary poems as either great or otherwise. However, it does give us a new way to understand contemporary poetic metaphor.

Rebecca Watts' recent and controversial article in PN Review (Watts 2018) ostensibly redraws the line between art and populism for the internet generation. This article is poetry criticism, written for a non-academic audience, and it is perhaps unfair to subject it to philosophical scrutiny. However, it demonstrates how the account of language promoted in the article and the one it critiques both depend on the literal/figurative distinction. I will show how Heidegger's view of language and metaphor provides a more illuminating way to view the language of the poets under consideration. Watts, a poet herself, critiques the rise of what she terms 'noble amateurs', which are described as 'a cohort of young female poets who the poetic establishment is currently lauding for their "honesty" and "accessibility"'. She is referring to poets such as Canadian Rupi Kaur, whose sales figures far exceed those of more traditional poets. However, the article's primary focus is two UK poets, Kate Tempest and, specifically,

Hollie McNish. In fact, the article was initially commissioned as a review of a collection by McNish.

Watts' critical characterization of the noble amateur is three-pronged. First, she notes that poets such as Kaur build their reputations on social media platforms, notably Instagram, before going on to substantial book sales. McNish and Tempest emerged from the Spoken Word scene in the UK, and both made significant use of YouTube Channels to promote their work. Watts points her finger squarely at the internet and social media with their 'deleterious effect on our attention spans and cognitive abilities' (Watts 2018). Poetry, according to Watts, has not escaped this widespread dumbing down. In the hands of the noble amateur poetry, she argues, has become nothing other than 'short-form communication', designed for the age of soundbites and Twitter. As with every other art form, in the contemporary world, poetry is now just another consumer product. Watts' second and perhaps most damning complaint concerns how both Tempest and McNish have been welcomed unreservedly into the poetry establishment in the UK. Both are published by Picador, and both have received the Ted Huges Award for New Work in Poetry.

Finally, and most pertinent here, Watts, critiques the noble amateur in terms of language use. She is not being unfair when she says the noble amateur's use of language is simplistic and clichéd. She quotes poet Don Paterson, who edits both Tempest and McNish, speaking about the appeal of McNish in terms of the 'direct connection with an audience' and the 'disarming honesty of the work'. Watts asks, 'When did honesty become a requirement – let alone the main requirement – of poetry?' (Watts 2018). McNish's work is very light on metaphor and image and Watts' describes it as merely an 'assemblage of words'. It uses everyday language without artifice, and thus it communicates clearly with its audience. Watts claims that it is not the work of a poet but rather that of a personality.

It is not my intention to defend McNish from Watts' fairly vitriolic attack, but I do want to make explicit the account of language that Watts' is working with. Watts' critique of McNish implies a particular characterization of poetic language. She sets up a distinction between poets who prioritize honesty and immediacy and others who prioritize craft. The noble amateur achieves honesty with non-poetic language. For example, she hardly uses metaphor, but when she does, she immediately falls into cliché. Traditional poets, however, augment non-poetic language with metaphor and other poetic tropes. For the sake of contrast, I will use Susan Millar DuMars, as an example of poet concerned with craft. Given this, we end up with an implicit distinction between honesty and immediacy on the one hand and craft on the other. While, on the face of it, this seems like an apt distinction, it implies an aesthetic understanding of both language generally and poetic language specifically.

So that we can see the difference, here are examples of how both poets use metaphor. First is a poem by McNish (2015). It is worth noting here that McNish is a spoken word poet, and the performative aspect is central to her poetry. On the other hand, Millar DuMars (2019) is undoubtedly, what is sometimes referred to as a page poet; her work is not performance-driven. Thus, it is important to bear in mind that we are not comparing like with like.

Cocoon

This is as close as I'll ever be to a butterfly
raincoat zipped up to my chin
for the half hour bike ride
to work

Hair bunned
at the back
to fit in the hood
helmet clipped tightly
– I am waterproof

Now pace reaches peak
the streets are attacked
Cold frosts the trees
but the sweat coats my back

until one minute left
I let myself go
cycling slow

as I unbutton clothes
jacket unzipped
helmet unclipped
from beneath
hood stripped from my forehead
hairband released

Hair ruffled with hands
to be free in the wind
body to elements
cool down my skin

At that moment
I open
and peel myself free

I feel as close to
a new butterfly
as I'll ever be

For the sake of contrast, the Millar DuMars poem (2019):

Near the End

Her face all bone and eyes.
She always looks surprised.
Sucks the air's marrow,
pushes beans around her plate.
I push words around
this page. Both have gone cold.

All this white space
is where we pause,
fight for breath.

As we can see, these poems use metaphor in very different ways. The cocoon/butterfly metaphor in the McNish poem is familiar to the point of cliché. It does not tell us anything new. In fact, we could argue that it is dead and may not even still function as a metaphor. If there is anything different about this use of the butterfly metaphor, it is that rather than being associated with some personal transformation, it is used to describe the action of loosening clothes while cycling and thus, it certainly remains squarely within a convention that uses the image of the butterfly emerging from its cocoon to stand in for some sort of human transformation. While the poem captures a feeling of exhilaration, which would be intensified in a performance of the poem by the poet, its use of metaphor remains within metaphysics.

In the second poem, there are a number of metaphors; for example, the air has 'marrow', words are pushed around the page and they have gone cold. These are fresh uses of language, intended to show things in a new light. While they may not make Heidegger's criterion of greatness, they are unexpected and yet true. We grasp what Millar DuMars means when she says 'Sucks the air's marrow'. For Watts' the difference between the two poems is that one uses metaphor in a clichéd way, whereas the other uses it in a skilled way. While this may seem like the right characterization, it does not seem right to say the first poem is more honest or immediate than the second.

To understand this, it is worth asking what immediacy means in this context. It seems fair to suggest that Watt uses the term to mean something like 'immediately graspable'; that is, she uses it to mean something akin to 'easily comprehensible'. This implies that poetry is a use of language which is less than immediately graspable. In this way, Watt's use of 'immediate' can be viewed as an aesthetic use of the term. The McNish poem is considered more immediate because of its reliance on everyday language. Thus, everyday language is considered more basic in some sense than poetic language. Poetic language is, therefore, seen to originate in everyday language. Aesthetic accounts understand the poem as a sort of distortion of common or everyday language; everyday language, which is distorted in order to make it more beautiful or to fit it into a form of some sort or another. From an aesthetic viewpoint, a poem is a piece of natural language that is augmented or to which aesthetic qualities are attached. Because everyday language already serves perfectly well as a vehicle of meaning, the process of making it into poetry, in some cases at least, impacts negatively on this ability to convey meaning adequately.

Such a view can be clearly contrasted with Heidegger's thought. For Heidegger, poetic language does not originate in everyday language; in fact, the opposite is true. When it is great, poetic language is a founding; thus, everyday language derives from it, rather than the other way around. As language moves down the scale, from its most essential use in the words of a great poem, towards deception, the tendency to objectify becomes more pronounced, and language itself recedes from view; rather than unconcealing truth, it represents the world as something present-at-hand. Below the level of the poetic, there is the tendency of language to objectify things and conceal itself. However, it is worth bearing in mind that this analysis does not preclude the possibility of a great poem that utilizes everyday or simple language or the possibility of poetic language that deceives. At every level of the scale, language has the possibility of being authentic or inauthentic. However, to be great art, a poem must unconceal truth and because truth requires an original appropriation, then the process of writing poetry is an undeniably 'metaphoric' process. To achieve a more original appropriation, the poet must work at the level of essence. From an aesthetic perspective, the essential always seems metaphoric because it inevitably redescribes reality or disrupts metaphysics as it is presented by the distinction between the literal and the figurative.

Thus, the McNish poem is only honest and immediate in the sense that it is an unambiguous description, in the first person, of an event which probably took place. If it is true, it is true in the simple sense of correspondence. Thus, it is true in the literal sense; the event described is simply a testimony of an actual occurrence. Even the use of the metaphor, if we consider it dead, barely interrupts the literal meaning of the poem. If poetic immediacy simply means a literal description of an actual event, then this poem is certainly immediate. However, from a Heideggerian perspective, the language of this poem is trapped entirely within metaphysics. Moreover, because of its banal content, it is an inessential use of language. Because of its use of ordinary, everyday language, it is, in fact, simply on the same level as everyday language. If we agree with Heidegger that poetic language is more essential than everyday language, we must concede that McNish's language discloses reality simply as everyday language does. In addition, if we view immediacy in terms of essentiality, then we have to concede that it is actually the Millar DuMars that is more immediate. We can also maintain that it is more honest because it resonates with something closer and less easily articulated than the McNish poem. The second poem says something for the first time. To be fair, Watts does not explicitly preclude the possibility of honesty and craft within the same poem, but her characterization implies that honesty and immediacy are perfectly achievable with everyday language and that the poet must take this raw material and craft it to make poetry. Given our examples, this seems wrong. The second poem cannot simply be seen as everyday language to which something additional has been added.

Watts acknowledges that the effect of the McNish poem

> is limited to recognition, which merely reinforces the reader or audience's sense of selfhood. As McNish and her critics agree, her fans are drawn to the poems by the themes – sex, relationships and perceived social inequalities – as well as by McNish's 'unpretentious' presentation, where unpretentious means abundant in expletives and unintimidating to anyone who considers ignorance a virtue. (Watts 2018)

The immediacy Watt ascribes to McNish's is simply recognition. This recognition is not of something new, but rather it is recognition of the already known, the already agreed upon. McNish mirrors the concerns of her public, and they, in turn, are gratified to see them aired in the public realm. In this way, the McNish poem must be seen as representation.

A great poem allows the reader or listener to inhabit the subject matter of the poem directly. A poem is not a description of an experience or something ready-to-hand, but rather it is the experience. We could argue that what is unique is, in fact, poetry's immediacy. I, the reader or listener, am brought along on an experience. Though it is not my experience, the poem allows me direct access to the experience of the poet. So, to use a vivid example, consider Louis MacNeice's 'Snow' (MacNeice 2016).

Snow

The room was suddenly rich and the great-bay window
Spawning snow and pink roses against it
Soundlessly collateral and incompatible:
World is suddener than we fancy it.

World is crazier and more of it than we think,
Incorrigibly plural. I peel and portion
A tangerine and spit the pips and feel
The drunkenness of things being various

And the fire flames with a bubbling sound for world
Is more spiteful and gay that one supposes –
On the tongue on the eyes on the ears in the palms of one's hands –
There is more than glass between the snow and the huge roses.

In this poem, the language departs entirely from everyday language, and yet we see the shared experience of poet and reader; we garner something of the essence of language as showing. It is fair to say this poem represents a more authentic showing than the McNish poem. It is not in the 'fallen' mode of semblance. The language of the poem does not objectify the experience. Rather the reader is brought along with the poet. In a way that is analogous with Heidegger's way to language, the language in this poem does not follow a pre-existing path; but instead, it makes its own way. Watt's implicit account of language, while it can be used to separate the McNish and the Millar DuMars poems, cannot fully account for the quality of the MacNeice poem. We cannot view the MacNeice poem as everyday language, which has been augmented by the skilful use of metaphor. Instead, it makes more sense to see it in terms of essential language. Despite this, we can still recognize and isolate instances of both figurative and literal language within the poem. However, just as Heidegger's way to language is, on first reading, an undoubtedly metaphorical journey, this path making necessarily transcends any literal/figurative distinction. The way to language is signposted by a series of seemingly metaphorical terms (design, language as showing, owning, (or appropriation) etc.), but these cannot be metaphorical in the sense we commonly understand the term. Because, as Heidegger points out, the concept of metaphor only makes sense in the face of a distinction or separation between the sensible and the nonsensible. Any such distinction implies a given or set path for language. Language, as a set of signs which signify, is a path or a set of paths linked to the sensible. We may deviate into the figurative from time to time, but to make any sense of this, we must get back on the 'real' path. In this way, we can subject the MacNeice poem to an aesthetic analysis, but to do so prevents the poem's showing; in fact, the poem becomes irrational. A Heideggerian analysis gets at what is happening in the poem in a way that an aesthetic account simply cannot.

In contemporary poetry, however, metaphor use often seems to run wild in a way that resists the aesthetic view. In many contemporary poems, the literal and figurative elements cannot be isolated. In cases like these, it does not make sense in terms of a sensible/nonsensible distinction. For example in the Ted Hughes poem Crows Undersong (1972), we find the following lines,

> She comes with the birth push
> Into eyelashes into nipples the fingertips
> She comes as far as blood and to the tips of hair
> She comes to the fringe of voice

We can claim it does not make sense to consider these lines as metaphorical. It would seem an impossible task to reverse the transposing from one realm to another. We cannot view such a poem in terms of a literal/figurative distinction. The poem can only be seen as nonsense by those who would defend the distinction. Yet the poem undoubtedly says something that could not have been expressed in more literal language. The use of metaphor in Hughes' poem prepares us for a movement in contemporary poetry, where it becomes difficult, if not impossible, to untangle the metaphoric content of the work. To illustrate this, consider this poem by John Shoptaw (2023).

Near Earth Object

> Unlike the monarch, though
> the asteroid also slipped
> quietly from its colony
> on its annular migration

between Jupiter and Mars,
enticed maybe by
our planetary pollen
as the monarch by my neighbor's
slender-leaved milkweed.
Unlike it even when
the fragrant Cretaceous
atmosphere meteorized
the airborne rock,
flaring it into what might
have looked to the horrid
triceratops like a monarch
ovipositing (had the butterfly
begun before the period
broke off). Not much like
the monarch I met when I
rushed out the door for the 79,
though the sulphurous dust
from the meteoric impact
off the Yucatán took flight
for all corners of the heavens
much the way the next
generation of monarchs
took wing from the milkweed
for their annual migration
to the west of the Yucatán,
and their unburdened mother
took her final flit
up my flagstone walkway,
froze and, hurtling
downward, impacted
my stunned peninsular
left foot. Less like
the monarch for all this,

the globe-clogging asteroid,
than like me, one of my kind,
bolting for the bus.
(reprinted with permission)

How are we to understand this poem in terms of metaphor? We can argue that an aesthetic account based on a literal/figurative divide cannot adequately grasp this poem. While it would seem reasonable to say this poem is metaphorical, it would be hard to define these metaphors in terms of separate linguistic categories. It is indeed difficult, if not impossible, to identify the metaphors in this poem from a comparison view of metaphor because it is hard to unpick this poem and say where exactly one thing stands in for another. The poem, for example, uses the motif or image of a butterfly, but it cannot be considered metaphorical in the sense that the metaphor is a puzzle which is solved when its meaning is understood in literal terms.

In fact, we can argue that this poem results from a deliberate dissolution of the literal/figurative divide. In the face of this dissolution, the poem can be seen as simply incomprehensible. For example, the poet Robin Robertson claims, '[t]he world of poetry is small and currently polarized: it is often either simplistic or incomprehensible' (Robertson 2018). He goes on to say, 'I find myself in the middle, vaguely appalled. I'm allergic to "light verse" because it seems a betrayal of the purpose of poetry. Equally, poetry that sets out to be deliberately opaque is betraying the purpose of language.' Without the ability to divide language into the literal and the figurative, poems like the Shoptaw poem can be considered at best as pretty nonsense and, at worst, a betrayal of the language.

As we have seen, for Heidegger, great poetry is not subject to metaphysics; thus, it cannot be understood in terms of figurative tropes. It is a necessary requirement of great poetry that it transcends the literal/figurative divide. However, it is not a sufficient condition for great poetry. For Heidegger, as we have seen, great poetry speaks Being. As we see in the examples of art used, by Heidegger, in 'The Origin', a great work is epoch-defining, and by this criterion, it is too early to say whether Shoptaw poem will be considered great, but what is the value of this work, given these Heideggerian considerations?

Poetry of this sort is now common, and it would seem reasonable to claim that the 'betrayal of language' we see here is actually a betrayal of the linguistic categories of metaphysics. Yet this betrayal does not always necessarily lead us to a speaking of Being.

While there are notable examples of poetry in this style, for example, Wallace Stevens' 'The Idea of Order at Key West' (Stevens 1990), there is certainly poetry of this type that transcends metaphysics but does not speak Being. This is a relatively contemporary movement, and it is interesting to ask what it says about language. From an extreme positivist viewpoint, such poetry can be considered as nothing more than nonsense. While such viewpoints are no longer in currency, it is still obviously possible to speak of a betrayal of language. The literal/figurative distinction is as central to metaphysics as the subject/object distinction; as we will see in the following chapters, an overcoming of these distinctions is an overcoming of metaphysics from a Heideggerian perspective. But there is also the possibility of the dissolution of these metaphysical dichotomies in technology, which is not an overcoming of metaphysics but, rather, a situation where both subjects and objects lose their significance and become standing reserve. In the following chapters, we will consider how technology allows these metaphysical binaries to be eroded without being overcome.

3.8 Conclusion

Heidegger's account of language implies a radically different understanding of metaphor. While the failure of the logical atomists to create a language free of metaphor forced philosophers to accept the inherently metaphorical nature of language, metaphors are still generally understood as a figurative trope. Heidegger, however, does not privilege any part of language, be it the literal or the sensuous. Thus his account still represents a challenge to many contemporary accounts of language and aesthetic accounts of poetry. What is at stake, for Heidegger, is the literal/figurative distinction itself. Obviously, the philosophical implications of this are significant. As we can see from Heidegger's own language use, it is precisely what is generally understood as metaphoric, which has the ability to challenge metaphysics. A great poem, like those of Hölderlin, discloses reality or speaks originary Being. In order to grasp reality in this way, we need a constantly fresh appropriation. A great poem discloses reality in an authentic way. A poem which fails to do this operates within the received metaphysics and can only objectify reality. Moreover, the great poem cannot be fully understood in terms of an aesthetic account of language because such an account deems this disclosure metaphoric, that is, as a deviation from literal language. From the perspective of the reader or critic, what is required to understand Hölderlin's speaking of Being is 'the gentle force of the singular and innocent capacity to hear' (Heidegger 1972: 101). The poem can fail either because the poet is trapped within metaphysics or because its readers do not possess the innocent capacity to hear.

It is possible to view some contemporary poetry in terms of the erosion of the literal/figurative divide. As we have seen, there is a trend within contemporary poetry that cannot be understood with respect to either distinct linguistic categories or in terms of a transposing between these categories. In fact, it would be impossible to 'solve' the metaphorical puzzles of a poem, such as 'Near Earth Object', by replacing metaphoric terms with literal ones. While it seems right to view this poem as metaphoric, an aesthetic view cannot adequately account for it. Leaving aside the question of greatness, we can see this poem, more fruitfully, as an attempt to transcend linguistic categories and as an attempt to speak being. However, a dissolution of the literal/figurative divide does not necessarily represent a transcending of these categories. It is possible to dissolve these categories and not speak being. In fact, it is not unfair to describe a great deal of contemporary poetry in this way. How are we to understand this tendency in contemporary poetry? As we shall see in the following chapters, technology can be viewed as an intensification of metaphysics, which erodes the binaries Heidegger associates with metaphysics without transcending them.

4

Technology

4.1 Introduction

Heidegger's account of technology comes in the later period of his writings, after 'The Origin', and it has to be considered in its own terms. Heidegger's characterization of metaphysics in the earlier works is rethought in the later works in the face of his engagement with technology. Technology, as Heidegger comes to understand it, is an understanding of being, which requires a new approach. Both language and art are fundamentally altered in an age of technology. As we have seen, language and art are understood by Heidegger in terms of truth disclosure. Technology is that which threatens the very unconcealment of language and art. This book aims to apply Heidegger's ontological analysis of truth, language and poetry to contemporary poetic movements. To do this, we must also understand technology from within this Heideggerian framework. Heidegger uses the term 'technology' in an ontologically broad way; that is, this account goes beyond a description of the development of technological devices to an understanding of the historical epoch in which we now live. Like language, technology is prior to us and holds sway over us. Ultimately, it is a way in which things are revealed to us or, simply put, how they are. In this way, technology is related to the truth-disclosing capabilities of language, including poetic language. As we will see, for Heidegger, technology negatively influences the possibility of poetic truth. This book is concerned with digital technology. Thus one question that arises immediately is whether Heidegger's account is still relevant, given that he died in the 1970s, just as digital technology began to come into its own. We will argue that his account still provides an appropriate framework by which to understand the digital age. Be this as it may, Heidegger's extensive influence on the philosophy of technology is undeniable.

Notwithstanding this influence, there is much debate within the literature on how to characterize and understand Heidegger's contribution. Some theorists describe Heidegger's account as technological determinism, where technology is understood as a historical force which both opens up and limits the range of possibilities for a historical people. Generally, determinism is contrasted with technological neutrality, the notion that technology is merely instrumental, exerting little or no substantive influence on humanity. Given the sudden ubiquity of handheld devices and internet technologies, it becomes increasingly difficult to play down the impact of technology in practically every aspect of our lives. This influence can be couched both in positive and negative terms. Negatively, there is a growing literature on addiction to various internet applications, including online role-playing games, online gambling or online pornography. For example, in 2013, Internet Gaming Disorder was classified as a particular problem in need of further study in the revised *Diagnostic and Statistical Manual of Mental Disorders* (Young 2017: 228). The benefits of internet technology are myriad, and while there is clearly no way back to a pre-internet society, Heidegger, writing before the onset of the digital, implores us to develop a 'free relation' to technology. This entreaty is perhaps significantly more urgent now than it was at the time of his death.

Given Heidegger's ontology of concealment and unconcealment, technology is, then, another mode of unconcealment; it is the way we understand being in the present age. Central to his account is the concept of *Gestell*, variously translated as 'enframing' or 'positionality'. For Heidegger, as we shall see, *Gestell* is the essence of technology. In this chapter, I will investigate the claim that Heidegger's account of technology as 'enframing' can be viewed as a deterministic view. Central to any such investigation is an understanding of Heidegger's epochal view of history, where an epoch is a historical period in which a particular understanding of being comes to dominate. Technology is, then, the current understanding of being.

Heidegger characterizes this epoch in a primarily negative way: technology is the epoch where being, including the human being, is understood, at the ontological level, merely as orderable stock or 'standing reserve' (*Bestand*). Heidegger is not the only theorist who points to technology's danger. Different commentators, often taking Heidegger as a starting point, characterize technology in various ways and prescribe different responses. In some accounts, such as Anders (Scollo 2017), the outlook is bleak, perhaps even beyond remedy. In others, such as Borgmann's (1992), there are different possibilities which may allow us to retrieve a more meaningful connection to human life. Heidegger himself asks us to develop a 'free relation' (Heidegger 1978: 311) to technology. By this, he means that by developing an understanding of technology, in its essence, we can ameliorate its negative consequences. In a seemingly paradoxical move, Heidegger tells us to say 'yes' and 'no' to technology. He suggests that we take up a comportment of releasement or *Gelassenheit* towards it. In this way, we respond to technology, not with the action of turning away and focusing on something else as Borgmann suggests we do, nor do we passively accept our fate. Instead, we let this free relation to technology emerge. This is a difficult position for us 'moderns' to grasp as we are accustomed to understanding things in terms of binary oppositions such as subject and object, form and matter, and activity and passivity. In this way, Heidegger's view can be characterized as middle voiced. I will consider Scott's (1989) account the middle voice to illuminate Heidegger's thought in this respect. Scott shows us how art can be a middle-voiced enterprise. As Heidegger also tells us that art, especially poetry, is the realm where we find the essence of things, I will end this chapter by asking whether we can see the essence of technology in contemporary poetic movements.

4.2 Heidegger's account of technology

Heidegger's ontologically broad use of the term 'technology' includes the way things become intelligible to us. In his redefinition of the term, Heidegger distinguishes between technology and the technological. The technological refers to the instruments and processes we usually associate with the term, but technology is defined as the manner in which being is revealed. We are told, 'the essence of technology is by no means anything technological' (Heidegger 1978: 311). Moreover, to understand technology as simply the technological is to commit a grave error. Heidegger acknowledges that viewing technology in terms of human activity or as a means to an end may be a correct characterization, but such an understanding prevents us from recognizing the corrosive role of technology on humanity. Again, we are pointed to the difference between correctness and truth. A correct characterization may be valid, but it does not capture the essence of technology. We are told that truth is essential to achieve a 'free relationship'; that is, to grasp technology in its essence, we must go beyond the correct to the true. However, technology is dangerous for Heidegger precisely because it blocks off the truth in this sense of essence. Achieving a free relationship to technology is not a simple task; it is made more difficult because we are already caught up in a technological mode; that is, technology is already the way in which things come into presence for us, and therefore, it is concealed from us.

In every epoch, the manner in which things come into presence is concealed, but technology is unique in that, unlike other modes of unconcealment, Heidegger describes, the coming into presence or becoming intelligible of something is not poetic in the sense of *poiēsis*. The word 'technology' derives from *technē*, which refers not only to the skills and work of craftsmen but also to the poetic bringing forth of the arts and, therefore, of *poiēsis*. 'The possibility of all productive manufacturing lies in revealing' (Heidegger 1978: 318). The craftsman creating a chalice 'reveals what is to be brought forth' (Heidegger 1978: 319). Technology is a realm where revealing and concealment take place, and it is, therefore, the realm of truth in this sense of 'Aletheia'. Heidegger's point is that the revealing associated with modern technology is fundamentally different from all other modes of revealing because it challenges (*Herausfordern*) rather than reveals. For this reason, Heidegger tells us, it cannot be considered a part of *poiēsis*.[1]

Thus, Heidegger understands *Poiēsis* as a bringing forth. While enframing is a mode of revealing, its challenging character means that it cannot be considered part of *poiēsis*. Technology, then, is a corrupted mode of unconcealment that reveals without bringing forth. Again, we can understand this in terms of truth. Enframing derives from a way of representation associated with modern science, especially physics. In physics, Heidegger tells us, 'nature presents itself as a calculable complex of the effects of forces' (Heidegger 1978: 331), 'as such it can indeed permit correct determinations, but precisely through these successes, the danger may remain that in the midst of all that is correct the true will withdraw' (Heidegger 1978: 331). Because enframing reveals without bringing forth, it cannot reveal the truth. It is this that makes enframing the supreme danger.

We can roughly identify several arguments against Heidegger's account and its application to contemporary technological applications. First of all, it can be denied that technology is a mode of unconcealment. Richard Rorty, for example, defends a traditional, liberal view of technology as a collection of neutral tools. These tools may exert some influence in human affairs for good or for ill but reject the idea that technology is an ontohistorical process; such a position can be termed the instrumental view (Rae 2012: 311). Moreover, even if we accept that technology is some sort of ontohistorical process, we need not agree with Heidegger's characterization. Some commentators, such as Gunter Anders (1978), argue that Heidegger's account of technology does not go far enough by arguing, for example, that democracy becomes impossible in a technological age. Given this, we can arrange responses to Heidegger's critique of technology along a continuum with a strong technological determinism on one end and instrumentalism on the other. Heidegger himself is not at the furthermost extent of the determinist end of this continuum because of the possibility of *Gellassenheit* or the idea of the correct use of technology.

In what sense is Heidegger's account determining? Technology determines not in the sense of depriving us of our free will, but instead, it decides how we understand being. In an age of enframing, things become standing reserve, and this calibrates our response to them. In a technological age, we understand everything as subject to our manipulation. In order to comprehend the technological epoch, we must first understand Heidegger's account of the history of being.

4.3 Epochality

From the 1930s onwards, Heidegger began to isolate different historical periods in terms of the understandings or 'truths' of being that held sway. This historical approach leads to his attempt to provide philosophy with a new beginning in the *Contributions*, where Heidegger announces the transition from metaphysics to the thinking of beyng. To understand this, we must first understand Heidegger's account of history. He tells us, '[t]his being [*Sein*] – historically – is never the same in every era. It now stands on the verge of an essential transformation, inasmuch as it is given the task of grounding that domain of decision, that nexus of the event' (Heidegger 2012: 24). In this quote, Heidegger is attempting to think a transition between the first beginning of Western philosophy, a beginning in wonder, and a new beginning concerned with beyng rather than beings. Essential to this endeavour is the requirement to think of history not as 'the object and the sphere of a spectating but as that which first awakens and brings about thoughtful questioning' (Heidegger 2012: 7). What is at stake is how beyng occurs (Heidegger 2012: 8), to approach this, we must first recognize the current 'worldview' as what it is: simply the current understanding of beings. For Heidegger, then, history is understood as a sequence of worldviews, each characterized by a different understanding of being. In each of these epochs, the question of Being itself is concealed. The transition into the thinking of beyng requires that we move from the level of beings to the level of beyng and to do so requires a 'penetration into something well guarded'. (Heidegger 2012: 8)

In this way, Heidegger turns from an analysis of history (*Geschichte*) to historicality or historiography. In each epoch, the understanding of being is 'well guarded' in that it resists our comprehension; it is beyond our questioning. Each epoch is, thus, built on a concealed understanding of being. Historiography is, then, concerned with what Wrathall calls the 'background understanding that shapes and constitutes foreground activities' (Wrathall 2011: 181). While it appears self-evident or necessary, this concealed background understanding determines how things are for us, and in this way, it is generative of the epoch. Historiography is an account of this sequence of background understandings. These understandings do not determine in the sense that they are hidden forces that decide the outcome of historical events. They do not determine the outcome of, for example, the Battle of Waterloo, but they provide the context in which the Battle of Waterloo makes sense to those fighting it. Heidegger describes how these understandings allow things to come to presence in different ways in different epochs. But in each epoch, the way in which things come to presence that defines it recedes so that its mode of bringing things to presence is concealed.

This ontohistorical picture is not without ambiguity, and there is scope for differing interpretations. What is clear, however, is that some account of being holds steady for a time and within that time, it allows beings to be understood and grounds all practices. Different commentators characterize epochs in different ways. Dreyfus conceptualizes it in terms of skills for coping with things (Dreyfus and Spinosa 1997: 159). Thompson terms it 'ontological epochality or *epochality*' (Thomson 2011: 8), or '*constellations of intelligibility*' (2011: 9). Different commentators give different estimates of how many distinct epochs and sub-epochs are discussed by Heidegger and then characterizes them in different ways: Dreyfus discusses three distinct epochs in terms of being (Dreyfus and Spinosa 1997: 160) as *physis* (springing forth on its own), being as *poiēsis* (things that are brought forth), as created beings and finally, the technological understanding of being. These can also be characterized in terms of the '*pre-Socratic, Platonic, medieval, modern and late modern*' (Thomson 2011: 8), as Thomson does. In 'The Origin', as we have seen, Heidegger comes to see that it is great art that founds an epoch and that different epochs are exemplified by the works Heidegger uses as examples in the essay. For example, his choice of van Gogh's painting, as Babette Babich points out, is 'an illustration not of painting but of the kind of thing that the artwork is qua manufactured or poietic thing' (Babich 2003: 153).

One of the strengths of Heidegger's view in this respect is that it implies philosophy can never be considered ahistorical. As Wrathall shows in his description of the famous spat between Heidegger and Carnap, the twentieth-century attempt by analytic philosophers to eliminate metaphysics only increased their entrenchment in a metaphysical understanding to which they were blind. In fact, Heidegger claims, the desire to eliminate metaphysics in the way Carnap proposes is itself a sign of the 'technological' understanding of being. The attempt by analytic philosophers to eliminate metaphysics, he claims, might be more appropriately called the 'passing of Metaphysics', where 'passing' means the simultaneous departing of metaphysics (i.e. its apparent perishing and hence being remembered only as something past), even while the technological understanding of being 'takes possession of its absolute domination over what is' (Wrathall 2011: 179).

As we have seen, central to metaphysics are several seemingly self-evident binary distinctions, the most important of which is the Cartesian split between subjects and objects. These distinctions are inexorably linked with science and technology. In 'What Are Poets For' (Heidegger, 1971: 110), Heidegger says, '[e]ven this, that man becomes subject and the word object, is a consequence of technology's nature establishing itself and not the other way around'. A consequence of a scientific world view is that the domain of philosophy shrinks as the domain of science expands. At best, the philosopher is left with questions of normativity and aesthetics. The link between science and metaphysics ensures that the basic Cartesian precepts of science are viewed as self-evident and accepted without question. However, as Heidegger explains in 'The Origin of the Work of Art', it is precisely the subject/object dichotomy that makes art confusing. Art becomes difficult to account for in an age of subjects and objects. Therefore, in the first instance, technoscience is determining insomuch as it makes subjects and objects out of everything.

4.4 Old and new technology

The ambiguity mentioned earlier in Heidegger's account derives in part from the fact that he appears to use the term 'epoch' in different ways in different places. Ma and van Brakel (2014) contend he employs it, 'sometimes more on the ontological, sometimes more on the ontic side'. This has caused some commentators, such as Ihde (2010), to think that the current technological age can further be subdivided into different ontological epochs. Notwithstanding these debates, the move from old to new technology, a move related to science, is clearly delineated by Heidegger.

Despite this, some commentators have critically interrogated this distinction. Some of these criticisms constellate around the relationship between science and technology. In some passages, it seems that Heidegger suggests that science, particularly physics, is the basis of the new technology. In other passages, he suggests that science and technology are the same (*das Selbe*) (Ma and van Brackle 2014: 2). The question of the relationship between science and technology was one that concerned Heidegger right until the end of his life. In a 1976 letter, he claims that reflection upon this relation could help prepare a transformation of man's dwelling in this world (Forman 2007). The distinction between old and new technology is central to Heidegger's view of technology as enframing. He characterizes the difference between the two in terms of the challenging nature of modern technology. While some philosophers, such as Riis (2011), suggest that Heidegger's demarcation line is overstated because it is easy to find examples of old technologies that challenge nature, be it in the form of land or humanity, slavery, for example, is certainly challenging to the humanity of the enslaved person. Heidegger tells us that the challenging of modern technology is 'a challenging, which puts to nature the unreasonable demand that it supplies more energy that can be extracted and stored as such' (Heidegger 1978: 320). In this quote, we see two elements, the unreasonable demand or challenging of nature and the extraction and subsequent storage of energy. The upshot of focusing on these two elements is that nature enframed becomes *nothing more* than stored energy standing by to be ordered at will.

This challenging of new technology is linked with science, especially the 'exact' science of physics. Heidegger seems to reverse the traditional or common sense view that science fosters modern technology by claiming that in fact, technology proceeds science. This somewhat surprising claim is understood in different ways by different commentators. For example, Rae (2012: 315) defends Heidegger by enumerating three ways in which Heidegger uses the term 'technology', first, as a collection of machines and devices, second, as the 'work processes' (2012: 314) that create these devices and third, as a mode of unconcealment or a way of disclosing being. Rae argues that Heidegger's claim that technology comes before science refers only to technology in this third sense. However, while it is clear that the modern devices that we commonly associate with technology flow from developments in science, it is just as true that developments in physics rely on technology, and therefore, Heidegger's use of one term for all three senses is not incidental. Rather, Heidegger uses the term 'technology', as he uses some other terms, in an ontologically broad sense. As Wrathall points out, 'Heidegger sees words in their familiar or everyday sense as an ontic and thus derivative (*abgeleitet*) use which are properly understood in their authentic ontological sense' (Wrathall 2011: 2). This ontological sense cannot be fully exhausted by giving a taxonomy of the senses which are gathered by the term. Otherwise, Heidegger would distinguish between the senses of terms himself. As Wrathall also points out, 'he typically alerts the reader when . . . he is using the word in the usual sense (*im gewöhnlichen Sinne, im üblichen Sinne*) or in the contemporary sense (*im heutigen Sinne*)' (Wrathall 2011: 2).

We can further illuminate this point by noting that methodologically, the advances in physics rely on what some commentators within the philosophy of science, such as Nancy Cartwright (1999), term 'experimental closures'. Experimental closures rely on a technological intervention. For example, the effects of gravity are isolated in a vacuum. Early examples include Otto von Guericke's Magdeburg Hemisphere experiments, which took place in 1671. The results obtained in the closed system of a laboratory cannot be replicated in open systems or the world at large. The experiment brackets off the subject under investigation, abstracting it from the world in which it is generally manifest. Where a physical closure cannot be achieved, for example, in some social sciences, mathematics is employed to isolate one aspect of a phenomenon. It is the ontological claim of physics that the laws of the natural world should be understood in terms of these mathematical or experimental closures. As physics was traditionally considered to provide the methodological standard for all other sciences, including the social sciences, then this process of technologically facilitating closures becomes a way of demarcating science from other inquiries. Part of science's remit is to decide what is properly considered science, and yet the laws of physics require mathematical or experimental closures. The laws of physics are *ceteris paribus* laws; they depend on technological intervention to hold off countervailing factors. Thus, in a purely ontic sense, science both requires and fosters further technological innovation. For this reason, science and technology develop in tandem and are inexorably linked with one other. It is not necessary, therefore, to claim that technology is prior to science only in the ontological sense.

The challenging aspect of new technology is linked with a cutting away of prior meaning rather than just the brute force required to deforest a swath of land or use enslaved people to build a monument. To use Heidegger's example, once the Rhine is dammed to generate electricity, it is not simply physically thwarted; its previous significance is cut away. The river becomes isolated from its context and represented as *only* a means of generating electricity. In this challenging, it loses the truth unveiled in Hölderlin's poem. It becomes an exploitable resource, which is understood in terms of the force of water per cubic metre and its potential to generate power. In this way, enframing does not simply strip away prior meaning, but it also replaces it with the idea that everything in nature is stored energy or a potential resource to be used as required. Everything is reduced to standing reserve like the airliner standing by on a runway in Heidegger's example of stored potential. Science and technology cut away poietic meaning or truth and view all phenomena this way. Thus, even a river not used in the generation of electricity is, nonetheless, no longer a river in any traditional sense. It is now a potential power source or, perhaps, a resource to be exploited by the tourism industry. It is this recasting of the natural world as an interlocking sequence of laws and objects, each element of which can be isolated and used by means of technological intervention, that demarcates new technology from old technology. While the revealing associated with enframing reveals things as standing reserve, this challenging is also associated with truth, but now the truth is in danger of withdrawing.

> [T]he unconcealment in accordance with which nature presents itself as a calculable complex of effects and forces can indeed permit correct determinations, but precisely through these successes the danger may remain than is the midst of all that is correct the true with withdraw. (Heidegger 1978: 331)

In 'The Origin', van Gogh's painting is chosen because it lets us know what the shoes are 'in truth'. The shoes poetically depicted in the painting are used to contrast our usual circumspect engagement with tools. The shoes are technology in the old sense. The example of the shoes demonstrates the relationship between old technology and truth. In the account of the painting, we see that truth is a rare or uncommon occurrence; like authenticity in *Being and Time*, it is not usual or even common for humans. For the most part, we are circumspect and are only pushed out of circumspection when a tool breaks. However, the tool's essence is still concealed in its broken state. Truth only happens in great art when, for example, the peasant's shoes are shown as a locus of meaning, which enables the peasant's work. Enframing threatens this possibility of great art because it limits the way in which a thing can be unconcealed to one possibility, that of stored potential.

Thus, the movement from the old to the new technology is a move from truth to the validity or correctness associated with science. While something can be correct in the sense that a scientific fact is correct, there is no longer a way for the truth to be brought forth. As we can see, the relationship between enframing and truth is complex. Heidegger tells us, 'Enframing blocks the shining-forth and holding sway of truth' (Heidegger 1978: 333). In this way, enframing is not just one mode of unconcealment that coexists with others; it actually prevents other modes, such as art, from unconcealing. 'Enframing threatens man with the possibility that it could be denied to him to enter into a more original revealing and hence to experience the call of a more primal truth' (Heidegger 1978: 333). In short, while art and enframing are both unconcealment, their relationships to truth differ significantly.

It is the very possibility of truth that is concealed in the unconcealment of technology. 'Enframing conceals that revealing which, in the sense of *poiēsis*, lets what presences come forth into appearance' (Heidegger 1978: 332). In this way, we cannot view enframing as simply a choice about how to view the world. It is 'no mere human doing' (Heidegger 1978: 324). Like language, it is prior to us. We are already trapped within it and can take up a relationship with it 'only subsequently' (Heidegger 1978: 329). With respect to poetry, the consequences of such a view are obviously drastic. If art is truth and enframing can drive out truth and replace it with correctness, then the possibility of art is threatened. Where the correct is the only truth, art becomes mysterious and aesthetic accounts are proffered as a way of understanding art, but these are doomed to failure.

To sum up, Heidegger's account understands technology as determining to the extent that things become standing reserve. He is clear that this mode of unconcealment prevents any other possibility of truth. The Rhine enframed is *only* standing reserve: it has lost the poetic significance assigned to it by Hölderlin.

4.5 The digital

The question of whether Heidegger's account is appropriate to the digital age is not a simple one. One immediate concern is that Heidegger's engagement with technology does not extend to the technological advancements we associate with personal computing; rather, it culminates with a metaphysical account of the atomic. This account is ontological in that as Mitchell points out, 'his worry is not so much over atomic destruction as the pervading threat on the nature of being that this threat has already set into play' (Mitchell 2015: 25). Moreover, Heidegger's account of technology is developed throughout his later writings from the 1930s onward. It is important to note that in this work, Heidegger moves beyond the understanding of metaphysics of subjectivity. In a technological age, the object of metaphysics becomes enframed; thus, the Cartesian dichotomy is no longer an apt way to understand the technological thing. This thing ceases to be an object for a subject and instead becomes standing reserve. Indeed, Heidegger's focus on simple things in his later writing is developed in tandem with his account of technology as enframing. While the thing is ontologically understood in terms of its 'thinging', a piece of standing reserve is understood, precisely in terms of its inability to thing, in the sense of opening up the fourfold. In this way, the critique of metaphysics is substantially revised in this later account of technology. Both subject and object become standing reserve in the age of technology and, in this way, the ontological gap between them is eroded or collapsed. As we will see, the digital is a realm where this enframement of the subject becomes obvious.

Originally, the term 'digital' refers primarily to data expressed by values of a physical quantity, typically numerically. It has come to be mainly associated with binary digits. It now refers to the practice of using or storing data or information in the form of signals and thus the use of computer technology. The digital age began in the 1970s and is primarily associated with the introduction of personal computing, which provided the means to transfer large amounts of information freely and quickly via the internet. The onset of the digital age has had undeniable and profound consequences for all aspects of society. Economically, it marks the shift from a post-industrial revolution industry to an information-based economy. The term 'digital age', like the technology it describes, continues to develop and change, making the definition of the term a complex matter.

Of particular interest here is the rise of Web 2.0 software in around 2004–5. Often heralded as the 'second stage' of the development of the internet is characterized by the move from static HTML web pages to user-generated, interactive content. Web 2.0 is a descriptive term initially used in a conference brainstorming session by industry experts in the wake of the 2001 dot-com bubble (O'Reilly 2009). Web 2.0 allows for a non-hierarchical collaboration in that users can share information online, irrespective of technical knowledge. This collaborative aspect is primarily associated with social media but also with blogging and other web-based communities. Web 2.0, in part, describes the exponential growth of social media and a more participatory online culture, especially in terms of social media. It is undeniable that every type of social relationship is affected by the rise of social networking. Yet, philosophical responses, particularly ethical responses, tend to lag behind the speed at which the technology evolves.

Given these considerations, how are we to understand the digital age with respect to Heidegger's analysis of technology? Some commentators, such as Ihde (2010), claim that developments in the digital or information technology are revolutionary, moving us beyond the epoch of enframing and into a new epoch of technoscience and quantum physics. In contrast, others such as Ma and van Brakel (2014) argue against this, claiming that Heidegger speaks powerfully to contemporary technological advancement. In this section, I will defend the view that Heidegger's account of technology is appropriate to the digital age and that in fact, the digital represents an intensification of the metaphysics of technology.

Capurro employs a Heideggerian framework in order to ground information ethics. He describes the intensification of metaphysics as digital ontology or the move towards the ability to understand things only 'as far as we are able to digitise them' (Capurro 2006: 179), where all possible phenomena can be recast as digital information. This movement towards digital ontology is made inevitable by certain developments in Western metaphysics, such as

> the procedure of separation (*chorzein*) or abstracting points and number from 'natural beings' (*phsei onta*) as analysed by Aristotle in his 'Physics' and largely discussed by Heidegger in his 'Sophists' lectures. (Capurro 2006: 197)

Thus, technology's isolating and representational tendency is expressed more emphatically in the digital. According to Capurro, the intensification of metaphysics into digitalization can be understood as a further consequence of man's forgetting temporality in the face of three-dimensional presence or 'standing presence-at-hand' (Capurro 2006: 178).

> If the digital casting of Being by holding only to the one-dimensional sense of presence forgets the question of Being in its full three dimensionality it 'changes over' into digital metaphysics. (Capurro 2006: 178)

In this way, Capurro argues for an ontological interpretation of the digital given Heidegger's account.

Both Dreyfus (2001) and Borgmann (1992) offered early responses to digital technology in terms of social networking. Their accounts primarily focused on pre-Web 2.0 social networking platforms, which were dominated by chat rooms, newsgroups, online gaming and email. Borgmann, for example, considers the ethical and social consequences of social networking in terms of his concept of *hyperreality*. His critique focuses on how social networks may replace real-world social interactions, but as these interactions are between stylized versions of the users, often involving mock identities, something essential of real-world social interactions is lost. Eventually, Borgmann predicted the 'disconnected glamour' of these online personas would divert us from the realities of everyday life. Moreover, this 'glamour of virtuality' is lacking for a number of reasons, including the fact that the presence of network users is corrupted in that no one is 'commandingly present' because, for example, the fact they can be deleted or blocked at will. As we have already noted, these accounts are critiqued by Feenberg (1999), and Verbeek (2005), among others, precisely in terms of their appeal to what is understood as Heidegger's technological determination, which, they claim, prevents Borgmann from recognizing the specific implications of individual technologies. Some of these criticisms have been seemingly vindicated by history because certain features Borgmann associates with hyperreality have not persisted in the wake of Web 2.0. For example, the anonymity and identity play of online chatrooms and MUDs (multi-user dungeons) gave way to social media sites, such as Facebook, where real identities are used. Moreover, Borgmann's view that social networks lead to 'immobile attachment' to online reality failed to predict current networking applications that encourage users, for example, to seek out and join friends at concerts and events, not to mention the capacity for political mobilization.

However, these types of arguments against technological determinism generally fail to recognize the work Heidegger's ontologically broad use of the term 'technology' does. Given this, it is more useful to view Heidegger's account as 'destining' rather than determining. Once we agree that Heidegger's understanding of technology is appropriate to the digital, then changes and developments in web-based specific technologies are, as we have seen, relevant only if they represent essential, epochal-defining differences. For Heidegger, the essence of the new technology is enframing. In this way, the differences between chatrooms and social media platforms are superficial, and the internet can be considered an enframing technology in all its iterations. In other words, to defend the thesis that the digital is simply a continuation, or intensification, of technology in Heidegger's sense, one must hold the differences between various pre and post-Web 2.0 digital technologies are not substantive because these technologies share basic ontological features. This is true of digital technologies and technologies that predate the digital era; that is in essence, television is the same as Facebook.

Thus, while users in pre-Web 2.0 chatrooms may have used aliases, whereas Facebook uses real identities. It can be argued that real identities now function as empty aliases, that is, that personal identities are enframed as social media becomes ubiquitous. Perhaps, it is only online identity that matters now. Leighton Evans (2010: 219) argues people in social networks are transformed into resources and, as such, they become standing reserve. Such a claim is not difficult to defend in the face of online dating sites, where the concept of swiping left or right has become a criterion for assessing someone's value. Moreover, as Babich (2018: 1113) points out, commentators such as Anders, Adorno, Horkheimer and Postman argue that there is no possibility of democracy where there is television, let alone the internet. Or indeed, as Jean Baudrillard (Babich 2018: 1113) argues, actual communication becomes impossible in an age of mass media because there is no longer a possibility of a real response. Moreover, the option for political mobilization afforded by social media has failed to materialize as a widespread force. However, the manipulation of elections using the same tools is well documented and probably widespread. No matter how disconcerting the reality of electoral manipulation, some commentators claim it is irrelevant because we are already too distracted to be politically motivated. For example, as Babich argues, our dependence on technology leaves us politically impotent. From a Heideggerian perspective, it is not the potential uses of any particular technology that is the problem but rather the way in which reality is now understood as something to be manipulated or exploited. Electoral manipulation is possible because the electorate is now revealed as standing reserve. Once this is the case, the technologies that enable this manipulation follow naturally. In this way, we can argue that any difference between digital and pre-digital technologies are differences of degree rather than kind and that the digital is simply an intensification of the process of enframing because it effectively enframes humanity itself. Of course, writing before the digital age, Heidegger saw the enframing of humanity as an integral part of technology.

> As soon as what is unconcealed no longer concerns man even as an object, but exclusively as standing-reserve, and man in the midst of objectlessness is nothing but the orderer of the standing-reserve, then he comes to the very brink of a precipitous fall; that is he comes to the point where he himself will have to be taken as standing-reserve. (Heidegger 1978: 332)

The danger associated with enframing is twofold. First, the human being becomes standing reserve; second, she begins to see everything else as a human construct and thus only ever encounters herself. In all this, humankind loses the connection with its deeper essence, and every other possibility is driven out. In this, Heidegger uncannily predicts the way in which web-based technologies continually reflect us back to ourselves, for example, in direct response advertising where increasingly widespread harvesting of seemingly innocuous data is processed in order to build models of individual consumers so that they can be effectively targeted for advertising. The digital is the realm where everything about us, including our emotional responses, becomes data and, therefore, quantifiable. The internet is the tool that facilitates this transformation and converts us into resources, standing by for commercial or political interests to exploit.

The digital, expressed in the internet, is the arena where the modernist subject becomes something else. While, arguably, this could be viewed as a positive development from a Heideggerian perspective, it is not. Heidegger views the Cartesian subject/object dualism as central to metaphysics. Subjectivity is, perhaps, the paradigmatic feature of our entrenchment in metaphysics. As we saw in Chapter 1, it is precisely this subjectivity that obscures the essence of art and prevents its authentic showing. Given this, wouldn't Heidegger applaud something that could interrupt this metaphysical picture? No. In the digital, the subject is transformed into standing reserve. It merely stands by in order to be exploited. Thus, while the Cartesian subject may lose its pivotal position, it does so by becoming enframed and, therefore, just standing reserve in the midst of more standing reserve. The transformation of the subject into standing reserve represents a change in the metaphysical landscape, whereby the modernist subject is reduced to mere stock, which only differs from other modes of standing reserve in that it can order them, but despite this, it is also, itself, always orderable.

It is not difficult to justify a characterization of the digital as the realm where this transformation is completely accomplished. The digital age is the time when the human being of modern subjectivity becomes a complex of consumer desires that standby to be exploited by various interests. Dreyfus and Spinosa point out, in his final analysis of technology, Heidegger was critical of those, who still caught in the subject/object picture, thought that technology was dangerous because it embodied instrumental reason. (Dreyfus and Spinosa 1997: 161)

Heidegger claims that the new technology becomes 'something completely different and new' (Heidegger 1978: 320). The change between the new and the old technology is inexorably connected with the enframing of the subject. As we have argued, the internet is the realm where this transformation is completed. The question then is does the enframed subject even have the ability to formulate a response to the danger posed by technology? Different commentators approach this question in different ways. Dreyfus and Spinosa (1997: 162) agree that unless we accept that subjectivity is compromised by technology, we cannot formulate a response to it. Borgmann entreats us to look away from the technological and focus instead on the 'focal', which are non-technological or traditional events such as the ritual of a family meal. But, as we will see, such action becomes less possible in the digital age where information replaces objects, and the subject is diminished. According to Dreyfus and Spinosa, the difference between Heidegger and Borgmann lies in how we understand the technological subject. For Borgmann, even though the subject's status is demoted from the 'modernist subject' with its 'long-term identities and commitments' (1993: 162) to merely a collection of arbitrary desires. For Heidegger, as we have seen, the subject in the technological age does even meet this minimal criterion and instead becomes standing reserve.

4.6 Gelassenheit

If we accept that the subject is enframed by the digital, then we cannot simply look away; we cannot just avoid technology, as Borgmann suggests. The question is still whether there is still a possibility of forming a response to the digital. Heidegger describes two interrelated ways in which to confront technology. First, he invokes the possibility of *Gelassenheit* leading to a free relation with technology and second, he discusses the possibility of a poetic confrontation with technology. The poetic approach is more pertinent to the current book, but we will first consider the possibility of *Gelassenheit*. However, the question remains: does Heidegger's insistence that technology can be confronted conflict with his characterization of technology as a mode of unconcealment prior to the human being? Once the human being is transformed into standing reserve, can it hope to formulate an approach to that which initially enframed it? Can we respond to technology once we have been altered so profoundly by it? Moreover, the continuing developments of digital technologies further challenge the possibility of a confrontation in a way Heidegger could not have fully envisioned. It is fair to ask whether Heidegger's proposed solutions are a capitulation on his part and whether this capitulation is now a more serious matter than it was at the time he was writing. Heidegger's solutions must be considered in terms of these considerations.

Notwithstanding this, in the *Discourse on Thinking* (1996), we are told what is required is for meditative thinking to 'awaken'. This awakening will ultimately allow for the possibility of using technical devices without falling into bondage.

> We can use technical devices as they ought to be used, and also let them alone as something which does not affect our inner and real core. We can affirm the unavoidable use of technical devices, and also deny them the right to dominate us, and so to warp, confuse, and lay waste our nature. (Heidegger 1966: 54)

In this way, Heidegger views meditative thinking as a way to think past the unconcealment associated with technology and to develop a 'free relation' with it. However, in the digital age, this call to let technology alone must be seen in reference to devices, such as smartphones, laptops and tablets that we keep with us at almost all times. His call to leave or let (*Lassen*) them be is obviously pertinent. This is an age where letting devices alone becomes more and more difficult, yet Heidegger tells us we must say both 'yes' and 'no' (1966: 54) to technological devices; and that meditative thinking is one way to achieve this. However, if the digital subject is little more than an arbitrary collection of desires, how is it possible to prevent technology from dominating us or laying waste to our nature? Can we say either yes or no to technology when our devices continually command more and more of our attention in a way that Heidegger could not have predicted? We spend more and more time engaging with devices for a whole array of reasons, but whatever the reasons, we call this time 'screen time'. There has been a lot of research on levels of screen time, especially among children. For example, in 2019, the World Health Organization recommended that children under five spend less than an hour on digital devices. By the time these children become adults, will the potential for meditative thinking leading to *Gelassenheit* be possible? If not, *Gelassenheit* cannot represent an effective way to confront technology.

Attempts to limit screen time are pointless if we understand technology as mode of unconcealment, which is always prior to us. While we are under its sway, things will show up for us as standing reserve; that is, things will *be* technological, no matter how little time we spend on screens. So an approach to technology based simply on limiting screen time is ultimately impotent and probably doomed to failure. As a mode of unconcealment, technology negatively affects people's capacity to engage meaningfully with each other and with things. By definition, this impacts our ability to develop a free relation with technology. As our reliance on digital devices increases, we can reasonably ask if meditative thinking is still possible; and if it is, will it remain so for future generations? Without the possibility of meditative thinking, we cannot take up a comportment of releasement towards devices. But what exactly is meditative thinking? Heidegger contrasts it with calculative thinking. The difference between the two can be understood in terms of what is possible for each. Calculative thinking is not limited to numerical calculation, but it does limit itself to 'conditions that are given' (Heidegger 1966: 46). This means that all the options are known and set out before the calculation takes place. Because all the conditions or premises are known from the outset, the result of the calculation is definite and predictable. Heidegger does not argue with the practical applications of such thinking, but he points to its ungroundedness.

> Calculative thinking computes. It computes ever new more promising and at the same time more economical possibilities. Calculative thinking races from one prospect to the next. Calculative thinking never stops, never collects itself. Calculative thinking is not meditative thinking, not

thinking which contemplates the meaning which reign in everything that is. (Heidegger 1966: 46)

Calculative thinking is closed in that it is the manipulation of a set of pre-existing variables. In contrast, meditative thinking is open because it is concerned with meanings and significations not previously set or understood. Reminiscent of the account of metaphor in the previous chapter, meditative thinking involves previously unrecognized similarities, like the terms of metaphoric statements. If it is possible to approach our current devices meditatively in order to release them, we do this by claiming back an 'openness to the mystery'. Calculative thinking is closed and ungrounded, whereas meditative thinking is open and yet grounded. While, in the *Discourse on Thinking*, Heidegger grounds meditative thinking in the soil of the Swabian homeland, it can also be seen as grounded in things such as the jug, which opens up the fourfold in the essay on things. However, the point is not to return to 'old' objects such as the earthenware jug but to approach our internet-enabled devices meditatively. Given that these devices can be seen as expressions of calculative thinking, the question is can we take up a meditative relationship towards them? Whether or not such a relationship is indeed possible, it is clear that we cannot return to the world of the earthenware jug. What is at stake here is not a way to return to the old world or the old technology but rather a new 'possibility of dwelling in the world in a totally different way' (Heidegger 1966: 55), where we can use technology without 'being imperilled by it'.

4.7 A saving power

In the 'Question Concerning Technology', we are pointing towards a saving power that is poetic in nature. Heidegger quotes Hölderlin, who tells us in his poem 'Patmos':

'Wo aber Gefahr ist mächst
Das Rettende auch'.

(Hölderlin 1826: 271)

This can be translated as where the danger is, the saving one is also. While we know the unconcealment associated with enframing is not just a point of view or a way of looking at the world that can be easily changed because man 'merely responds to the call of unconcealment, even when he contradicts it' (Heidegger, 1966: 55). However, we are told that though enframing is the extreme danger, it cannot 'exhaust itself solely in blocking all lighting-up of every revealing, all appearing of truth' (Heidegger, 1966: 55). While enframing drives out truth, it cannot drive it out completely. The danger of technology is not total; within the essence of technology, there is the seed of its own undoing. While enframing renders objects objectless, if we look deeply into the essence of technology, we can find this 'saving power'. But to do this is not a simple task. It requires preparation and a consideration of exactly what makes enframing the essence of technology.

As we have seen, it is not essence in the sense of a universal category under which examples of technology, such as computers and sawmills, fall. In 'The Question Concerning Technology', Heidegger links essence with destining, and destining is linked to the way that Being is unconcealed in a given epoch. Just as the essence of the peasant's shoes reveals the life of the peasant and her connection with the land, destining, more generally understood, is inherently linked to what it means to be human and thus to receive being. The peasant's life makes sense to her in terms of a network of significance. This network is her world, and shoes are an integral part. Moreover, destining must be understood in terms of two elements, language and historicity. As we know, the danger of technology is not the consequence of using technological devices; rather, it must be understood in terms of language and historicity. Consequently, the saving power must also be understood in terms of these elements.

In short, Heidegger is telling us that the essence of technology is its ability to unconceal being in this epoch. To harness the saving power, Heidegger extolls us to 'look with yet clearer eyes into the danger' (Heidegger 1978: 334). The challenging of enframing blocks the granting of *poiēsis*, but it cannot block it altogether:

> the saving power lets man see and enter into the highest dignity of his essence. The dignity lies in keeping watch over the unconcealment – and

with it, from the first, the concealment – of all essential unfolding on this earth. (Heidegger 1978: 337)

The saving power comes from keeping watch over the unconcealment. What is required is,

> essential reflection upon technology and decisive confrontation with it [this] must happen in a realm that is, on the one hand, akin to the essence of technology and, on the other, fundamentally different from it . . . . Such a realm is art. (Heidegger 1978: 340)

In this way, there is a sort of reciprocity between art and enframing, just as enframing makes it difficult to account for art because it drives out truth, an understanding of the essence of technology must happen within the realm of art. The essence of technology must be captured in art. While technology drives out art as truth, it cannot drive it out altogether. There is a truth of technology, even though this truth is related to the technology's concealment of truth. We must understand this truth in order to protect ourselves from its danger. For Heidegger, the possibility of art is seriously threatened by the danger of technology; it is driven out by calculative thinking, but it still remains because calculative thinking cannot entirely exhaust thinking. From a Heideggerian perspective, the role of art in this age is to bring the essence of technology into view.

4.8 The middle voice

No matter how we approach the dangers of technology, it is clear that the issue cannot be understood from within the existing metaphysical framework; for Heidegger, technology is metaphysics. While new technology may mark a departure from the metaphysics of subjectivity that concerned Heidegger up till the 1930s, it is still inherently metaphysical. We cannot think past this danger of technology from inside the metaphysical view that engendered it in the first place. In order to deal with the problems associated with technology, we have to address the full scope of what is covered by

Heidegger's ontologically broad use of the term. As we have seen, the danger of technology is not that our children spend too much time in front of screens; rather, it is a consequence of the technological understanding of being. From within this metaphysical view, we cannot take action in the form of policies that limit, for example, screen time, nor can we simply look away and focus on something else and expect to resolve the danger. First, we have to understand the truth of technology as the current epoch. Some commentators suggest that the middle voice may provide a way to get beyond the metaphysics of technology. Scott (1989), for example, heralds the middle voice as a step towards the end of metaphysics. Theorists, such as Scott, hold that this epoch is characterized in terms of a number of binary dualities, such as subjects and objects, form and matter, activity and passivity and along with Heidegger, they hold that from within this framework, we can only strengthen the hold that this metaphysics has over us. What is needed to release us from this grip of metaphysics are ways to transcend these metaphysical dualities. The middle voice offers a possible way of overcoming the active/passive distinction, in particular, by offering a third option between action and non-action. In this way, it provides us with a potential way to undermine the conceptual machinery of metaphysics. While it can be argued that such accounts fail to fully recognize the distinction the later Heidegger draws between modernism and new technology, where some of these distinctions are collapsed, it still has value for the current discussion. As we have seen, one of the modernist dualisms collapsed by technology is the subject/object dichotomy. While the literature on the middle voice points to an overcoming of the active/passive distinction, we shall see in chapter 6 that the digital collapses this distinction in a similar way to how it collapses the subject/object distinction.

The middle voice is an antiquated verb form, uncommon in modern languages, where the active and the passive voices dominate. To illustrate these different voices, consider the active statement, 'Paul made a mistake'. It follows the subject-verb-object sequence, regarded as fundamental to modern languages. Such a statement is also paradigmatic of Cartesian dualism. As Heidegger points out, the Cartesian mind/matter distinction is self-evident precisely because it is expressed in this basic sentence structure, where an agent acts on something else. An example of a passive voice statement is 'a mistake was made'. In this formulation, the agent is no longer present but is still implied. Thus, 'a mistake was made (by Paul)'. In the middle voice formulation, 'mistakes were made' even this implied agent is no longer present.

The verb form carries a statement's voice. There is some confusion in English because the same verb form is used for both passive and middle voice formulations. While there are many instances of middle-voiced formulations in modern languages, these are generally interpreted as passive, where an agent is nonetheless implied. A good example is the statements of science, 'prices rise as quantity demanded increases' or 'metal expands when heated'. Such statements are technically middle voiced, but they are generally understood in terms of the actions of agents or natural laws. Such examples are also transitive in that they involve a direct object. Another common, contemporary example of a middle voice statement is reflexive statements, such as 'I wash myself'.

There is, however, a form of middle-voiced verb use that was common in ancient languages such as Greek or Sanskrit, but that is almost impossible to find in modern languages, namely the non-reflexive, intransitive. Charles Scott gives us examples from Sanskrit.

> In the case of the intransitive verb, the active of *drmhati*, for example, means 'makes (something) firm.' The intransitive middle *drmhate* means 'becomes firm,' or, we might say 'firming comes of its own action.' In the case of the middle voice of 'die' (*mriyate*) we translate dying occurs (of itself). (Scott 1989: 747)

As Scott points out, we tend to understand these examples in a quasi-self-reflexive way.

> We are inclined by our structures of expression to speak of an action doing something in relation to itself and thereby indicate an incipient subject-relation in the verbs action. (Scott 1989: 747)

These examples clearly resonate with Heidegger's attempt to use language in such a way as to try to wriggle free of the metaphysical restraints imposed on it. In a way that chimes with the earlier examples, Heidegger tells us that things 'thing' and that the nothing 'noths'. Scott suggests that we can understand this Heideggerian terminology with respect to the middle voice and highlights the importance of the middle voice in challenging modern subjectivity. Moreover, he argues that the tendency to interpret these Heideggerian statements in terms of an implicit subject/object relation has led to confusion in understanding Heidegger. For example, Moore argues that the turn in Heidegger has been mistakenly interpreted 'as a turn from the active voluntarist resoluteness of *Being and Time* and the writings of the rectorship to the passive, submissive releasement of his later works' (Moore 2017: 26). Rather than viewing the earlier works as active and the latter as passive, Moore suggests that we understand the entire corpus as middle voiced. In this way, he maintains that 'Heidegger's appreciation of the middle voice stands as a significant contribution to efforts to think outside of metaphysical binaries such as activity and passivity' (Moore 2017: 27).

While the middle voice is a grammatical construction, philosophers are quick to point out its significance at the level of discourse or metaphysics. Lewin, for example, suggests that the middle voice is a 'linguistic mode that places agency between activity and passivity' (Lewin 2012: 1), and Scott, in the influential paper 'The Middle Voice of Metaphysics' (Scott 1989: 747), talks about middle-voiced events such as the staging of Oedipus the King, as described by Jean-Pierre Verant. This staging is middle voiced because the ambiguity within the play's narrative mirrors the ambiguity in the audience's situation. What makes such events middle voiced, according to Scott, is their ability to express 'multiple values'. Scott claims that the non-reflexive, intransitive middle voice allows a 'word with several, even countervailing meanings' to be expressed without narrowing down these meanings. Middle-voiced events are events which allow a similar excess of meaning to rest. We can draw a parallel between this discussion of the middle voice and Heidegger's account of metaphor in the preceding chapter. Scott's claim that an event is middle voiced because it embodies multiple meanings resonates with the account of metaphor. We can understand this by noting that Heidegger's seeming metaphoric language is used precisely because it opens up multiple meanings. An aesthetic view of metaphor operates by trying to shut down this 'excess' of meaning by viewing them as figurative. This is similar to the way that the middle-voiced expression in modern languages tends to be understood in terms of an implied subject/object relation. Metaphysics can be understood in terms of the tendency to shut down the significance of things and to understand them as self-contained, discrete objects.

For our present purposes, however, it is enough to note that without thinking beyond metaphysics, we cannot get beyond technology. Developing a free relation to technology requires an overcoming of the activity/passivity dualism. Scott locates the discussion of the middle voice within a discussion of metaphysics. He asks, '[c]an Metaphysics come to an end? What could its ending mean? Is its ending found in the questionableness of its foundations?' (1989: 743). It is beyond the scope of this thesis to consider these questions, but they do point to the fact that we cannot address technology in the sense of devices and processes without addressing the metaphysical binaries that are continuous with them.

The following chapters question whether we can see evidence of this Heideggerian 'essential reflection' in contemporary poetic movements. In particular, we will consider those movements which deal explicitly with technology, specifically digital poetry and post-internet poetry. We have already seen that for Heidegger, great poetry must transcend metaphysics. When Heidegger speaks of great poetry, or indeed of *Gelassenheit*, he is attempting to speak beyond the technological into the realm of the poetic. One way to grasp this possibility is in terms of the middle voice.

4.9 Conclusion

Heidegger's ontological use of the term 'technology' captures technology's power to unconceal reality as standing reserve. This power is not separated from the devices and processes we usually associate with the term but is, rather, continuous with them. Technology is the epoch we are living through now, and thus, it is a way of revealing reality. In particular, Heidegger's account gives us a way to understand how technology is intensified in the digital. Technology, unlike other modes of unconcealment, reveals without bringing forth. It is not poetic. While the great art of the previous age had the ability to unconceal the essence of something by bringing us out of our usual circumspection, that is to bring something forth in its essence, this possibility is now past or, at least, under serious threat. This is because technology does not bring forth but rather unconceals everything, including the human being, as orderable and endlessly replaceable. In this way, it barely makes sense to ask what something is its essence. Given this, we must be critical with respect to Heidegger's claim that we can still confront technology. However, Heidegger offers us two options *Gelassenheit* or the poetic. In the rest of this book, we will examine, in particular, how the poetic may confront digital technology.

5
Eco-poetry

5.1 Introduction

Eco-poetry is a poetic movement in contemporary poetry that attempts to respond to the ecological crisis, where this crisis is understood as a change in environmental systems due to human interference. Heidegger's critique of technology, with its focus on how all things are recast as resources or standing reserve, seems to provide a philosophical entry point to discuss environmentalism and its relationship to poetry. Indeed, commentators often couch discussions of eco-poetry in terms of Husserlian or Heideggerian phenomenology. For example, in 2017, the University of Warwick hosted a symposium bringing phenomenology and ecology together in terms of the poetry of Peter Larkin (De Sousa 2019). Heidegger himself uses environmental examples, such as the Rhine River, to illustrate the corrosive effects of technology. Once the river becomes a resource, then its exploitation is inevitable. Thus, in the first instance, contemporary poetry cannot relate to things without acknowledging that things are now digitized. For example, Seamus Heaney's famous poem 'Postscript' was written before the coastline of Clare on the West coast of Ireland, which it describes, was rebranded as the 'Wild Atlantic Way'. We can argue that this rebranding means the coastline is no longer the landscape of Heaney's poem.

Given this, one way to understand eco-poetry is to view it as an attempt to affirm the natural world and natural objects, especially in terms of their prior significance. However, in the later works, Heidegger describes things in terms of the fourfold and contrasts the thinging thing with the technological thing, which is unworlded. In this way, the conceptual dualisms of metaphysics are eroded in technology but not overcome. An eco-poetry, which fails to acknowledge the enframement of the environment is ultimately impotent. In Heidegger's terminology, things, including the environment, no longer open the fourfold or 'thing'. This poses a particular challenge to eco-poetry, which can be characterized by an attempt to instil meaning back into things. Jane Hirshfield's recent collection 'Ledger' (2020) is a case in point. In this collection, Hirshfield describes the basic, everyday things that occupied the later Heidegger, such as buckets and paint. If Heidegger's account is apt, then Hirsfield's attempt to make a bucket 'thing' should be affected. In this way, a contemporary poet allows us to test Heidegger's account.

5.2 Heidegger and climate change

We hit an immediate problem when we attempt to interpret contemporary eco-poetry in terms of Heideggerian philosophy. For Heidegger, as we saw in Chapter 1, it is poetry that gets us to the truth of the matter, not science. At best, science merely represents the world and, at worst, is the engine of metaphysics, leading ultimately, in to the enframement of reality, including the natural environment. It is not difficult to argue, from such a perspective, that science, and its nefarious twin technology, are to blame for the current climate crisis. Yet it is also science that informs us about this crisis and without scientific measurement, we would be unable to understand the scale of the situation in which we find ourselves. Science also seems to hold out the greatest promise of solutions to this crisis. It is certainly not my aim to argue with the science of climate change but rather to point out the role that science and technology have played in this crisis and how we are to understand this philosophically. Of course, the ecological crisis is not something Heidegger specifically commented on, but it is not difficult to imagine a Heideggerian explanation for climate change and a possible Heideggerian solution. Indeed, Irwin (2011) links the climate change to technological enframing, and Padrutt (2009) points out that the word 'ecology' derives from the Greek word '*oikeos*', which means 'dwell' or 'home'. Ecology, then, is the science of how an organism relates to its surroundings. Pardutt connects this to how 'Heidegger's thinking opens up human dwelling'(2009: 18), in this sense of ecology, and attempts to bring Heidegger's thinking and ecology into 'proximity'.

In this way, it is plausible to see the enframent of the natural world as the key factor in climate change and argue that the ecological crisis is a consequence of technoscience. However, as we saw in a previous chapter, technology is prior to us; therefore, it is not amenable to human action. Given this, Botha (2003), for example, argues that we cannot invoke Heidegger's work as a basis for ecological activism. Thus, we can understand and explain the environmental crisis in terms of Heidegger's account of technology, but from a Heideggerian perspective, the solution to this crisis does not lie with action or activism.

This is not to argue that we should abandon ecological activism or the attempt to find scientific solutions to environmental problems. It is not even to claim that we cannot solve these problems within technological metaphysics. I do not disregard this possibility. However, we can see our inability to act decisively as a philosophical matter. Rosół (2016), for example, suggests a role for philosophy in developing an understanding of our collective reluctance to act, despite impassioned pleas by activists, such as Greta Thunberg and the consensus that the time for action is passing, if not passed. Still, this does not mean, from within our current metaphysical standpoint, we cannot address and effectively respond to this crisis. For Heidegger, the possibility of nuclear annihilation was not the only threat associated with the atomic; the most immediate threat was the technological enframing of reality. Up till today, we have managed to avoid a widespread nuclear disaster, but we have not managed to avoid the danger of technology, that is, the danger which recasts all things to standing reserve. Similarly, we could conceivably avoid a catastrophic ecological disaster while remaining trapped within technology. While activism and political action may halt the rise of global warming, it cannot change the role that technology, as mode of unconcealment, plays in this crisis.

It is beyond the scope of this book to say what this means for the future of humanity, but there is a point to be made here about the role of poetry in this respect. Without change at the level of metaphysics, perhaps the best we can hope for is to lurch from one existential crisis to another. Still, according to Heidegger, we can only address metaphysics at the level of metaphysics, and as we have seen in previous chapters, poetry is one way we can access this metaphysical level. Of course, it is deeply naïve to suggest that poetry can make a difference in terms of climate change, at the level of ontology, where activism is, perhaps, doomed to failure. We will leave this naivety aside for the time being, while noting that Heidegger is clear, great poetry is great because it challenges metaphysics. This suggests a very important role for eco-poetry in our efforts to avoid ecological disaster, but only great eco-poetry can play this role. However, in order for an eco-poem to be great, it must challenge the metaphysics of technology; it must disclose the natural world in a new way. An eco-poet who does not acknowledge the technological status of the environment cannot challenge the technology as mode of unconcealment.

5.3 Contemporary poetry and greatness

Again the question arises, how are we to understand this account of poetic greatness in terms of contemporary poetry or literature and art more generally? Can it really be helpful to think about poetry or art in terms of a sliding scale from greatness? Heidegger's analysis condemns the vast majority of poetic works to the less-than-great pile. In 'The Origin', Heidegger tells us that only great work is under consideration. Such a claim cannot be made without the presupposition that greatness is readily recognizable, at least to Heidegger. This seeming arrogance is tempered by the fact that as we have seen, Heidegger uses the term 'great' in a particular way. We can begin to approach what Heidegger intends by noting that his account challenges traditional accounts of art, where art can either good or bad but nonetheless remain art. Greatness for Heidegger is an ontological category rather than a value judgement. When we speak about greatness in this Heideggerian way, we do not imply that there is a scale by which a work can be measured. Greatness in art is future orientated – it opens up a world, making that world and all that is in it possible. While Heidegger does not explicitly speak of it, it is interesting to note that the etymology of great

(*Groß*) seems to come from West Germanic *grauta* meaning coarse or thick. In other words, the great is coarse in the sense of not yet refined, suggesting an earthiness, but also that which grates with the established conventions, which is not yet worn down, made smooth. This would make sense of Heidegger's choices, such as van Gogh's shoes, but also the temple at Paestum. Far from being a value judgement, greatness can be understood in terms of the making possible of a world in which subsequent poetry and art can happen and be refined. The role of art is not so much to make that world as it is to show that which is 'always already' there. It is coarse for us because it 'rubs us the wrong way', showing us the world we are in without knowing it. The idea that the authentic disturbs the familiar or the everyday recurs in Heidegger. It is present in the analysis of anxiety in *Being and Time* and is essential to the new beginning of philosophy described in the *Contributions*. It is in this sense of a new beginning that Hölderlin is seen as futural.

Thus, we can understand what Heidegger means by greatness by considering it in three interrelated ways: greatness in terms of metaphor, greatness as founding in the sense of epoch-defining, and the third, the engagement with Hölderlin as the futural poet. In Chapter 3, we discussed poetic metaphor and greatness, and in Chapters 1 and 4, we saw how great art is epoch-defining for Heidegger. The Greek temple, for example, defines its era; it is a significant node in a matrix of meaning. This matrix is formed by the work but it also supplies meaning to the work. Thus, the temple is not simply understood in terms of its context; rather, it unconceals the 'world' of the ancient Greeks. It is art's role in world disclosure that Heidegger calls 'founding', and it is this founding that makes a work great. We can further understand this by noting that greatness can be won or lost. When the Aegina sculptures are 'torn out of their native sphere' (Heidegger 1978: 166), for example, they lose their greatness. In fact, we are told that 'placing them in a collection has withdrawn them from their world' (Heidegger 1978: 166). The very act of moving a work into an art gallery or a museum can destroy its greatness. Heidegger calls this 'world-withdrawal' or 'world decay', and he claims it can happen even when the location of the work remains the same 'we visit the temple at Paestum at its own site . . . [but] the world of the work that stands there has perished' (Heidegger 1978: 166). Greatness in this Heideggerian sense is not set in stone.

Poetry as language is the most immediate founding, because all beings are first disclosed in language. We are unambiguously told that '[p]oetry is the founding of being in the world' (Heidegger 2000: 59). As we saw in Chapter 3, poetry is not ornamental. We cannot fully understand it, when we view language as referring to a pre-existing reality. Instead, poetry is the way in which language discloses what is most essential. '[A]bove all', Heidegger tells us, it is not 'a mere expression of a culture' (Heidegger 2000: 59). The great poet, for Heidegger, is Hölderlin. As Bernasconi points out,

> Hölderlin was for Heidegger the poet who, if the Germans decided in his favor by listening to the language of his poetry, could lead them to another place, a place where Western metaphysics no longer held sway. This is why Hölderlin was for Heidegger not one poet among others but a destiny for philosophy. (Heidegger 2000: 59)

Of course, this destiny is a particularly German one, and as Bernasconi points out, it is not one that can be easily separated from National Socialism. This is a complex issue which has been dealt with extensively by other commentators, such as O'Brien, (2022) and Mitchell and Trawny (Mitchell and Trawny 2017). I will not focus on this issue here. What is pertinent to the current discussion is that Hölderlin offers the German people a way beyond metaphysics. We do not need to agree with Heidegger's account of Hölderlin in terms of the destiny of the German people; we simply need to decide whether poetry can be instrumental in birthing a new metaphysics. However, the fact that Heidegger's account is limited to the destiny of the German people does tell us something about the scope of his account in this respect, namely that it is not universal. It deals with a specific culture at a particular point in time. Given its unfortunate entanglement with National Socialism, it is, perhaps, folly to think that it could or should be universalized, or used in any way to understand contemporary poetic movements. However, at the base of his account is the idea that metaphysics is given in the language and culture of a people and that poetry has the power to be the most immediate and authentic expression of this.

What, if anything, can Heidegger's reading of Hölderlin say to the English-speaking world of the twenty-first century? In the first instance, the German culture of the 1930s, 1940s and 1950s radically differed from today's globalized and multicultural English-speaking world. If poetic or artistic greatness is related to the founding of culture, how could we possibly assess it when numerous cultures coexist? This diversity of cultural voices is applauded and widely encouraged in contemporary poetry and art. This diversity becomes apparent in the various types of poetry that now coexist, represented by their own journals and anthologies. Each of these has its own internal standards and norms. Any attempt to impose a single standard of greatness on these diverse voices would seem misguided at best and, at worst, a backward move to a time when marginalized voices were routinely excluded. Because of this, commentators on contemporary poetry tend to shy away from the notion of poetic standards because these standards were regularly used to exclude female poets, poets of colour, poets from the global south and LGBTQ+ poets. Indeed, the decisions to exclude certain groups were often defended in terms of maintaining standards. The triumph of contemporary poetry has been the drive towards inclusivity. Given Heidegger's account of Hölderlin and its unpleasant associations, it seems obvious that Heidegger is talking about another time, a time that is thankfully gone.

While it may be naïve to suggest that Heidegger's ontological account of greatness does not line up, to some extent, with a conservatism regarding poetic standards, it is certainly not identical to it. My contention is that Heidegger's ontological understanding is essential to an account of contemporary poetry. Despite the wealth of new and previously excluded voices, contemporary culture is a digital culture. If we agree with Heidegger's characterization of this age as a technological one, then technology, as the way things are, underlies the diversity of the current age and is, in some sense, homogenizing. The apparent differences that make up the world of contemporary poetry exist and proliferate within the digital. If technology, expressed as the digital, challenges the possibility of great art, one way to understand this is to say there is no longer a single cultural standard. Thus, it is now impossible to say what greatness is. We cannot have an epoch-defining poem in an age of diversity and globalization simply because no one thing has the power to define this epoch. However, this proliferation of poetic styles is facilitated by the digital. It is worth considering how digital technologies enable this divergence of poetic voices and how it presents them as just more content. The notion of the social media echo chamber, where agents are only ever confronted with their own political biases, is now familiar among political theorists. However, there are also cultural and artistic echo chambers. The diversity of contemporary culture can also be strangely exclusionary because it exists in a digital field that separates people into their relevant groups. A poem or any other work bouncing around in its echo chamber cannot be great in this Heideggerian sense.

Perhaps for a poem to be great in this age it has to disclose the echo chamber. In fact, in a digital age, this is the very purpose of art, and Heidegger's account lets us see this. In the following chapters, we will consider more thoroughly the question of how poetry may disclose the digital.

5.4 What is eco-poetry?

How are we to understand eco-poetry? We can begin by noting how it is related to other poetic movements. Eco-poetry can be understood in terms of its relationship with nature poetry or political poetry or in terms of activism. Eco-poetry originates in the late 1980s when, as Terry Gifford (1994: 2) notes, everything turned green. A new awareness of ecological matters allowed for a resurgence of poetry dealing with nature. Up till that point, according to Gifford, nature poetry was having a bad time. Writing in 1995 he claims '"nature poetry" has become a pejorative term and it is therefore difficult to use the phrase without inverted commas' (1994: 3). Gifford describes how the poetry of poets, such as Ted Hughes, had been replaced with the poetry of urbanization and confessional poetry. However, this trend was reversed and by the early 1990s there was a renewed and substantial interest in poetry about the environment.

> The summer 1990 issue of *Poetry Review* declared itself to be the green issue. . . . At the same time *Poetry Wales* also produced a 'Special Green Issue' which reviewed four new anthologies of green poetry. One of the

reviewers, Hilary Llewellyn-Williams noted '[p]oets need no longer apologise for writing about Nature.' This new nature poetry was not simply descriptive of nature, but it concerned the relationship between humanity and the environment. (Gifford 1994: 3)

Interest in eco-poetry has grown exponentially since then and there are now many anthologies and journals dedicated to poetry about the environment. How are we, then, to characterize the difference between nature poetry, pastoral poetry and eco-poetry, or between eco-poetry and other contemporary poetic genres? It would seem like a good idea to start with a definition of eco-poetry, and while the matter of a definition is by no means settled. The poet John Shoptaw attempts one in the January 2016 edition of 'Poetry'. He claims,

> an ecopoem needs to be environmental and it needs to be environmentalist. I mean first that an ecopoem needs to be about the nonhuman natural world – wholly or partly, in some way or other, but really and not just figuratively. In other words, an ecopoem is a kind of nature poem. But an ecopoem needs more than the vocabulary of nature. (Shoptaw 2016)

It is not my purpose here to question the veracity of Shoptaw's account or to argue that his account is better than another account. My aim is merely to say that this account is typical within contemporary poetics and to examine the metaphysical presuppositions on which it relies. In this way, we can indicate how a Heideggerian analysis can change how we think about eco-poetry and its possibilities.

5.5 Eco-poetry and metaphysics

While Shoptaw's definition is clearly a reasonable one, it does not fit well into a Heideggerian view for two immediate reasons. First, Showtaw's definition concerns the nature of the relationship between the poet and the natural world. It also says something about what this relationship should be if the poem is to be considered an eco-poem, namely, that the eco-poet cannot merely describe the natural world. This definition, thus, relies on a distinction between the human and the non-human, in this case the 'natural' world. For Shoptaw, it is the particular nature of this relationship that makes a poem an eco-poem. In very simply terms, Shoptaw's definition gives us a metaphysical picture containing a poet, who is distinct from the natural world, the natural world itself and the relationship between these. He fully acknowledges that poetry investigates the relationship between the natural world, perception and culture. He says 'eco-poets cannot be naive about matters of perception and poetic representation' (2016). However, despite this, he goes on to claim,

> that nature exists not only in the sensorium of the beholder; it's really 'out there.' There are, for instance, environmental facts – such as the unnerving one that the level of atmospheric carbon dioxide has now reached an unsustainable 400 parts per million – that we know objectively and can render independently of our personal or cultural perceptions, in an essay or a poem. However self-aware and self-reflexive it may be, an ecopoem must be tethered to the natural world. (Shoptaw 2016)

While Shoptaw's account is formulated to show that eco-poetry must refer to the world in a particular way, it includes an implicit metaphysical picture where scientific facts are independent of what he describes as the 'sensorium of the beholder'. The poet, in this picture, is required to use his art in order to address these facts in a responsible way.

That the world is 'out there' is evidenced by the facts of science. Thus, the language of science must be distinct from our personal or cultural perceptions. The language of science is given primacy in this implicit metaphysics. However, as we saw earlier (in chapter 2) Heidegger does not privilege any part of language as scientific evidence, and he does not see language as referring to an unambiguously pre-existing world. For this reason poetry does not come 'after' our relationship to world, but rather it discloses the world. Great poetry, as we saw earlier, discloses the world in the most authentic way possible in language. Shoptaw's definition implies that when we write poetry, we write about the world in much the same way we write other things such as scientific theories or reports or travel guides etc. As we have seen, the difference between these writings and poetry can be accounted for in terms of aesthetic categories such as beauty, or in terms of the use of figurative tropes like metaphor.

5.6 Eco-poetry and metaphor

This brings us to the second reason why Shoptaw's definition is unamenable to Heidegger's account. The figurative nature of poetry leads Shoptaw to, immediately, refine his definition by saying that the use of nature in an eco-poem cannot be figurative. From a Heideggerian perspective, such a claim is ultimately metaphysics and, as we have seen Heidegger associates the literal/figurative divide with Cartesian subjectivity, which we are told explicitly in 'The Origin', inhibits the disclosure of poetic truth. Of course, what Shoptaw means here is that we have to distinguish, in overly simplistic terms, between a poem that uses a rose as a symbol of, for example, human love, from a poem which presents a rose simply as a rose (a nature poem) or a poem which uses a rose to make some point about the environmental crisis (an eco-poem).

The objects of nature are, of course, often used by poets in a figurative way. The Hollie McNish poem in the preceding chapter is a simple example. The poem uses the image of a butterfly, not to say something about butterflies, but to say something about the poet. The Shoptaw poem in the preceding chapter is also about butterflies, but the butterflies in this poem are not standing in for some human transformation. Rather, in this poem, we get some sense of where we are with respect to butterflies. The Shoptaw poem acknowledges that many species of butterflies are in danger of extinction due to climate change and the destruction of natural habitats and so on. Eco-poetry brings our attention to these facts. The question becomes how do the metaphysical underpinnings of Shoptaw's poetics affect the environmentalist aim of his poem?

At base, this can be seen in terms of an ontological question, which asks, 'what is a butterfly?' Given the quasi-scientific realism at work here, a butterfly is, according to a Google search, 'an insect in the macrolepidopteran clade Rhopalocera from the order Lepidoptera, which also includes moths'. Shoptaw's implicit metaphysics refers to scientific objects, such as butterflies, which are independent of us, and which can be known by our scientific theories (scientific realism) and a human sensorium. Metaphorical transference happens within the realm of this sensorium. As we saw in chapter 3, such a metaphysical outlook precludes Heidegger's rich understanding of poetry as truth, and leads, ultimately, to an inability to philosophically account for poetry, or art more generally. We cannot fit great poetry into the metaphysical picture that Shoptaw is promoting. Thus, Shoptaw's 'Near Earth Object' cannot be accounted for by his own poetics of eco-poetry. As we saw in Chapter 3, if we see this poem in terms of the dissolution of the literal/figurative divide, the pertinent question becomes whether this dissolution allows being to speak, or to put it another way, does it represent the erosion of metaphysical categories associated with technology?

5.7 Metaphor and the fourfold

What is clear is that we cannot use an aesthetic analysis of metaphor as a transposing, to unlock the literal meaning of Shoptaw's poem, because it is simply difficult to isolate the boundary between the literal and the figurative in the poem. Our normal, aesthetic understanding of metaphor requires this divide. Such an account of metaphor is inextricably bound up with the metaphysics described earlier. The line between the sensuous and the non-sensuous is the same as the science/sensorium picture on which Shoptaw's definition of eco-poetry relies. In such a picture, science provides us with objective facts untainted by the subject's anthropomorphizing. Also, as we saw earlier, few philosophers of science would attempt to strictly defend such a metaphysical picture nowadays. There is a general acknowledgement of the influence of the cultural context within which science takes place and, as we saw earlier, an acknowledgement that scientific models themselves can be considered metaphorical. Despite this, the fact that Shoptaw's account relies on this metaphysics seems to show that it is ubiquitous and, to some extent, inevitable.

This metaphysical construct consigns metaphor to the realm of the subjective, where it is independent of the object itself. Because this view is so engrained, it is difficult to imagine an alternative, but this is what Heidegger means when he says 'that up till today we have not yet sufficiently pondered what the sunliness of the eye consists of' (Heidegger 1996: 48). Pondering the sunliness of the eye means considering an alternative account of metaphor. The fourfold is Heidegger's attempt to think this alternative. A Heideggerian poetics would use the idea of the fourfold where aesthetic accounts refer to metaphor. The fourfold is the later Heidegger's attempt to give a metaphysical account of things, especially everyday things, that doesn't collapse into Cartesian subjectivity. The thing of the fourfold is 'inherently relational' as Mitchell (2015) puts it. Things are only conceivable, in the first instance, as part of a world; they stand in a reciprocal and symbiotic relationship to one another generating the world in which they have meaning. A specific thing both contributes to and receives meaning from the world and it cannot be the thing it is, in isolation. As we saw in the previous chapter, the fourfold cannot be explained away as figurative, or as literal. Heidegger's jug points to meaning beyond its 'objectivity'. These meanings are grouped, by Heidegger, as world, earth, god and man. We understand things in terms of these categories. In this way, the fourfold includes the phenomena we describe as metaphor. Rather than seeing things solely in terms of their physical dimensions and characteristics, the later Heidegger understand them in terms of their relational significance. Things ring out with meanings, which interlace and interact with other meaningful things to weave the world, into which Dasein finds itself thrown. It is only because we are so accustomed to viewing objects as self-enclosed entities, that we require separate metaphysical categories in order to understand or conceptualize metaphor. Of course, this is not to say that the concept of the fourfold is isomorphic with the idea of metaphorical transposing between categories. The fourfold is an attempt to overcome these very categories.

Given this, how are we to understand our example of a butterfly in terms of Heidegger's fourfold ontology? We start obviously by saying that a butterfly is not exhausted by its scientific definition, or by an account of its physical characteristics simply stated. While these are instrumentally useful, they result in a linguistic representation of a butterfly. This representation necessarily comes after the experience of disclosing butterflies in our day-to-day life. To express this initial disclosure, we also use language. We might say 'butterflies are beautiful, delicate creatures that flutter into our gardens during the summer'. This short description expresses our actual experience of butterflies better than the earlier scientific description, but it hardly gives us the intensity that experiencing a butterfly can sometimes engender; this intensity comes not only from the butterfly but also from our associations, be they personal or cultural. For Heidegger, these cannot be untangled from the butterfly's being, but they are inherent to it. To capture this we need a poetic language. In fact, the most authentic way to capture this is in a poem: the being of a butterfly is most authentically expressed in poetic language.

5.8 Subjectivity and the aim of eco-poetry

This analysis has powerful consequences for eco-poetry. We can see this by asking what is the purpose of eco-poetry? There would be no point in writing such poems if they could not have a positive influence on how we interact with the natural world. Indeed, Shoptaw makes an optimistic claim about the possible impact of eco-poetry. 'Even if we can never specify its means or results, eco-poetry can also help make environmentalism happen' (Shoptaw 2016). In order to have a positive effect, eco-poetry must influence behaviour in relation to the environment. But poetry is not legislation, it cannot force a change in behaviour. It can only persuade us in some way. One obvious way that poetry may do this is by changing how we know or understand the environment; to make it somehow more important to us. But if we accept the metaphysical implications of Shoptaw's definition, any attempt to change how we feel about environmental things is limited to the realm of the subjective.

However, the objective butterfly of science, the insect of the definition given earlier, is not the butterfly of our experience. Without arguing against the science, it is fair to say that the butterfly of the scientific definition is not the butterfly of our experience. Perhaps we cannot change our behaviour towards this butterfly because it is not changeable, unless the scientific theories in which it is embedded change. It is the butterfly in our garden that we need to consider, the butterfly that perhaps still can be the butterfly of the fourfold. If we see our experience of butterflies as merely subjective, then they are not that important. In the realm of the subjective, I may not care for butterflies, or I may think butterflies are merely sentimental things. You may assign a particular significance to them, but this significance, like my ambivalence, is subjective; just as my preference for tea and your preference for coffee. Ultimately, it is difficult to assign value to such preferences, all we can really say is that they are somehow equal. I am at liberty to dismiss your subjective appreciation of butterflies and see it as no more important than my preference for electronic dance music.

At the same time, science operates by isolating the butterfly, from all this subjectivity. The scientific definition unworlds the objective butterfly, isolating it from its place, both in nature and from our cultural and personal associations. This distinction between nature and our cultural associations is metaphysical. For Heidegger, it is simply not the case that there is nothing beyond the 'scientific' butterfly other than the subjective. We know this because we resonate with certain artworks and poems. This resonance is how we know great poetry, and without Heidegger's notion of poetic truth, we cannot explain our resonance. In this way, great art, for Heidegger is not subjective. Heidegger extolls us not to understand the world in terms of this dualism but rather to understand that we are, first, always disclosing the world. If poetry has the ability to overcome metaphysics, it is for this very reason. Poetry shows us that attempts to divide the world up into categories of natural and cultural, or literal and figurative are only ever provisional and arbitrary.

5.9 Eco-poetry and technology

Of course, as we saw in the previous chapter, according to Heidegger, Shoptaw's implicit metaphysics is no longer relevant in a digital age, where the Cartesian object becomes standing reserve. After the 1930s, Heidegger's critique of

Cartesian metaphysics gives way to his critique of technology. Heidegger's jug becomes the mass-produced, disposable product of late capitalism; such a product has no particular significance and, thus, it can barely be thought of as a thing at all. Technology, as ontohistorical process, supersedes the epoch where things are brought forth (*poiēsis*) and replaces it with a challenging mode of disclosure. The challenged environment stands by awaiting exploitation; it is a merely a resource or a product to be consumed. As we saw earlier, it is not just objects, which are enframed in technology, the subject itself is also reduced to exploitable standing reserve. Given Heidegger's account, and the foregoing account of the digital, the question becomes whether the enframed subject retains the ability to disclose anything but standing reserve.

How does this movement to technology affect our consideration of contemporary poetry and poetics? We can begin by noting that Heidegger's critique of Cartesian metaphysics constellates around art, finding its most elegant expression in 'The Origin'. As we have seen, great art is not subjective, and the work 'itself', in the sense of work material, cannot be adequately understood as an object. In this way, great art is the realm, which resists the subject/object dualism. If we insist on viewing a great work in terms of these Cartesian categories, we fail to grasp the work's ontological particularity, as unconcealment of truth. In terms of poetry, as we saw in Chapter 3, an aesthetic reading of a great poem similarly bypasses its Saying. However, in a technological age, this already bad situation deteriorates further. It is not simply that we misunderstand great art by forcing it into Cartesian framework, that is, by viewing it as subjective, but rather the very possibility of great art is eroded. To understand this point, we must remember that we cannot account for this erosion simply by considering some poem or another. Rather, any explanation must also refer to the preserving of the poem. In the digital, this preservation is also enframed. In a digital age, even the metaphysical misunderstanding of art becomes impossible. In 'The Question Concerning Technology', Heidegger tells us that truth is driven out. As we saw in Chapter 1, truth as unconcealment takes place in the interaction between the work and its preservers; the great work is preserved unconcealment. However, technology determines how the digital item is both concealed and how it is unconcealed; it can only be disclosed as standing reserve. A digital preserver can no longer even assign a subjective meaning to a work. The work can be understood *only* as standing reserve. The butterfly is no longer the butterfly of science, nor is it the butterfly of my purely subjective understanding; it is now the butterfly of a Google search, and thus, of even less consequence than before. If things, including natural things, become inconsequential in the digital age, then surely, the aim of eco-poetry can be viewed in terms of resisting the enframent of the natural world.

Technology, manifest as the digital, makes Shoptaw's definition more problematic than it originally seemed because it becomes difficult to distinguish between the natural and the human, when everything has become standing reserve. Also, the question of demarcation of eco-poetry becomes more difficult if we accept that the natural world has become enframed. So for example, Shoptaw goes on to give examples of poems that may or not be eco-poems, given his definition. He points out disagreements between commentators in this respect. While Shoptaw's definition puts strict limits on the poems we can consider as eco-poems, theorists such as Timothy Morten (2009) claim that any poem which deals with the ambient environment can be considered eco-poetry. Such a definition may be so broad as to make the term 'eco-poetry' meaningless. From a Heideggerian perspective, the issue at stake is whether poetry can still disclose the natural world to us as something important and worthy of our attention; as something true. A poet who can make things thing or open the fourfold will allow us to connect with our environment in a way that is not 'just' as a subject or as an enframed thing. It would seem, then, that one possible role for the poet in a time of environmental crisis is to make environmental things thing. That is, the role of eco-poetry is to instil meaning back into objects. The question, from a Heideggerian perspective, becomes whether this is still possible.

5.10 Jane Hirshfield and the eco-poetry of things

One poet who can be interpreted as attempting this task is Jane Hirshfield. Hirshfield's recent collection 'Ledger' (2020) is environmentalist in the sense that Shoptaw means.

The collection deals with many natural things, such as fish and pebbles, many of the poems are concerned with the sorts of basic things that occupied the later Heidegger, such as buckets and paint. Many of the poems deal with one simple thing, which is given in the poem's title: 'The Bowl', 'Vest', 'Paint', 'Dog Tag' and so on. One way to read this collection is as an attempt to recover these things into their worldedness, and in this way, the collection can be understood in Heideggerian terms. Heidegger's account of things provides us with a powerful way to understand this collection that aesthetic accounts cannot fully capture. For example, 'A Bucket Forgets Its Water' can be viewed, from a Heideggerian perspective, as capturing a bucket in its thinging.

Like the jug in Heidegger's essay, the poem opens up the fourfold, and in this way we could see it as a true Heideggerian eco-poem. The bucket is understood in terms of fabric of meaning of interlocking meanings that constitute the bucket as the thing it is. Like van Gogh's shoes, the poem interrupts our usual circumspect use of a bucket and shows a bucket in truth. The bucket is associated with a donkey, not in a metaphorical way, but rather in terms of the historical link between buckets and donkeys in terms of human work. Like the bucket, the donkey was used to carry and transport goods. In the past, buckets and donkeys were both part of a rural life. The poem seems to focus on the difference and similarities between the living animal and the inert tool, but it also links them as constituents of a world. Moreover, the bucket in its status as ready-to-hand is brought to light by the very notion of forgetting. The bucket forgets its water as it is forgotten in its use, but brought to truth or unconcealed in the poem. While we have focused on concealment as circumspection; concealment is also forgetting. Aletheia can be translated as un-forgetting (lethe). The poem brings the bucket out of its forgottenness and allows it to thing. It is easy to see how the language of metaphor could obstruct a Heideggerian reading. Furthermore, any attempt to objectify the bucket will prevent the poem's saying.

It is not just traditional everyday things that Hirshfield deals with, she also deals with things that are typical of the digital such as a ream of printer paper. The choice of technological items means Hirshfield's collection provides an interesting test case for our Heideggerian analysis. If Heidegger's warning about technology is valid, then Hirshfield's attempt to make things including technological things thing should be impacted. Yet both the poem about the bucket and the poem about the printer paper seem to disclose things as relational things. It would be certainly unfair, or simply wrong, to say that either of these poems had 'failed'. If they have not failed; if Hirshfiled's poem opens the fourfold of a technological object, then it would seem that Heidegger's account that can be questioned in this respect. We could, then, take a position similar to that of Dreyfus and Spinosa (1997), described in Chapter 5, and argue that technological things can be affirmed, and it is this that is captured in Hirshfield's poem. But as we saw, such a reading regards the fourfold as metaphorical. As we saw earlier, a metaphorical reading of the fourfold cannot support the idea of affirming technology and ultimately collapses back into subjectivity. The ream of paper is listed alongside other things, such as almonds and coffee, that we understand in terms of Hirshfield's subjective experience; that is, they are not essential things. There is also something nostalgic about Hirshfield's collection; the wool scarf which features in the poem is a nostalgic thing in the age of mass-produced disposable fashion. This is not to say that Hirshfield's poems do not work on their own terms, but that they describe a human life, which is in the process of being enframed. In some cases, at least, Hirshfield's poems do not acknowledge this digitization.

If we accept Heidegger's account, then we must hold that all things including the environment are digitized in a digital age. This claim goes beyond the banal claim that we are now surrounded, mostly, by disposable, mass-produced items, to the deeper claim that even a seemingly meaningful thing, such as an heirloom, can no longer 'thing', in the Heideggerian sense of opening up the fourfold. The significance of heirlooms is lost in the digital and replaced with nostalgia. The same is true of the environment. An eco-poetry which merely exemplifies this nostalgia is trapped within a technological metaphysics. If eco-poetry, such as that of Hirshfield, fails to challenge the digital, can poetic movements that deal explicitly with technology such as digital poetry and post-internet poetry provide us with a way to overcome the effects of technology?

6

Towards an ontology of digital poetry

6.1 Introduction

As we have seen in Chapter 2, Heidegger places poetry at the centre of his account of language. Language is that which makes things manifest, and poetic language brings things to manifestation in the most authentic way possible. However, contemporary poetry's ability to authentically uncover is subject to the influence of technology. In this way, Heidegger's accounts of poetry and technology offer us a conceptual framework with which to view movements in contemporary poetry. In Chapter 4, we saw how the digital is the realm in which technology, as the greatest danger, becomes more deeply entrenched, and in Chapter 5, we saw how this danger becomes apparent in eco-poetry. We can now ask how are we to understand poetic movements that directly involve technology. If technology is the way that things are, and language is that which makes them manifest, how is the language of poetry affected by the direct employment of digital technology? In this chapter, we begin our investigation of these questions in terms of digital poetry. While Heidegger describes poetry and technology as two opposing modes of unconcealment, he also claims that neither can entirely escape the influence of the other. The challenging nature of technology threatens art, yet the dangers of technology can be revealed by the saving power of the poetic.

It is a banality to note that the reach of digital technology now extends into practically every aspect of life, including the arts and poetry. For good or ill, poetry has become inexorably interwoven with technology. Poets have certainly critically confronted the technological as subject matter, but technology is also used in the composition and dissemination of poetry. In an age where natural language generators are being 'taught' to compose poems, do we need to concede that Heidegger's bleak warning with respect to technology did not go far enough, or does Heidegger's disdain for the technological seem ridiculous when we consider the fact that anyone who writes a poem using word processing software had unwittingly enframed the poem by using a technology based on the exact science of physics?

Given this Heideggerian picture, it would seem fruitful to examine the cultural practices that explicitly combine the digital and the poetic. In this chapter, I will consider digital poetry. To this end, I will briefly describe the difficulties inherent in defining and categorizing digital poetry, given the flexibility in the technologies used. Next, I will consider digital poetry in terms of Heidegger's categories of 'world' and 'earth'. In 'The Origin', the most contemporary example of an artwork used is van Gogh's painting of the peasant's shoes. The painting is used to demonstrate how art allows us to know the shoes in their essence, that is, their *equipmentality*.

The shoes depicted are an example of old technology. It is interesting to ask, what, if any, contemporary artwork would give us the essence of the new technology, especially as technology has become digital? Heidegger's account of technology can certainly be understood in terms of art. In 'The Question Concerning Technology', *we are told* that technology is the realm in which truth is driven out, and as a consequence, the nature of art becomes mysterious. I will attempt to extend Heidegger's account into the realm of the digital by asking what prevents technological devices or processes from functioning as the earth of a poem. To these ends, I will compare how earth operates in traditional and contemporary poetic modalities. I will show how the earth of digital poem operates and argue that because of its enframing essence, digital technologies do not conceal, and therefore unconceal, in the manner of traditional poetry and that this prevents the possibility of truth disclosure.

Heidegger exalts poetry because it is a language-based art form, and we will investigate how language is presented in digital poetry. In addition we will investigate how various elements common in digital poetry act as the earth of digital poems. I will employ Hui's (2016) ontology of digital objects to provide a conceptual framework for this discussion. I will focus on common elements of digital poems such as screens, computer programming languages and hyperlinks and how this affects their ability to open up a world. This discussion revolves around a number of case studies including Geoffrey Squires' poetry for screens and the Apostrophe Engine. In short, this chapter will ask, can we consider digital poetry as a confrontation with technology, or is it a realm where the poetic is further concealed by technology?

6.2 Can the digital gather the fourfold?

As we have seen, if we begin with a broadly Heideggerian characterization of the digital, there are two possible ways to confront it: *Gelassenheit* and the poetic. In terms of digital poetry, the question becomes whether it represents a way in which we can develop a free relation to the digital or simply an expression of how the digital enframes poetry. In this chapter, we will work towards a Heideggerian account of digital poetry. We will see how the analysis of Borgmann and Dreyfus and Spinosa can inform such an account. Notwithstanding the subtleties of their respective positions, we can understand them as different possible Heideggerian responses to technology. While these differences are possibly differences of degree rather than kind, they have substantive consequences for an account of digital poetry. Borgmann suggests that we should look away from technology towards focal practices, while Dreyfus and Spinosa suggest that we affirm technological devices themselves. These positions differ from Heidegger's solution because Heidegger asks us to both affirm and negate technology. Finally, we will ask whether digital poetry offers a way towards this.

While Borgmann acknowledges the advantages that some technological devices offer, as we have seen, he suggests that we can ameliorate the influence of technology by looking away from it and turning our attention to focal practices such as the ritual associated with a family meal. From such a perspective, digital poetry seems like a movement in the wrong direction. Rather, it would seem that the act of opening a book and reading a poem is exactly the sort of focal practice that could reorient us away from technology. From a Heideggerian perspective, the obvious problem with this type of solution lies in the assumption that we can turn away from technology in the first place. If technology is prior to us, it is not amenable to our will and, therefore, not something we can wish away. Furthermore, the idea that we can simply turn towards focal practices may actually blind us to the detrimental effects of technology and lull us into believing that we can sidestep its influence. We may seek out authentic experiences, but these are provided to us by market forces and are ultimately kitsch, for example, a pub rebranded as a traditional Irish pub.

Alternatively, we have seen that Dreyfus and Spinosa suggest that we learn to affirm technology itself. This seems a more hopeful candidate for developing a Heideggerian-free relation to technology and a way to philosophically defend digital poetry. But how exactly do Dreyfus and Spinosa propose that we affirm technology? Rather than becoming standing reserve, we must become disclosers of technology. 'We must first get a clear picture of exactly what it is like to be turned into resources responding to each situation according to whichever of our disaggregated skills is solicited most strongly' (Dreyfus and Spinosa 1997: 170) and then learn to affirm this state of affairs. Tellingly, the example they give of how 'mortals' can 'morph' in this way involves a 'pack of today's teenagers' buying a CD. When a group of teenagers want to get a new CD, the one with the car (with the driving skills and capacity) will be the most important until they get to the store; then the one with the money (with purchasing skills and capacity) will lead; and then when they want to play the CD, the one with the CD player (with CD playing skills and capacity) will be out front (Dreyfus and Spinosa 1997: 170).

Of course, buying a CD is now a thing of the past. The only skill required now to acquire music is the skill to search the preferred tracks on Spotify and press play. Even this is not necessary as Spotify will suggest music, and the preferred way to listen to music is through earphones that minimize the need for the social interaction required to buy the CD. The notion that we can easily affirm technology by becoming disclosers of it seems to underestimate the power and momentum of digital technology. The example of buying a CD now only serves to demonstrate how the rapid evolution of the digital can overwhelm any attempts to disclose it.

Wrathall (2011) offers another possible explanation of why Dreyfus and Spinosa's solution is doomed to failure. This attempt to affirm technology cannot work because it does not fully acknowledge the essential role of the fourfold, especially the divinities, in Heidegger's account. Although the fourfold can be a challenging aspect of Heidegger's thought, some theorists such as Mitchell claim that it is 'nothing less than the inauguration of Heidegger's later thinking' (Mitchell 2015: 3). In the later work, Heidegger becomes more focused on the things of everyday life. A thing is the thing it is because it 'things'; that is it opens up the fourfold. In short, simple things are inherently relational. This is not an account of what things can do – that is, things can relate – but rather as an account of what they are: a thing is not something that possesses the ability to extend past 'itself' in a system of relations, but rather, a thing can only *be* with respect to these relations.

As Mitchell puts it, 'thanks to the fourfold, these things unfold themselves ecstatically, opening relations with the world beyond them' (2015: 3). Things in this sense are contrasted with the things of metaphysics which are 'unworlded'. We can understand this in terms of Heidegger's notion of finitude. For Heidegger, Mitchell tells us, '[f]initude is a kind of relational radiance'. The finitude of things can only be understood in terms of something 'beyond' the thing. This beyond is not the 'empty void' of metaphysics, but rather, it is capable of 'transmitting these radiant relations' (2015: 5). In this way, something is ecstatic, in a Heideggerian sense, when it is inexorably connected to this beyond so as to be 'unthinkable apart from it' (2015: 7). We cannot think the thing without this ecstatic relationality, and the thing, in its turn, helps to generate this relationality. Things are only the things they are in terms of this relationality, and it is precisely this relationality that technology challenges. It is important to note that the account of technology and the account of things thinging are developed simultaneously by the later Heidegger. These accounts represent a progression in his thinking about objectivity. Technology is, for Heidegger, an epoch where being is abandoned. In this time, objects cease to be objects and merely 'put on a performance of objectivity' (2015: 27). Objectivity and representation, the modes of unconcealment associated with modernity, are corrupted as standing reserve becomes the dominant mode of being.

While affirming technological devices is central to Heidegger's account of *Gelassenheit*. It is unclear whether a technological device or indeed a digital device can 'thing' in this sense. Things thing, for Heidegger, when they gather the fourfold of earth, sky, divinities and mortals. The idea of the fourfold undoubtedly challenges many contemporary commentators with its rather overblown metaphysical excess. However, the gathering of the fourfold is a central idea in Heidegger's later philosophy and one that cannot be simply glossed over without considerable violence to Heidegger's position. Wrathall suggests that Dreyfus and Spinosa's metaphorical reading of the fourfold cannot support their idea of affirming technology.

Dreyfus and Spinosa claim that when Heidegger speaks of the fourfold,

> his thinking draws on Hölderlin's difficult poetic terms of art; yet what Heidegger means has its own coherence so long as we keep the phenomenon of a thing thinging before us. (Dreyfus and Spinosa 1997: 166)

In this way, they describe the divinities in a way that reigns in Heidegger's extravagant language. They claim the language is poetic and makes sense on its own terms. While we may recognize the special quality of a focal event, such as a family meal, we need not take Heidegger entirely seriously when he suggests that the divine is an 'actual' part of this event. In this way, Heidegger's ascription of a divine aspect to a thing or an event is not literal and rather refers to the tendency such events have, to be graceful and to have a momentum of their own.

> When a focal event such as a family meal is working to the point it has a particular integrity, one feels one feels extraordinarily in tune with all that is happening, a special graceful ease takes over, and events seem to unfold of their own momentum – all combining to make the moment more centered and more a gift. (Dreyfus and Spinosa 1997: 167)

The divine aspect of a family meal is the feeling that a gift has been bestowed on the occasion. Traditionally, saying grace acknowledged the gift of a family meal. Even in the absence of the prayer, there is still the feeling of a gift. This feeling is what, according to Borgmann, creates a community from strangers, for example, in the context of a baseball game. So for Dreyfus and Spinosa, the divinities provide something that is, somehow, beyond the efforts of those involved in the focal practice and is dependent on the context in question. In this way, the divinities, as understood by Dreyfus and Spinosa, can be seen as simply a feeling of community or gratitude. Still, as we have seen in the earlier example of teenagers buying a CD, this 'feeling' is subject to erosion from the continuing progression of technology. It is not difficult to imagine a situation where a family meal becomes a rare situation and one that is increasingly encroached upon by technology.

Contrary to this, Wrathall gives a much more literal account of the fourfold. In fact, he claims that Heidegger describes the fourfold generally and the divinities in particular in an 'infuriatingly literal fashion' (Wrathall 2011: 205). While acknowledging that the metaphorical reading is 'certainly preferable' (Wrathall 2011: 205) to most contemporary philosophers, Wrathall's focus on Heidegger's seemingly literal account is compelling. As Wrathall points out, there are many instances of very literal interpretations of the fourfold by Heidegger; the earth of a jug, for example, is earth. The jug gathers the sky by holding and pouring the wine that results from the action of the rain on the earth. According to Wrathall, passages such as this are meant 'quite literally' (Wrathall 2011: 205); moreover, he claims, more metaphorical readings 'do violence to the text' (Wrathall 2011: 205). In fact, according to Wrathall, the sky is *the* sky, the earth is the earth used to make a jug, we are mortals, and the divinities 'are divine beings' (Wrathall 2011: 205). Without the ability to gather each element of the fourfold in this literal sense, things become meaningless and inauthentic.

However, we cannot read Wrathall's account without acknowledging that for Heidegger, metaphysics imposes the literal/figurative distinction onto reality. It is wrong to say Heidegger's account is mostly metaphorical or literal when it is precisely these metaphysical categories that Heidegger brings into question. These literal examples of the fourfold resonate with the thinking metaphor from the *Principle of Reason* discussed in Chapter 3, where thinking is described as an extension of hearing. According to Heidegger, there is no cut-off point after which it becomes figurative to call thinking a hearing. Similarly, the earth is that which the jug, as thing, is concealed. It is from the earth of its clay that the jug performs its task of holding and pouring wine; in this way, it mirrors the earth from which the vine grows but not metaphorically; the wine is from the sky and the earth. For a thing to thing, all this significance is apparent, implicitly or explicitly.

In terms of poetry, greatness is achieved by transcending the boundary between the sensuous and the nonsensuous. In a technological age, this limit is pulled tightly around the object itself so that the sensuous is understood in a very minimal way; the jug is represented by or framed within its measurable physical qualities, its monetary value or its orderability and exploitability. As the technological can only deal with things in this way, the figurative becomes the repository of anything beyond these brute physical or calculable dimensions. Poetry is the realm in which this boundary is transcended, or at least shown as arbitrary. In enframing, the earth, in its role as material, sucks up the other elements of the fourfold. The jug is a replaceable object that serves a simple purpose of pouring a liquid. It is earth, but in such a way that conceals itself and everything else except for its status as standing reserve, which is challenged forth from it. In this way, it cannot thing. The poetic is the realm in which the jug, or in this case the technological device, is reconnected to the sky, the earth, mortal and divinity if such a reconnection is possible. In this way, Heidegger's account of the fourfold should not be understood as either literal or metaphorical because our line of demarcation between the two is a driving force of metaphysics, a historical force that culminates in the digital.

If a digital poem can function as a way of developing a free relation to digital technology, then it must thing, and we cannot simply understand this thinging in terms of the figurative. In order to thing, a digital poem must open up the fourfold. If a digital poem can do this, then it provides us with a way to affirm digital technology, and if it cannot, we must ask what it is about digital technology that prevents this world opening. To investigate these questions, we will begin with an ontological analysis of both traditional and digital poetry. However, because this book concerns art, specifically poetry, the most crucial aspect of the fourfold for the present purpose is that of earth. Therefore, I will focus on the account of earth as it is presented in 'The Origin'. As we saw in the chapter on metaphor, Heidegger's critical attention is focused on the literal/figurative distinction, which he associates with metaphysics. In 'The Origin', as we shall see, Heidegger links metaphysics with a collection of conceptual dualisms, in particular, the subject/object dichotomy, but also and relatedly, the notion that an artwork work is comprised of a material substructure to which aesthetic qualities adhere. Heidegger replaces this conception of the work with his account of world and earth and the strife between them. In the later work, earth becomes one of the fourfold and, therefore, a part of what it means for a thing to thing. Heidegger's account of things is developed further as he comes to understand technology in terms of the danger it poses. Technology is an intensification of metaphysics. The conceptual dualisms of metaphysics are eroded in technology, but they are not overcome. Thus, in 'The Origin', Heidegger uses the categories of world and earth to critique elements of metaphysics. Later, he uses the fourfold as a foil against which we can understand how technology enframes the object rendering it as standing reserve. In this way, it is important to note that the discussion of earth in 'The Origin' is not identical to the discussion of earth as a part of the fourfold.

6.3 The earth of an artwork

To understand if or how the digital can operate as the earth of a poem, we need to first examine how Heidegger understands earth in terms of the art of previous epochs. In 'The Origin', Heidegger attempts to give us an account of what art is, or more specifically, what great art is. As we have seen, he contrasts his view with what he holds to be the dominant aesthetic view, where an artwork is viewed as a thing to which aesthetic qualities are somehow attached. While a painting is a piece of stretched canvas to which pigment has been applied, we miss the point if we focus on this element. Instead, the aesthetician looks past the canvas and considers the work in terms of aesthetic categories such as beauty. From this view, Heidegger tells us, 'the work makes public something other than itself; it manifests, something other' (Heidegger 1971: 19). This 'other' is brought together (*sumballein*) with the work. The work is, then, a symbol bringing a thing and something other together. Heidegger claims, 'Allegory and symbol provide the conceptual frame within whose channel of vision the artwork has long been characterized' (Heidegger 1971: 20).

For Heidegger, the aesthetic view is problematic for several reasons. First and foremost, it is based on philosophical notions of thinghood that are inadequate for artworks. If we begin an analysis of art with an unexplored presupposition about what a thing is, we get off on the wrong foot straight away. Things come with a lot of philosophical baggage. According to Heidegger, we tend to see 'mere' things or things in an 'almost pejorative sense' (Heidegger 1971: 21) as paradigmatic of thinghood or even of existence more generally. To understand the work, we must first get beyond this sense of a thing that is basic to the metaphysical world view of this epoch, where an artwork is simply another thing, albeit one to which aesthetic qualities adhere. Aesthetics, as Heidegger defines it, fails to make this move beyond metaphysics.

Heidegger tells a philosophical story about the shift from the Greek *Hupokeimenon/ta sumbebekota* to the Latin *subjectum/accidens* and how this move conceals a movement away from understanding things as beings to an understanding of things as substances with accidental qualities. The Latin concept of thing mirrors the basic propositional structure of a sentence, a structure where a quality is generally predicated to a subject. According to Heidegger, the question of which came first, the structure of propositions or the concept of things, is unanswerable. However, the relation between the two makes this thing-concept appear self-evident. Despite this, Heidegger considers it 'rash' because it 'would have to explain how first such a transposition of propositional structure into the thing is supposed to be possible without the thing being already visible' (Heidegger 1971: 24). Moreover, such a concept of thinghood cannot capture what is particular about given things because it applies itself equally to every sort of thing. In this way, it does violence to all things because it does not 'lay hold of the thing in its own being' (Heidegger 1971: 24) as van Gogh's painting of the shoes does.

Similarly, if we conceive of the thing as *aistheton*, 'that which is perceptible by the senses' (Heidegger 1971: 25), we hit another problem. Harking back to Heidegger's account of categorial intuition, we are told that it is not sensations we encounter but things. We do not perceive a 'throng of sensations', but we hear the sound of a car approaching. Moreover, this account, like the concept of the thing as a bearer or traits, captures all things and none. 'In both interpretations the thing vanishes' (Heidegger 1971: 26).

Heidegger, then, considers things as matter (*hule*) and form (*morphe*), a conceptual framework with obvious attractions for those interested in artworks. However, these 'hackneyed' concepts again allow everything to be subsumed under them. Moreover, Heidegger links the thing as formed matter with equipment rather than artworks. Historically, it may seem that the concept of formed matter originates from the 'workly character of the art work' rather than the 'thingly character of the thing' (Heidegger 1971: 27), but Heidegger offers an alternative story.

> Form as shape is not the consequence here of a prior distribution of the matter. The form, on the contrary, determines the arrangement of the matter. Even more, it prescribes in each case the kind and the selection of the matter-impermeable for a jug, sufficiently hard for an ax, firm yet flexible for shoes. The interfusion of form and matter prevailing here is, moreover, controlled beforehand by the purpose served by jug, ax, shoes. (Heidegger 1978: 154)

It is usefulness that according to Heidegger, underlies the notion of things as formed matter. Equipment is formed to do something, and so the concepts of form and matter do not precede equipment, but rather they flow from it. In this way, we cannot clump all things together under the banner of formed matter. Instead, we have a continuum, with the fact of being produced by humans on one end and self-sufficiency on the other. Equipment is midway. Like the artwork, equipment is made, but unlike equipment, the artwork is self-sufficient in the way that a 'mere thing', such as a boulder, is self-sufficient. The dominant concept of things as formed matter is too clumsy to allow us to recognize these distinctions. Moreover, by accepting them, we cannot grasp how close equipment is to us while, at the same time, making equipment the very paradigm of thinghood. Yet, 'the interpretation of the "thing" as matter and form, whether it remains medieval or becomes Kantian-transcendental, has become current and self-evident' (Heidegger 1971: 29).

The important point is that all three concepts of the thing represent an encroachment of the individual thing. A given thing loses its unique thinghood and then becomes hidden under a layer of conceptual analysis. Whether we see the thing as a bearer of traits, a gestalt or as matter and form, we 'assault' it. 'This preconception shackles reflection on the being of any given entity' (Heidegger 1971: 30). When we try to understand a given thing, we are immediately concerned with general thingness. We lose the thing under consideration. These philosophical failures are not accidental; they stem from the things themselves. It is the very nature of things to thwart our efforts to understand them. The individual thing, in its self-refusal, resists us. This self-refusal fuels philosophy's failure to apprehend the particular thing. Even if we manage to leave aside the usual philosophical 'assault', we are still confronted with the entity's own self-refusal.

Famously, Heidegger claims where philosophy fails, art has traditionally succeeded. The self-refusal of the peasant's shoes yields in van Gogh's painting. It is only in the painting that we come to see the equipmental nature of equipment in its self-refusal. The shoes' self-refusal is their usefulness. Like the hammer in *Being and Time*, the shoes disappear into usefulness when they are worn. But now, rather than the language of ready-to-hand and present-at-hand,[1] we are told, '[t]his equipment belongs to the *earth*, and it is protected in the *world* of the peasant woman' (Heidegger 1971: 33). It is the painting and Heidegger's poetic description that brings the shoes 'out of this protected belonging' so that the 'equipment itself rises to its resting within itself' (Heidegger 1971: 35). We do not reflect on equipment when we use it. Thus, we do not see its essence, which is its usefulness or reliability. The work brings us 'somewhere else than we usually tend to be' (Heidegger 1971: 35). This somewhere else is in the vicinity of truth.

For Heidegger, we cannot locate the reality of the work in its 'thing'. The reality of van Gogh's painting does not reside in canvas and paint for as long as we understand this as equipment. '[W]hat we tried to treat as the most immediate reality of the work, it's thingly substructure, does not belong to the work in any way at all' (Heidegger 1971: 37). This is, in part, because we see things as equipment, and the work cannot be understood as a 'piece of equipment that is fitted out in addition with an aesthetic value that adheres to it'

(Heidegger 1971: 38). In this way, Heidegger discards the traditional aesthetic account of art as *sumballein*. The work cannot be understood as two distinct elements that are somehow gathered together. Moreover, this does not lead to a denial of what is 'thingly' in the work. Heidegger is nudging us towards a new understanding of the material substructure of the work and the relationship between it and work. As we have seen in Chapter 1, this new understanding is concerned with truth. In the same way, as we force a poem into a metaphysical framework when we view it in terms of metaphor, considering the work via a 'preconceived framework' blocks our access to the truth of the work. Not only does the aesthetic approach misunderstand the nature of the work, it actually prevents us from seeing the truth that is the nature of the work.

The truth of the work is linked inexorably but not reducible to its context. Heidegger begins his discussion of the 'world' and 'earth' of art with a discussion of 'world withdrawal' or 'world decay'. Once a work is removed from its context, either by being physically removed or by time passing, its status as truth is eroded. Great art is epoch-defining or founding rather than the consequence of its historical context. Once this epoch wanes, the truth of the art is lost. In any epoch, the artwork is the exemplary thing. In the work, we find the 'sheltering agent' (Heidegger 1971: 41) of earth, the world set up by the earth. The artwork exists as the strife between the two. Such an account is incompatible with a representational account of art. The statue in the temple *is* the god and not a representation. In a tragedy, 'nothing is staged or displayed theatrically' (Heidegger 1971: 42); it is not something 'referred to' but rather something experienced directly. Much as we do not encounter a thing as a gestalt of sense datum, we do not experience great art as representation. 'To be a work is to set up a world' (Heidegger 1971: 43). The relationship between earth and world is one of 'setting up'. The earth sets up the 'ever non-objective' worlding of the world. Rather than the work being symbol or representation, it is paradigmatic of truth. The earth of the work sets up the world, which can be understood as unconcealment. Thus, 'space' is made by the work. The shoes are part of the peasant woman's world. They facilitate her work and her understanding of her life. The painting of the shoes opens the space for us to view the shoes in their essence; they appear from out of their 'covert' usefulness. The work appears while equipment in use disappears.[2]

As we saw in Chapter 1, the role of the artist in making the work is one of winning the open area or of making space. As different art forms involve different processes, the role of earth in winning the open space is crucial. 'Earth is that which comes forth and shelters.' This happens in two ways. First, earth allows 'historical man' to ground his dwelling in the world; second, it sets up the work of art. What happens within the artwork reflects the world-forming activity of human life. The work is not a thing that cannot be adequately captured by traditional philosophical concepts; rather, it is, in microcosm, the activity of all historical humanity. In addition, the work allows '*the earth to be an earth*' (Heidegger 1971: 45); the earth is not something from which world simply emerges. The dependency works in both directions. The world requires earth, and the earth requires world; the work allows each to be. 'The work moves the earth itself into the Open' (Heidegger 1971: 45). It is the artist's job to 'set forth the earth' (Heidegger 1971: 46). We are told that the sculptor uses stone as the mason does. She may use the same tools and work in the same workshop, employing similar techniques, but she does not use up the stone. The painter uses pigment, and the poet uses words. Each art form employs a different earth. The artistic process involves using a medium that can be used equipmentally but not using it up.

In this way, Heidegger views the work as the site of struggle between world and earth or unconcealment and concealment. Rather than viewing the canvas as an object or thing to which aesthetic qualities are added, Heidegger views it as a locus of strife between concealment and unconcealment. The world opening that results from this strife is truth in Heidegger's alethic sense of truth. So, as we saw in Chapter 1, great art is truth, in the sense of essence, but for this truth to be, it must struggle into the open from some sort of concealment. These considerations allow us to see how Heidegger's account of earth functions both to conceal and unconceal an epoch-defining artwork. This relationship between essence and unconcealment is a central theme of Heidegger's work from the 1930s onwards. It is expressed in terms of the strife between earth and world in the work in 'The Origin', but it is also a central theme of his later writings on technology, where the thing is understood in terms of the fourfold. In the epoch of technology, the object is understood precisely in terms of its availability, which is understood as a failure to conceal.

For Heidegger, there cannot be great art without concealment. If technology pushes out truth, it is for this reason.

As Mitchell points out, 'availability targets the concealment of essencing' (Mitchell 2015: 38). In a discussion of Heidegger's engagement with the Heraclitus fragment, *'physis kryptesthai philei'* explores further the notion of a reciprocity between concealment and unconcealment. Mitchell expounds on Heidegger's translation: 'that is to say, unconcealment let's concealment show itself. And without this showing of concealment, there would be nothing concealed, for concealment would go unremarked, a lapse into oblivion' (Mitchell 2015: 38). As in 'The Origin', the idea is that if unconcealment allows concealment to be shown and, concealment allows unconcealment to be shown. Both are required for the strife in which essencing arises, be this in terms of works or things. In this way, concealment is not just something which unambiguously hides something else, but it is instead a sheltering. 'To essence is to engage with concealment, to emerge in a way not entirely present.' Without concealment, essence is impossible. We must examine digital poetry in terms of these considerations and ask whether a digital earth allows for space or a world opening. In particular, we can ask, does the digital allow us to make space in terms of world disclosure? Can we ground our dwelling with digital technologies? And, finally, does the digital poet use but not use up the digital so that it first comes to shine?

6.4 The earth of poetry

Before attempting to answer these questions, we must ask how the earth functions in traditional poetry. By elucidating this, we can contrast traditional poetic formats with digital ones in order to understand the consequences of composing poems using digital technologies. We are told in 'The Origin' that language is the earth of a poem; however, a discussion of language does not exhaust the discussion of earth in this respect. Heidegger points out that during the First World War, soldiers on the front kept books of Hölderlin's poetry in their knapsacks, along with cleaning gear. A poem can be an object in the sense that it comes in a book or on a page, but we are told that language is fundamentally the earth of a poem; the linguistic work originates in the speech of a people. The earth of poetry is language, but language is not as simple a phenomenon as the pigment of a painting or the marble of a statue.

Language can be presented in a number of ways: in a book stored on a shelf, on the page when a poem is read quietly by a reader, but also in the sound of speech. Earth is the accent of the poet, the tone of her voice, but it is also the choice of font and the ink on the page. The earth of the poem is language displayed in one or more ways. No matter how it is displayed in the poem, language must, like the paint in a painting or marble in a statue, be displayed in a 'wholly distinct way'. The words used in a great poem are used differently from their use in other domains. This is, in part, because they do not disappear into usefulness. In everyday speech, language rarely becomes an issue. In fact, generally speaking, to the extent that language becomes an issue, it fails to serve its purpose. In order to serve its function, language must withdraw. But in the poem, language becomes apparent. Heidegger tells us that when a word is set up in a poem, it 'first' comes to sound. In poetry, we hear or see the words *as* words.

All the different ways poets present language, as written word, as sound, or as books, are employed variously to wrest language from the unconcealment of everyday written or spoken language and bring it into appearance. Heidegger tells us that it is in poetry that the 'word only now becomes and remains truly a word' (Heidegger 1971: 46). If this effort fails, then the work has 'miscarried'. The world opening has been lost, and the earth has swallowed up the words into their usual everydayness. In terms of poetry, this is the case when the language used is banal or clichéd. In these cases, the poetry cannot be considered great poetry. In everyday language use, written or printed words only become apparent as words if something happens to interrupt their meaning, such as bad handwriting or a typo.

The grammatical rules that govern language arrange words into clauses, clauses are arranged into sentences, and sentences are arranged into paragraphs. These rules facilitate the disappearance of language. While they are in place, language serves its purpose as a self-refusing vehicle of meaning. In the act of listening to or reading, we do not consider language itself. However, the poet is not bound by the rules of regular language use. The presentation of words on the page is important in poetry. Poets present words in many ways; they write formal poems, organize poems into stanzas, consider line length and alignment and write concrete poetry with shapes to reflect the poem's meaning. Even when poets write in a prose style, the decision to do so is a style choice, which must have some rationale, and when it does, it makes the prose style itself visible.

Similarly, when language is considered as sound, the sound of words also disappears into usefulness. Unless there is something to interrupt the sense of the spoken word, like a heavy accent or a speaker's unfamiliarity with a new language, most speakers never 'hear' or are generally unaware of the sound of the words used. In poetry, however, sound becomes key. The poet brings the word to sound through rhythm, rhyme, assonance and dissonance. Perhaps to an extent, more than any other linguistic art form, the poet is concerned with the sound of the words. For example, the use of rhyme allows the rhyming word to be heard in its sound. It emphasizes the sound and consequently the meaning of the word and the word with which it rhymes. It connects these words in sound and meaning. The breaking of a rhyming scheme can have the same effect. Even a bad rhyme can have the effect of bringing a word in its sound into view.

The fact that poetry comes in books or pamphlets is perhaps the clearest notion of the poem as an object. A book of poetry is the same sort of thing as a textbook on physics. They both have ISBN numbers. A book is a thing in the basic or 'mere' sense; it can be picked up, measured and weighed. But what about the book's role as an earth for poetry? Do the words printed on the page come to shine? Certainly, books can be equipment, but can we say that the paper and card of the book are not 'used up' in the reading of a book of poetry? As a book is read, doesn't it simply disappear into usefulness, even if it is a book of poetry? The role of the book as the earth may not be as important as the role of sound or the presentation of words on a page. It may seem that the paper the poem is printed on is incidental to the poem. Arguably, the book as thing does not influence the world of the poem in a significant way. However, on closer inspection, this is not the case. Most poetry books are A5, which constrains the poems' length, width and spacing. It has long been commented that the use of word processors has limited poetry to what can be rendered in an A4 word document. It is interesting to ask how modern word processing is linked to the dominance in contemporary poetry of the short, rather neat lyric. Despite this, the question remains whether the book serves as an earth for the poem in the same way language does. As I turn the pages of a book of poetry, does the book itself 'come forth'? There is certainly some degree of strife between the book and the world brought forth by the poem. Sometimes this is related to the size of the book. Poets are generally limited in terms of line lengths, but poets use various devices that make the book itself explicit. For example, some poems such as Ann Carson's 'XXVII. MITWELT (from Autobiography of Red)' (Berry Carson and Collins 2016) are printed on their side to allow for longer lines so that the book has to be turned on its side to be read. In this way, the limitation of the book form is brought into the reader's awareness.

6.5 Digital poetry

Central to the history of any given art practice are the technological developments associated with it. The limitations imposed on an art practice have always been subject to change in the face of technological advancement. So, for example, the development of different types of pigment influences the possible subject matter and durability of painted works. Similarly, advances in technique, such as the development of perspective, broaden the possibilities of artists working in visual arts. Up until the modern age, the pace of this technological progress has been relatively slow, but the advent of digital technologies has dramatically changed this in practically every artistic domain. The development and widespread dissemination of new technologies has led to a dizzying pace of technological development in all the creative arts.

In poetry, the influence of digital technologies has manifested in a number of ways. As with other art forms, the internet allows for greater access to poetry than ever. As with music and film, this has prompted a revaluation of traditional publishing methods. The ease with which poetry can be published on the internet has led to a profusion of new internet-based journals. Spoken word artists use video to record performances or make poetry films, which may be widely shared on Facebook, Twitter and other social media platforms. One viral video can build a profile for a poet who would have been excluded from traditional publishing pathways. It can be argued that the democratization of poetry by the internet has opened up the art form to an exponentially larger audience and that interest in poetry is greater than it has been in decades: out of three million Irish Facebook users, 430,000 list poetry as an interest. The internet also gives readers access to vast poetry databases such as Poetry Foundation.

However, the philosophical implications of the internet for contemporary poetry go far beyond the dissemination of content. Digital poets also use these technologies in the composition and presentation of digital poems, and thus we must add these technologies to our consideration of the earth of contemporary poetry. Furthermore, technology offers poets freedom from the limitations of the printed page and, in some cases, freedom from language in any traditional poetic sense. Given this, it is important to ask what the implications are of understanding these technologies as earth. This question is not an easy one, not least because the question of how to define digital poetry is a vexed one. Digital poetry (electronic poetry or e-poetry) is an emergent literary form, with much of it written since the 1990s. Seiça (2016) however, traces the roots of digital poetry in various historical art movements such as Dada, conceptual art and concrete poetry. The difficulty in defining digital poetry is further hampered by its relation to visual and film poetry.

Furthermore, and central to this discussion is the multitude of ways the digital poet can use technology to create poetry. The term 'digital poetry' is employed to describe works that are different in literally every aspect. Funkhouser describes digital poetry as follows:

> The creative task of digital poetry often involves an artist observing and making connections between separate but poetically associable entities and then using technological apparatuses to communicate to an audience through compelling presentations. (Funkhouser 2012: 1)

Central to a definition of digital poetry is the engagement with technology, but this engagement can manifest in myriad and ever-evolving ways. Digital poetry is not necessarily limited to works presented on PCs, tablets or mobile phones but can include performances and installations. Funkhouser points out that digital poetry's 'ever-present variability' (Funkhouser 2012: 3) is its primary attribute, inviting 'vibrant, transformative multi-modal engagement for its practitioners and audience alike' (Funkhouser 2012: 3). Notably, digital texts allow readers to interact with texts in a way that has been impossible until the advent of digital technologies.

Despite the variability of digital poetry, some commentators have attempted a classification. Leonardo Flores (2014), for example, gives a seven-part classification as follows:

- Generative Poetry is produced by programming algorithms and drawing from corpora to create poetic lines. This is the oldest e-poetic genre and remains relevant today through e-literary genres like the bot.
- Code Poetry is written for a dual audience: computer and human readers.
- Visual Digital Poetry arises from visual, concrete and Lettrist poetic traditions includes concrete poetry
- Kinetic Poetry uses the computer's ability to display animation and changing information over time.
- Multimedia Poetry incorporates audio, video, images, text and other modes of communication in its strategies.
- Interactive Poetry incorporates input from the reader in the e-poems expressive strategies.
- Hypertext poetry uses nodes and links to structure the poem into spaces for the reader to explore.

6.6 The earth of digital poetry

Two interrelated problems arise when attempting to interpret digital poetry within a Heideggerian scheme of world and earth. First, as we have seen, Heidegger's account only applies to great poetry. The world opening that characterizes great art is not a feature of less-than-great art. As we know, a piece of art that fails to overcome the concealing tendency of its work material, whatever that work material may be, does not qualify as a great work. Thus, as we have seen in Chapter 3, the question of greatness in poetry is ontological. To subject digital poetry to a Heideggerian treatment, we must first ask whether it is, in principle, possible for a digital poem to overcome the concealing tendency of its earth and if it can, has it done so up till now? If we argue it cannot, then we are making the bold claim that there has been no great digital poetry. But even if we claim that there is yet to be a great digital poem, this does not necessarily preclude the possibility of their being great digital poetry in the future. Questions of greatness cannot be avoided here. If a digital poem can, in fact, overcome the concealing nature of the technology employed in its construction, then such an overcoming would certainly qualify as a Heideggerian confrontation with technology. In this way, the question of digital poetry's greatness (potential or otherwise) is one that has significance beyond the somewhat insular world of contemporary poetry.

The other difficulty we encounter is, as noted earlier, the complexity involved in defining and classifying digital poetry. It is difficult to know how to approach the earth of these poems, given that they are rendered in so many ways. In some respects, the digital poem can be viewed simply as a result of some novel and unique combination of software and equipment. While, as we have seen, a rough classification is possible, the poem's meaning often resides in its particular use of digital elements. If the combination of software and equipment used in the poems varies from poem to poem, then it is difficult to generalize a discussion of the earth of digital poetry.

Finally, before we can begin to ask whether a digital poem can be great in this Heideggerian sense, we must consider how we are to understand digital poetry in terms of Heidegger's ontology. There are a number of ways we can approach this task. We can, following Hui, see a digital poem as a digital object (or as a collection of digital objects), or we can investigate various elements of technology that are often utilized in digital poetry and see how they specifically conceal and unconceal in terms of poetry. Hui (2016) defines digital objects as

> objects that take shape on a screen or hide in the back end of a computer program, composed of data and metadata regulated by structure or

schemas. *Metadata* literally means data about data. Schemes are structures that give semantic and functional meaning to the metadata; in computation they are also called ontologies – a word that has immediate associations with philosophy. (Hui 2016: 1)

Hui provides a fascinating account of digital objects based on a synthesis of Simondon and Heidegger. He begins with the insight that objects exist in different 'orders of reality' (Hui 2016: 24). While we tend to approach digital objects in terms of data, Hui points out, 'at the level of programming, they are text files; further down the operational system they are binary codes, and finally at the level of circuit boards they are nothing but signals generated by voltage values and the operation of logic gates' (Hui 2016: 27). In terms of the current investigation, all of these levels can be viewed as the earth of digital poetry.

Therefore, we must ask how voltage values and logic gates act as an earth in digital poetry. As Hui asks, are they 'the substance of digital objects'? He makes sense of this situation in terms of 'orders of magnitude'.[3] Hui's central insight is that an object can only be observed once an order of magnitude has been specified. Each order of magnitude may require different instruments and theoretical presuppositions and may lead to non-overlapping bodies of knowledge. Hui is centrally concerned with how to understand the connections or 'relations' between the orders of magnitude of digital objects. Such an approach has obvious benefits in terms of analysing digital objects, where there is a clear causal relationship between the different orders of magnitude. His account provides an elegant framework to investigate how these levels interact with each other. Hui isolates a number of 'spectrums of orders of magnitude with respect to digital objects, for example, from microphysics to that of representing on-screen' (Hui 2016: 23) but he focuses on the spectrum from code to phenomena 'because it is this that forms the intermediary between calculation and human existence' (Hui 2016: 23).

Following Hui, we will focus on the spectrum from code to phenomena. The phenomenon that is a digital poem is typically presented on a screen, and almost all of it utilizes computer software and programming languages, so I will begin by considering these elements in their role as the earth of poetry. However, it must be borne in mind that these elements cannot exhaust an account of digital poems.

6.7 Screen as earth: The poetry of Geoffrey Squires

To investigate the use of the screen in digital poetry, I will focus on the work of Irish poet Geoffrey Squires. While language is central to his poems, the traditional book format is longer present in the work we will consider here, which is exclusively presented on a screen. There are two ways to look at the use of screens in Squires' work. In the first instance, this work breaks from what Seiça (2016: 96) calls 'static linearity of the printed page'. Thus, it challenges the canon in new, valuable ways. In the second instance, we can hold that the use of the screen as earth prevents the world opening that it is poetry's aim, and therefore, it represents an enframing of the poetic. We will consider both of these ideas.

Traditionally, poetry that seeks to challenge traditional formats is considered avant-garde or experimental and therefore as 'other', as Kenneth Keating (2017) points out. Irish poetry is a case in point. Keating claims that experimental poetry 'has been falsely homogenized and segregated from "traditional" or "conventional" Irish poetry' (Keating 2017: 196). In this way, digital poetry is generally considered outside of the canon. Squires is an example of this. While he is not a digital poet in a strict sense, his texts share 'certain elements with electronic literature [but] they do not fully adhere to conventional understandings of what constitutes contemporary electronic literature' (Keating 2017: 196). His works could, in principle, be rendered in book form. Though this is not the poet's intention, and to do so would be to lose some element or experience of the work as it is. The poems are described, by Squires himself, as 'texts for screens' (Keating 2017: 196). Despite this, the difference between Squire's work and more traditional poetic forms can be characterized almost solely in terms of how it is published. Throughout his career, Squires has published poetry in several formats, including e-books and flash videos, and a few in the 'conventional page format'(Keating 2017: 196). Here, I will focus on the collection 'Abstract Lyric and Other Poems' (2012), which is only available as an e-book on Kindle.

The book consists of words on digital pages without any other visual elements or sound elements. However, as Keating points out, 'these texts amount to more than a digital conversion of an original text to an e-book, instead embracing the technology central to their construction' (Keating 2017: 196). The poems consist of short phrases; each of these phrases is presented on a single page. They are spread out over a number of pages. There are 918 pages or 'locations' in the book. The phrases are related across the pages but not sufficiently for linear meaning. The turning of the virtual page further disconnects the text. The selection of text and its layout disrupt the possibility of lyrical meaning. The 'I' of the lyric is interrupted, and with it the subject-object duality. According to Keating, Squires 'attempts to foreground a destabilization of singularity, particularly in relation to subjectivity and identity' (Keating 2017: 196). For this reason, Keating claims that Squire represents a significant challenge to the 'Yeats-Joyce-Kavanagh-Heaney' (Keating 2017: 195) canon of Irish poetry. While Beckett and indeed Joyce mounted their own challenge to a pre-existing cannon with old-fashioned paper and ink, in contemporary poetry, the use of digital media is a central part of this challenging.

From a Heideggerian perspective, the disruption of the subject-object duality is necessary to overcome metaphysics, and overcoming metaphysics is the hallmark of great poetry. But the question remains whether this overcoming can happen on a technological instrument such as a computer screen. For Heidegger, the screen would certainly be an example of new technology. Thus, its capacity to function as the earth of an artwork is compromised at best and impossible at worst. The earth of a work must become apparent and withdraw simultaneously so that the strife in which art happens can be present. While technology conceals and unconceals, it unconceals things only as standing reserve. To take Heidegger's account seriously, we need to ask whether a screen prevents the world opening that defines poetry. For work, such as Squires, to be great, it would have to overcome the concealing tendency of the screen. Like paint or paper, a screen is equipment which generally disappears into usefulness. The question is whether it can become apparent in its role as the earth of a work. In the case of Squire's poetry, we can view the screen as analogous to the page. The screen page works much as a paper one does. The poems are presented sequentially, and in order to access the next segment of the poem, a virtual page is turned. Because the turning of the page adds to the fragmented aspect of the poem, the poem's presentation as an e-book is central to the poem's structure and form and thus central to the possibility of the poem's world opening. While, on the face of it, the e-book merely replaces an older technology, we must ask if Squire's work acknowledges the consequences of moving between these formats. If we see technology as a danger, then we cannot simply move between formats without taking into consideration how these formats function as earth. The screen does not operate as a page does because it conceals in a different way. Thus, we cannot simply write poetry for a screen without asking what it would mean to overcome the concealing tendency of this format. To do so is not to look deeply into the essence of technology, as Heidegger asks us to do, but rather to treat technology as simply instrumental. It can be argued that Squire's collection does not overcome the concealing tendency of the screen. One way to do this is to suggest that there is no possibility of *Spielraum* in these texts. As a technological apparatus, the screen unconceals text as standing reserve. This means that the concealment required for art is not at work. Heidegger tells us that '[t]he essence of truth, that is, of concealment is dominated throughout, by a denial' (Heidegger 1978: 179). This denial is, arguably, missing from the experience of Squires collection.

6.8 The earth of a hyperlink poem

It is also important to note that 'digital poetry functions as something other than poetry presented on a computer, involving processes beyond those used by print-based writers' (Funkhouser 2012: 1). In many cases, a digital poem is based on the ability of digital technologies to manipulate and reconfigure data. Much of the functionality employed by digital poets is used in other applications. It is, thus, familiar to the reader of the digital poem. For example, anyone who uses the internet knows how to navigate a hyperlink. A hyperlink is simply an icon, graphic, word or chunk of text that links to another file, object or Webpage. Hyperlinks are an integral part of the internet's architecture, linking trillions of pages and files to one another. Digital poets have also employed hyperlinks in the composition of digital poetry. In order to understand the philosophical implications of hyperlink poetry, we will use an example.

The Apostrophe Engine (2006) by Bill Kennedy and Darren Wershler-Henry is an early example of a hyperlink poem. It is a website which presents the poem 'apostrophe' written by Bill Kennedy in 1994 on its home page. Each sentence of the poem is a hyperlink. Clicking on a sentence instructs the site to send the sentence to a search engine. The search results are then 'edited' by five virtual robots, which then harvest the results for phrases beginning with 'you are' and ending with a full stop. This means that the phrases are often not complete sentences, giving the generated poem a fragmented, disjointed aspect. As with Squire's poems, this has the effect of disrupting linear meaning. The new poems are complete when the search yields a set number of phrases, or the robots have worked through a limited number of pages, whichever happens first.

The 'engine' then removes any anomalies, such as HTML tags, and presents the findings as a new poem. Every phase of this poem now functions as a hyperlink, giving endless possibilities for new poems. The Apostrophe Engine has, at any given moment, the potential to be as big as the internet itself. Also, as the content of the web changes continually, the subsequent poems change with each click. Like much post-internet poetry,[4] the Apostrophe Engine is a poem composed of fragments collected from the internet using a simple randomizing method decided upon by the poet. However, in this case, the software used does the harvesting and editing. This poem cannot be rendered in book form. The technology employed is essential to its structure.

There is an obvious tension between the original poem and the subsequent 'poems', which are generated entirely by software. We can assess the original poem as we would any poem. It is a prose poem that uses fragments in order to generate some sort of emergent meaning or tone. It either succeeds or it fails. It is great, or it is not. What about the subsequent poems? Can they possibly 'world'? Can we understand this poem with respect to a Heideggerian scheme of world and earth? If so, what is the earth of this piece? It is clearly not a case of simply swapping a paper page for a screen page. The poem is not merely presented on a website; it is a website. Thus, we must consider the website along with the hyperlinks that connect it to a search engine as the earth of the poem. In this case, a search engine along with hyperlink technology and the programming languages that run it[5] are elements of the poem. The question again is, can something that is inherently enframing, from a Heideggerian point of view, be an earth for a poem?

In the Apostrophe Engine, the words used serve two purposes. First, they function as all written language does; they carry the meaning of the words. Second, as the hyperlinks are embedded within the text itself, the words act as a tool by which the reader can generate another poem. Does this second function overwhelm the first? The purpose of poetic language is to Say, according to Heidegger, but can this poem bring language to shine or does it simply enframe it? If the poem enframes language, how are we to understand this? Undoubtedly, the generated poems can be interesting in that the sequences of sentences or phrases can chime off each other in unexpected ways. However, once the reader grasps the functionality of the poem, she knows that she can click on any phrase and generate a different but similar poem. Knowing this fact makes the act of generating another poem practically irrelevant. Once the concept behind the poem is grasped, there is no real need to read more than the first couple of poems. In this way, it can be argued that while language becomes apparent in the poem, it does so in the mode of standing reserve. The language in the Apostrophe Engine stands by awaiting further manipulation, but in this way, it ceases to be meaningful as language. Clearly, the language in this poem is present in a way which is entirely different from a traditional book of poetry. In a book of poetry, the written word ideally serves as the site of strife, from which a world is wrested. In the Apostrophe Engine, language is framed as a resource standing by to be endlessly reconfigured or manipulated. Heidegger tells us that the revealing associated with technology 'simply never comes to an end' (Heidegger 1978: 322). The Apostrophe Engine generates endless poems, but they are hardly worth reading. In defence of the Apostrophe Engine, it can be argued, however, that the meaning of this poem is the concept on which it is based. This concept can only be rendered in a digital format, and thus, an assessment of the poem must be focused on this concept. However, even if this is the case, the language used in the poem still becomes secondary to this concept. The language of this poem becomes just so much text, harvested from the internet and arranged. Language does not 'first' come to shine in this poem; rather, it is swallowed up by its use. The use of hyperlinks as earth is central to this 'swallowing up'.

6.9 Software and computer programming languages as earth

It may be argued that the use of software and its source code in the creation of a poem is obviously paradoxical from a Heideggerian point of view. D. Berry, for example, points out that software 'transforms everyday life into data, a resource to be used by others, usually for profit, which Heidegger terms *standing-reserve*' (Berry 2011: 2). However, the possibility of digital poetry offers a new possibility for digital technologies and the software that runs them, presenting 'poetic alternatives to the WWW's general ontology of promoting products and serving up data at rapid speeds' (Funkhouser 2012: 5). If we are to take the Apostrophe Engine as a piece of poetry, then we cannot deny the role of software and, therefore, programming languages in its creation. But if search engines are inherently enframing, then the software and programming languages that underlie them must be seen as enframing too? The question, again, is, can something that is inherently enframing be the earth of a poem? As we noted earlier, we could simply argue no by claiming that Apostrophe Machine is not a great poem and Heidegger's account only concerns great poetry. However, it is still worth questioning whether such poetry could act as a confrontation with technology. Two difficulties emerge when we propose computer software as the earth of a poem. The first involves the ontology of computer programming languages, and the second revolves around the notion of strife. If search engines, and the programming languages that run them, are enframing, can they be the sites of a world opening? If digital poetry struggles to overcome the concealing tendency of its technological earth, can we locate this tendency in the computer programming languages (CPL)[6] that are essential in the construction of so much digital poetry? We can isolate several difficulties with respect to using CPLs as the work material of a poem. The first difficulty is ontological. Most digital poets use some sort of software to compose a digital poem. This software is created using CPLs. But when we say 'language' in this context, we mean something very different from what Heidegger means by language. It is worth pointing out the differences between Heidegger's account of language and CPL.

To do so, we ask, in what sense is a programming language a language? We can begin by noting the historical link between programming languages and ideal logical languages. As we have seen in Chapter 3, the logical positivist's famous attempt to design an ideal language scrubbed clean of metaphysics and metaphor failed. The logical positivist's aim was philosophical. They wanted a language which would dissolve stubborn, long-standing philosophical problems, which they had recast as problems of language, for once and for all. To this end, they attempted to formulate a formal language. This language was designed to capture only the logically valid inferences of natural languages. If such a project is possible, natural languages must be understood, including sound inferential properties and logically constant elements. In other words, to abstract an ideal language from a natural language, there must be the possibility of formal validity within the natural language, to begin with. This, in turn, presupposes that some inferences will always be valid as long as the representational or semantic features of certain parts of the representations are kept fixed. In this way, the meanings of words like 'some' and 'all', for example, are held to be constant. These fixed elements are then abstracted from the natural language, while other elements, such as representational features, are ignored. As we saw in Chapter 2, the languages that emerged from this project could not adequately describe the world, and twentieth-century philosophy turned back to an analysis of natural languages.

However, the work on ideal languages did not go to waste. Some of it contributed to the development of computer programming languages. Indeed, 1930s logicians such as Alonzo Church and Alan Turing were involved in laying the foundations of the theory of computation. Also, as Colburn points out:

> [T]he development of predicate calculus by Gottlob Frege has been drawn on extensively by researchers in software engineering who desire a formal language for computing program semantics. Predicate calculus is also the formal model used by many of those implementing automated reasoning systems for mechanical theorem proving. These theorem proving techniques have even formed the basis for a style of general purpose computer programming called *logic programming*. (Colburn 2015: 3)

Computer science, like mathematics, is a formal science, and computer programming languages are formal languages, like the ideal language described earlier. While it must be noted that computer languages are in the imperative mode rather than the descriptive, and in this way, we are not comparing like with like, it is, however, still fruitful to examine CPLs in terms of their ontological status. As we saw in Chapter 1, Heidegger completely rejects logical accounts of validity because they view a proposition as the locus of truth. For Heidegger, this leads to an ontological difference between the actuality of the true proposition and the actuality of things. Thus, the actuality of the truth is not equal to the state of affairs it relates to (the Logical Prejudice). From a Heideggerian perspective, a language based on logic is necessarily a language that presupposes an ontology of being as presence. Russell's Logical Atomism is a case in point. The world is composed of simple discrete entities or atoms that are somehow combined to form complex states of affairs, which are unambiguously present to and captured by language.

Unlike the logical positivist's ideal languages, CPLs are not limited by the need to refer to or describe the everyday world in which we live. Since the 1980s, philosophers and computer scientists have been working on the concept of ontology with respect to programming languages. Of course, ontology in this sense means something quite different to its various philosophical conceptions. It is, however, akin to the ontological conceptions of other formal sciences. In terms of computer science, formal ontologies are viewed as designed artefacts, which comprise formal naming, representation and definitions of categories, relations and properties of data, concepts and entities that make up domains. In the early 1990s, Tom Gruber offered this definition.

> An ontology is a description (like a formal specification of a program) of the concepts and relationships that can formally exist for an agent or a community of agents. This definition is consistent with the usage of ontology as set of concept definitions, but more general. And it is a different sense of the word than its use in philosophy. (Gruber 1995: 908)

Given these ontological considerations, we can characterize the differences between programming languages, and Heidegger's conception of language, in several ways. First, as we saw in the discussion of metaphor in Chapter 3, Heidegger maintains that we cannot split off some portion of language as steady or fixed, be it the literal, the sensible, or some inferential component or even evidence. Language is not representational, and therefore, no section of it is prioritized or held fixed, and thus, natural languages cannot satisfy the conditions for formal validity. In this way, and certainly from a Heideggerian account, a programming language cannot be understood as a language in any meaningful sense.

Second, the 'fixedness' of programming languages is not frustrated by a messy metaphorical world, which resists their assumptions. Instead, programming language ontologies refer to 'artefacts' built up from the very assumptions inherent within a given programming language or set of programming languages. So, while some theorists, such as Turner and Eden (2007), suggest that certain elements of the Quinean ontological framework are pertinent in terms of programming languages, these languages do not entail Quinean ontological commitments because they do not describe an independently existing reality.

However, the question is not whether any meaningful comparison can be made between CPLs and natural languages, but rather it is a question of how our attention to the 'world' generated by these languages affects us. As the digital encroaches on more and more aspects of everyday life, this artefactual ontology, with its fixed array of possibilities, exerts increasing influence. The more time we spend online, the more this online reality competes with or blends with 'outside' reality and, subsequently, the more we understand everything in terms of the digital. Of course, from a Heideggerian perspective, the causality here works both ways. Because we are already under the sway of technology, we build and use devices that reflect this mode of unconcealment, and these devices, in turn, reinforce this mode of unconcealment. The historical story that traces the move from the logical positivist ideal language to its use in CPLs is an example of this move. While the logical positivist program failed, it helped to generate a world where a computer language does refer to an atomistic, pre-manifest reality. And this world increasingly offers an alternative to a non-technologically generated reality.

6.10 Digital poems as world openings

Given these considerations, we can ask whether digital poems can ever serve as the site of strife between world opening and earth concealment. Without strife, there cannot be great art, and without concealment, there cannot be strife. Concealment is central to Heidegger's philosophy. As we have seen, In *Being and Time*, the hammer, concealed in its usefulness, is ready-at-hand until it breaks. In this broken state, it is unconcealed, but merely as something as present-at-hand; its equipmental essence remains concealed. It is only art that unconceals the essence of equipment. A peasant's shoes are concealed in their use, but we come to see their essence in van Gogh's painting. Despite this, in the essay on things, we are given an account of a jug, which though it is undeniably equipment, its essence is not entirely concealed in use. Like the artwork, the jug is self-sufficient or self-supporting. It opens up the fourfold or 'things'.

> In the gift of the outpouring earth and sky, divinities and mortals dwell *together all at once*. These for are one because of what they themselves are, belong together. Preceding everything that is present, they are enfolded into a single fourfold. (Heidegger 1971: 171)

In this sense, the jug is a work, but not in the sense that art is a work. The thinging of the jug does not unconceal anything beyond the jug's own opening up of the fourfold. The thinging of the jug opens up a space in which the jug itself shows up in its own thinging. The jug unconceals a horizon of intelligibility in which the jug becomes understood as a jug. The jug unconceals itself, whereas the artwork, can unconceal something other than itself.

By comparing the artwork to the jug, we can isolate different senses of concealment. In van Gogh's painting, there is pigment and canvas, but also the tendency of the peasant's shoes to be concealed in their use. The world opening of the painting is won from both of these senses of concealment. In the case of the jug, we are told that the earth of the jug is earth, 'the potter makes the earthen jug out of the earth that he has specifically chosen and prepared for it. The jug consists of that earth' (Heidegger 1971: 165). But in this essay, the jug's world opening is mainly contrasted with yet another sense of concealment. This is the concealment of science. This concealment threatens the jug's status, and presumably the artwork's, as self-supporting; it threatens a thing's status as a thing. 'The thingness of the thing remains concealed, forgotten' (Heidegger 1971: 168). Thus, we have three different senses of concealment: the concealment of the work material, the jug's earth, that is, the actual material a work is made from; the concealment of the peasant's shoes in their usefulness, that is, the concealment that is only unconcealed in art; and, finally, the concealment of science, that is, concealment in the sense of 'annihilation' (Heidegger 1971: 186). For the time being, we can term these three modes as (1) concealment of earth, (2) concealment of essence or truth and (3) concealment of science. It is probably impossible to distinguish unambiguously between the first two modes of concealment in terms of demarcating works from artworks. For example, the temple at Paestum is an example of art that does not refer to something beyond itself. However, it does serve to demonstrate that the concept of a concealing earth is a complex one and that Heidegger's 'categories' are complex enough to capture individual works. What is important to note here is that the concealment of science is of a different nature in that it also is a mode of unconcealment, but it is the mode of unconcealment which annihilates things.

As we have seen, Heidegger links this annihilation of things by science with modern technology and technological devices. As we saw in Chapter 4, Heidegger links physics, the experimental method and technology. This link can be understood in terms of an isolating tendency within physics. Physics isolates causal relationships of the type whenever y then x, which require an experimental closure. As we have seen, this closure is provided by some sort of technological intervention and manipulation. This technological manipulation of nature is a challenging rather than an unconcealment. The experimental method serves as a sort of metaphor for how science conceals the jug's opening of the fourfold. Rather than allowing a jug to thing in this way, science treats the jug as separate from its context and any associations beyond its brute physical dimensions. However, this is not simply a metaphorical assertion; the experimental method actually strips things from their context. For Heidegger, this is a process which begins in the laboratory but then spreads out into and permeates the culture. In enframing, the jug, as thing, is isolated from its own significance; it is cut from its context. However, in this sense, context is not simply a constellation of significance that bestows meaning on this jug, but the jug is also something which is constitutive of the culture in which it has meaning. The jug and the cultural context in which it exists are inseparable. Science and technology destroy this context and show the jug as only an object with a set of measurable properties. In this way, this jug becomes a jug, entirely replaceable and interchangeable with anything that has similar properties. Therefore, as we have seen, technology is shown not only as a mode of concealment but also as a mode of unconcealment. From the standpoint of science or technology, the jug is enframed, the wine becomes liquid, and the horizon of intelligibility in which it is understood as an artefact of a culture and as a generator of a culture is shut down. The leeway or *Spielraum* is covered over by this third type of concealment. So while science and, therefore, technology unconceal, this is an unconcealment that conceals. It presents the actual as endlessly orderable standing reserve. The objects of technology are entirely interchangeable; in this way, they are isolated from any possible context. This isolating mode of unconcealment requires and fosters technological devices. As a mode of unconcealment without *poiēsis*, technology is the mode of the correct rather than the true. It is the unconcealment that blocks truth. This means that the technology associated with technology cannot, from a Heideggerian perspective, thing in the sense that the jug does, and therefore it cannot unconceal essence, which is the function of great art.

6.11 Conclusion

The digital poet faces a different sort of challenge from traditional artists. She must not only wrest a world opening from the concealment of the work material (concealment in the first and second senses) but also from the concealment of science (concealment in the third sense). This concealment is of a different order because it conceals things by simultaneously unconcealing them as standing reserve. This unconcealment threatens or destroys the very possibility of any other unconcealment. While we have considered only a few poems here, we have seen that in these cases, a Heideggerian analysis provides us with a way to express something about them that other accounts of contemporary poetry miss. There is something inherently different about using digital technology in the composition of a poem. Without investigation of the particular ontological status of technology as earth, it is not clear whether digital poetry can overcome the concealing tendency of its work material. While the requirement to wrest unconcealment from some earth is the task facing every artist, this task is inherently different for the digital poet. Given Heidegger's account, it is fair to question whether it is ever possible to wrest any sort of authentic world opening from a digital earth. If it is possible to overcome the digital in a digital poem, this would certainly represent a confrontation leading to a free relation to technology with all the promise that that entails.

7
Post-internet poetry and the essence of technology

7.1 Introduction

If digital poetry must overcome the particular challenges posed by its work material in order to function as art, we can ask if there are other contemporary poetic forms or movements better placed to disclose the essence of technology and allow us to formulate a free relationship with it. However, we must bear in mind that technology does not just threaten the possibility of a great digital poem; it threatens the possibility of any great poetry, regardless of format. Technology, as a mode of unconcealment, fosters devices, which in turn strengthen technology as the way things are. The devices reinforce the mode of unconcealment, which enables them. Thus, while devices are a necessary part of technology's unconcealment, this unconcealment spreads beyond the direct influence of these devices and into every aspect of our lives, including the capacity to write or appreciate poetry. Even if we try to avoid using digital devices, every aspect of our lives is, nonetheless, enframed.

In Chapter 3, we saw how Heidegger distinguishes between great and lesser with respect to metaphor. Poetry, which fails to transcend the literal/figurative distinction, cannot be great in the sense of unconcealing essence. Essence in this Heideggerian sense cannot be understood from within metaphysics. Given this, it is interesting to ask how the literal/figurative distinction operates in digital age poetry. While Heidegger's idea of an aesthetic philosopher may be a straw man, it is fair to say that philosophers of art tend to interpret a work in terms of symbol or metaphor. To give a crude example, the shoes in van Gogh's painting can be viewed as a metaphor for the life of the peasant or of the peasantry in general; that is, the shoes are symbolic in that they stand in for something else. Of course, this analysis does not exhaust the symbolic nature of the painting. The work itself is structurally understood as an object to which aesthetic qualities are attached. From a Heideggerian point of view, such a reading is insufficient, in part because it is based on a conventional separation between the sensuous and the nonsensuous. A Heideggerian reading understands the value of this work in terms of essence. In the painting, the essence of the shoes is shown. Similarly, with the painting in its actuality, the work material is not a thing to which aesthetic qualities are attached; it is an earth which allows world to come forth. In both cases, Heidegger's alternative reading relies on the dissolution of metaphysical categories. Heidegger tells us that in order to grasp the nature of art, we must overcome these categories, be it the literal/figurative divide or the distinction between art objects and aesthetic qualities. However, Heidegger also acknowledges that most artistic works fail to overcome these categories. Such work, however, can be adequately accounted for in terms of metaphor. In short, aesthetics impedes the essential saying of even great works, in this case, van Gogh's shoes. Heidegger's poetic interpretation, however, can retrieve the painting's truth.

The move from the old technology to the new technology, discussed in Chapter 4, also influences this analysis of art. In an age of enframing, it is not just that we fail to understand art; it's that how things *are* becomes further diminished. In the age of new technology, things can no longer be understood as literal or figurative but rather only as standing reserve. Things are challenged; they become enframed. They no longer hold the possibility of standing in for something else, even though it was a mistake to view them this way in the first place. The example of the peasant shoes shows us that while an aesthetic reading may have concealed the painting's ability to unconceal truth, this ability was still there as potential, and this potential was brought forth in Heidegger's analysis. In the digital, however, things are only standing reserve. Standing reserve can be seen as a corrupted version of the literal or the sensuous. While the literal holds the possibility of standing in, metaphorically, for something else. The transformation of things into standing reserve disrupts this possibility. In a technological age, the literal is only ever unconcealed as a resource awaiting manipulation or exploitation. This analysis has profound consequences for an account of contemporary poetic metaphor. If it is contemporary poetry's role to disclose the nature of the digital, the question becomes, is this still possible given the enframing nature of the digital? Can any poet be an essential poet in the digital age, and if not, what is the role of the poet now?

Furthermore, as we saw in Chapter 1, For Heidegger, great art exists as a strife, which is preserved. We have seen that the subject who interacted with old technologies is itself enframed in the digital. We can further argue that such an enframed subject loses the ability to either compose or preserve great art. Heidegger tells us the enframed subject is continually thrown back on itself so that all it experiences is itself. This means that an essential engagement with things becomes impossible because the enframed subject only ever encounters a reflection of itself. To confront the digital, the poetry of this age must disclose this relationship between a subject, which has become standing reserve, and objects which are also standing reserve. In this chapter, we will consider the post-internet poetry of Sam Riviere in this respect. Another way to understand this relationship between subject and things is in terms of boredom, which Heidegger holds up as the mood of the age. In deep or profound boredom, as in enframing, things are revealed as meaninglessness. I will argue that Riviere's poetry illuminates this deep boredom while ultimately remaining trapped within it. Thiele (1997) argues that deep boredom underlies the dominance of the technological, and its mode of revealing and that it challenges the very possibility of philosophy. I will examine Riviere's work in terms of boredom and technology and consider how things are presented in this work. Specifically, I will argue that this work cannot be understood as metaphoric and that Riviere's poetry discloses the enframement of things by digital technology, especially Google. Finally, I will conclude by claiming that Riviere's poetry unconceals the essence of search engines, such as Google, as enframing or as the essence of technology.

7.2 What is post-internet poetry?

Post-internet poetry is one way contemporary poets have responded to the influence of the internet and social media on modern life. It refers to the practice of reformulating internet content to compose poems. Much of this poetry, though not all, is rendered in predominantly non-digital formats. Of course, the practice of using pre-existing text as poetry is not new in poetry or art more generally. It can be traced back to Marcel Duchamp's ready-mades (Tomkins 1996). In poetry, there is a well-established technique of found poetry, the literary equivalent of collage, which involves reformatting old text in order to create new meaning. Maedbh McGukian (2013), for example, used this technique to powerful effect in the 1990s. Post-internet poetry uses the internet as its raw material. It is not exactly a new phenomenon: in 2015, Harry Burke edited an anthology of post-internet poetry called *I Love Roses When They're Past Their Best* (Burke 2015). Each of the poets featured has developed their own method of engaging and interacting with computer or web-based technologies; these range from poems consisting of sequences of online search results to works that take as their starting point the content of social media. While post-internet poetry is still very much in the experimental category, it is a technique showing up more and more in the world of contemporary poetry.

A prominent example of post-internet poetry is *Kim Kardashian's Marriage* (2015), the second full collection by English poet Sam Riviere. Riviere's first collection, *81 Austerities* (2012), won the Forward Prize for the best first collection. At first reading, there is nothing to point to the collection's distinctive methodology, but like the poems of his first collection, they all appeared first on Riviere's blog. There are seventy-two poems, one for each day of Kim Kardashian's first marriage. The book is divided into eight sections. Each section is named after a stage in Kardashian's famous make-up routine: PRIMER, CONTOUR, HIGHLIGHT, POWDER, BLEND, SHADOW, LINER, GLOSS. The Introduction to the collection claims that these elements are employed 'to explore surfaces and self-consciousness, presentation and obfuscation' (Riviere 2015). The poems actually have very little to do with the ill-fated marriage. They are created by Googling the titles and then piecing together the results in a way reminiscent of the Flarf poetry movement.[1] The titles themselves are chosen by employing an elaborate process of recombining chapter headings from Riviere's previous books in order to generate a number of keywords such as 'girlfriend', 'grave', 'hardcore' and notably 'sincerity'. These titles were then fed into Google. The poet took the first ten results of each search and edited them into poems. There is not one added word in the entire collection. The Introduction explains this by stating that Riviere 'eschews a dependence on confessional modes of writing to explore what kind of meaning lies in impersonal methods of creation' (Riviere 2015). So, for example, we have the following:

the new dust

I meet Franklin Delano Roosevelt.
He's been walking for three days.
He makes necklaces of refined sugar,
human hair is toxic now.
Melted plastic in plants is OK,
leather is sugar, metal sugar,
and sometimes rope or wool.

The poems are bland yet compelling. Commentators are divided as to their value and how to understand them. Leontia Flynn sums up this confusion by asking 'whether *Kim Kardashian's Marriage* marks a critique of contemporary tastes or merely a reflection of them' (Flynn 2016). Can a Heideggerian approach answer this question and provide us with a new deeper way to understand this collection?

7.3 Boredom

There is something deeply boring about the language used in *Kim Kardashians's Marriage*. The work does not avoid cliché or banal language but is, in fact, composed of such language. There is nothing vivid in Riviere's descriptions; they are entirely bland. For example, in *the new sunsets*, we are told:

Sunsets thru the trees.
It's always beautiful.

And in *spooky weather*, we read:

> Lightening and thunder send shudders
> through your spine. Late October rain.

Certainly, the language lacks vivacity or freshness of description that is generally regarded as a feature of good poetry. Viewed from one standpoint, these poems are just bad, yet there is something both unnerving and familiar about them. We are all subjected to the language of the internet, whether we pay attention to it or not. There is practically no escape from it. By presenting this ultimately boring content as poetry, Riviere points out the saturation of such language in our everyday existence.

The boringness of this content is essential to the experience of reading Riviere's collection, and it can be understood in terms of Heidegger's contention that boredom is the mood of the age (Heidegger 1995: 160). We can link the enframement of the subject in the digital to Heidegger's account of moods, particularly boredom. For Heidegger, we cannot understand moods as subjective psychological states; they are not 'at hand' but rather they are central to how Dasein discloses being and thus 'a fundamental manner and a fundamental way of being, indeed of being-there [*Da-sein*]' (Heidegger 1995: 167). Viewing moods as psychological states 'inside' the subject is a consequence of metaphysics. Just as we are never a context-free, Cartesian spectator of the world, we never encounter the world without a mood; moods come before and go beyond the capacity of the will to disclose the world.

In *Being and Time*, Heidegger confers a number of moods with particular ontological significance. Both anxiety and boredom are considered fundamental moods in that they remove everyday meanings from things and allow basic ontological structures to be apprehended. In fundamental moods, we are released from our everyday circumspection and instead experience our 'thrownness'. Anxiety or angst is perhaps the most discussed of the fundamental moods. Heidegger describes it as '*unheimlich*', which is generally translated into English as 'uncanny'. However, it is important to note that other connotations are at play in the German term, which are pertinent to

Heidegger's usage. '*Heimlich*' also means secret; thus, the *unheimlich* can also be understood, in some sense, as that which has been brought out of secrecy. Again this shows us that in anxiety, things are brought out of their everyday circumspection and made apparent in a different way. In their everydayness, things are hidden from us; they are secretive in that we are unaware of them. However, even though we are unaware, the things are still there, but in the way that a secret is hidden or unknown. Linked to this is the 'homeless' aspect in the meaning of '*unheimlich*'. In anxiety, we are rendered homeless in that our normal concerns and the intelligibility or meaning they supply to things are drawn back or stripped away.

In our ordinary, everyday interactions, we are at home in the world, but in anxiety, this at-homeness is no longer present to our awareness. For Heidegger, both states are natural for Dasein. As Thiele points out, 'human being oscillates between an ontic ensconcing in the world and an ontological alienation from it' (Thiele 1997: 501). Most of the time, Dasein is inauthentic, getting on with its everydayness. Occasionally, however, in anxiety, it becomes aware of the ungroundedness of its existence. It is not Dasein's task to transcend everydayness permanently so that it lives a more authentic life. We should not strive to live in constant awareness of the ontological uncanniness that is revealed by anxiety, but we should not try to suppress it permanently either. We need to be able to dwell, both in everydayness and in anxiety. As Thiele notes,

> Indeed, the uniqueness and greatness of human being lies in its capacity reflectively to experience its ungrounded contingency. What is dangerous, Heidegger maintains is the systematic effort to forego this struggle with contingency. (Thiele 1997: 501)

In the technological age, profound boredom becomes the fundamental attunement. However, Thiele relates this profound boredom with a refusal of anxiety and, therefore, the capacity to experience its contingency. While anxiety may render Dasein homeless, avoiding this entirely is dangerous, according to Thiele. He is arguing that the main danger associated with anxiety comes precisely from refusing it. Thiele suggests that the refusal of anxiety does not show up in a clinging to the everyday, as we may expect, but rather in boredom. He maintains that 'commentators are frequently mistaken on this' (Thiele 1997: 501). This is because they fail to see that for Heidegger, deep boredom is a refusal of anxiety. Thus boredom prevents one from finding a home within the homelessness of anxiety. Thiele describes deep boredom as 'a pervasive indifference to worldly existence as a whole' (Thiele 1997: 501).

7.4 Three types of boredom

To understand what is meant by profound boredom here, we can consider Heidegger's analysis of different types of boredom. Heidegger describes three types of boredom, culminating in the account of profound boredom; he explains each in relation to time and to things. While Heidegger primarily understands boredom in terms of time, it is the analysis of things that is most pertinent to the present thesis. He tells us boredom arises '*from out of things themselves*' (Thiele 1997: 501), a notion that is obviously difficult to square with the idea of boredom as a subjective psychological state. However, this idea does chime with everyday language use. For example, when we say a book is boring, we are saying something *about* the book. From the point of view of everyday language, boredom is an '*objective* characteristic' (Thiele 1997: 501). However,

> boringness is not some exclusively objective property of the book after all, such as its bad cover, for instance. The characteristic of 'boring' thus *belongs to the object* and is at the same time *related to the subject*. (Heidegger 1995: 84)

As Heidegger points out, this tendency to attribute subjective characteristics to objective things is generally explained away in terms of metaphorical transference. More strongly stated, in order to preserve the metaphysical distinction between subjects and objects, the idea of the book's boringness must be seen in terms of a transfer from the subject to the object. Obviously, such transference is common in poetic phrases such as 'the lonely hills'. However, as we have seen in Chapter 3, Heidegger critiques the idea that there are distinct metaphysical categories (the sensuous and the nonsensuous) between which characteristics can be transferred. Again, in the *Fundamental Concept of Metaphysics* (1995), he argues that this idea of transference is difficult to justify. But this time, he maintains that even from within a metaphysical view, subjective characteristics can only be applied to objective things where there is some rationale arising from the things for the application. Things cannot be randomly transferred between metaphysical categories. He asks,

> *why* do we transfer such characteristics of attunements onto things? After all this does not happen by chance, or arbitrarily, but evidently because we find something *about things* which demands of its own accord, as it were, that we address and name them in this way and not otherwise. (Heidegger 1995: 85)

For example, hills cannot be lonely in the poet's sense without there being some recognition of how hills can be lonely for the reader of the poem. The hills cannot be lonely unless they are lonely. What this means is that there is a relational quality between the hills and the self. We can characterize this relation, as Heidegger does, as a demand. The hills demand that we address them in a certain way. The poet, then, is in a dialogue with the hills. However, we can understand this relational quality in a more mundane way: the term 'boring' simply would not make sense if it did not capture something about the boring thing, that is, if it were just a subjective state attributed to an objective thing. Thus, boredom, along with every other attunement, is 'a hybrid partly objective, partly subjective' (Heidegger 1995: 88).

Heidegger describes profound boredom as 'it is boring for one'. On the way to the analysis of it, Heidegger analyses two types of 'everyday' boredom, 'becoming bored by something' and 'being bored with something'. In terms of the first type, he uses the example of having to wait for hours in a provincial train station. This type of boredom comes directly from things; that is, it is engendered by the boring thing or state of affairs. However, Heidegger tells us that once we become bored with something, the boredom starts to spread. '[T]he boredom is no longer nailed fast to something, but is already beginning to diffuse' (Heidegger 1995: 92), Heidegger tells us. Eventually, boredom diffuses and 'settles over everything' (Heidegger 1995: 92). In this case, we respond by trying to drive the boredom away by passing the time. In the example of waiting in a train station, we find ourselves reading the timetables or counting the trees. In this first type of boredom, time becomes long (*Langweile*) and drags. We, in turn, respond to this by trying to drive time on. Our response is a refusal of the boring situation. In fact, we attempt to avoid it altogether. But when this attempt fails, we find ourselves abandoned by things. This boredom may begin with some state of affairs or a thing, but the boredom soon spreads beyond this thing and onto things in general which, ultimately, leave us empty.

Heidegger illustrates the second type of boredom, or 'being bored with something', is illustrated with the example of attending a party. In this case, boredom is related to time and things in a different way. Now, time no longer drags. In fact, there is no awareness of the passing of time. In addition, this type of boredom does not arise out of specific things, 'in the first form we have a *determinate boring thing*, whereas in the second form we have *something indeterminate that bores us*' (Heidegger 1995: 114). The circumstance of being at the party leads us to forget our own concerns. In this way, we leave ourselves behind. 'We find *nothing that is boring*' (Heidegger 1995: 114). Instead, it seems to be the situation of the party itself that bores us. We give ourselves over to the time we will spend at the party and in this 'giving over' time becomes inconspicuous to us. The relationship with things is also different in that things do not abandon us or leave us empty. This boredom is characterized by what Heidegger calls casualness (*Lässigkeit*) towards things. Rather than see this instance of boredom as structurally different from the first type, Heidegger maintains it is a more profound level of boredom. What bores us in this case still leaves us empty, but now

> [b]eing left empty does not now first ensue in and through the absence of fullness, the refusal of this or that being, rather it *grows from the depths*, because its own precondition, namely seeking to be satisfied by beings, is already obstructed in such casualness. It now no longer even arises. (Heidegger 1995: 117)

We now no longer even look for things to satisfy us as they do in our circumspect everydayness, nor do we attempt to drive time on with them. In this type of boredom, we discover that we can be bored without the boredom arising from specific things. It is ourselves with which we are bored.

> We go along with things, we *chat* away, perhaps for some restful relaxation. Yet precisely our seeking nothing more from the evening is what is decisive about our comportment. With this 'seeking nothing more' something is *obstructed* in us. In this chatting along with whatever is happening we have, not wrongly or to our detriment, but legitimately, left our proper self behind in a certain way. In this seeking nothing further here, which is self-evident for us, we *slip away* from ourselves in a certain manner. (Heidegger 1995: 119)

In such situations, an emptiness forms and 'being bored with' is determined by this emptiness. In this passage in the McNeill and Walker translation, '*unterbunden*' is translated as obstruct, but it can also be viewed as a stifling. In this 'seeking nothing more', proper or authentic self (*eigentliches Selbst*) is stifled. Heidegger contends that this makes the second form of boredom more profound than the first. The casualness of 'being bored with' involves a leaving of ourselves behind and an abandoning of ourselves to the situation we find ourselves. We no longer even struggle against the boredom; in fact, we barely recognize it.

Profound boredom, or 'it is boring for one', is the third type of boredom identified by Heidegger. It is a further intensification of or a progression from the first two, but Heidegger does not use an example to explain it as he does with the first two types. In profound boredom, there can be no question of driving it away by passing the time. '[A]ll passing the time is powerless against this boredom' (Heidegger 1995: 135). Indeed, profound boredom 'conceals its temporal character and in this way it becomes overpowering' (Heidegger 1995: 136). This boredom is a fundamental mood because it manifests beings as a whole. It 'has in itself *this* character of *manifesting how things stand concerning us*' (Heidegger 1995: 136). We are told that they become manifest in a 'telling refusal [*Versagen*]' (Heidegger 1995: 136). However, it must be noted that the *Ver* prefix used in the term '*Versagen*' and in the other *Ver* terms in this section of the *Fundamental Concepts* (versagen, vertrieb, verschwinden, vewandlung, *verbringen*) is the equivalent of 'mis' in English, as in misspeak (*Versagen*), but it is also used for a transition to a new state – *verschwinden* – to disappear.

This refusal or failure does not conceal things; rather, they become manifest in their refusal. In this way, profound boredom determines all of Dasein's possibilities, in that beings as a whole become indifferent to it. Things are shown to us as a whole, but they are simultaneously refused to us.

> Accordingly this telling refusal on the part of beings as a whole merely indicates indeterminately the possibilities of Dasein, of its doing and acting, it merely tells of them indirectly and in general. (Heidegger 1995: 140)

In a way that is reminiscent of technological enframing, the telling refusal makes things manifest as insignificant.

> They recede into an indifference. Everything is worth equally much and equally little. Beings withdraw from us, and yet remain the as the beings they are. (Heidegger 1995: 145)

This withdrawal of things allows the temporal horizon itself to entrance Dasein. It is the essence of time that becomes apparent in profound boredom.

> The temporal horizon entrances Dasein so that it can no longer pursue those beings in whose midst it finds itself disposed at all times, so that it neither sees not seeks any further possibility at all of concretely reflecting about itself within these beings in whose midst it is set in place. It is not beings that properly refuse, but time which itself makes possible the mainfestness of these beings as a whole. (Heidegger 1995: 150)

In profound boredom, the apparentness of time means that beings withdraw, and this withdrawal of things is concurrent with and related to technological enframing. This link between profound boredom and technology becomes apparent in the digital. As things withdraw, the concerns which are a part of Dasein's structure are lost. But despite this, we are told, 'this profound boredom never leads to despair' (Heidegger 1995: 140). Thus, in the first type of boredom, we struggle to avoid powerful attunement of despair or anxiety by trying to drive time on, but in the profound boredom of the digital age, this struggle is further away from us. We do not need to pass the time and could not do so even if we wanted to.

It would seem then that the possibility of the first type of boredom is reduced or eliminated in the digital. In a time of profound boredom, where time entrances Dasein, there can, according to Heidegger, be no question of passing the time, and thus we should no longer have the experience of becoming bored and trying to drive time on. It is obvious to anyone who becomes stranded in a train station now that people use technological devices to distract themselves. The act of looking at a phone is not the same as reading the timetable or counting trees. Nowadays, when we sit in a train station looking at our phones, it does not seem appropriate to say that we are trying to drive on time to escape boredom. Rather we are held in a sort of stasis, neither bored nor interested. The engagement with our devices in a train station is not the circumspection that users of old technologies were taken up with. Rather, our devices function as a technological embodiment of deep boredom. We use our phones in part to access the internet in myriad ways. Thus when we look at our phones, we encounter everything as a consumer products, all manifesting as ultimately insignificant. Our devices allow us to encounter things as a whole in their telling refusal. While the act of taking out our phones in a train station seems to bring us before endless possibilities to pass the time, these possibilities are also present to us in telling refusal:

> [t]his telling refusal does not speak about them [the possibilities], does not lead directly to dealings with them, but in its telling refusal it points to them and makes them known in refusing them. (Heidegger 1995: 140)

We stare at our phones, with all the possibilities of the internet before us, and yet we can do nothing. However, this is not simply how people behave when they are stranded in train stations; it is also how the digital subject spends time more and more of their time in all situations.

7.5 The digital subject in poetry

We can now assess *Kim Kardashian's Marriage* from a Heideggerian perspective, especially in terms of its ability to let profound boredom 'arise' and to show things in their telling refusal. Profound boredom, as the attunement of this age, is difficult to apprehend because it seems like no attunement at all. We can argue that the value of Riviere's collection derives, in part, from the fact it allows us some awareness of or access to the attunement of profound boredom. While we can say that the poems are boring, they are not boring in the first or second senses of boredom. Rather, they are boring in the sense of 'it is boring for one'. The things presented in the poems do not bore us as a boring thing does, in the first sense of boredom; boredom does not arise from the things described in the collection. Rather, the boredom conveyed seems more like the casualness of the 'being bored with', where things are not encountered as boring in themselves. As we have seen, Heidegger sees these types of boredom as continuous with each other, culminating in profound boredom. The items mentioned in *Kim Kardashian's Marriage* are not just boring; they are somehow also engaging; they momentarily keep our attention. The fragmented narrator is not looking to drive time on. She is not looking for a deeper meaning in the things presented to her. She just passes over them in numb, casual interest. She does struggle against them. There is no anxiety. In this way, it is in Riviere's poem that we gain an insight into deep boredom, its relationship to time and the eroded subject of the digital age.

In *american sunsets* we read:

We are sorry, this thriller movie is under construction.
Picture twilight in Los Angeles: the city's labyrinth
of eight lane freeways is jammed with millions of cars.
It rises like a dream / in the fall from a feather
Trees shed all their summers / Washes away my peach

Which is your favourite?
Loading . . . Alert icon. Noam Chomsky error . . .

Each element of this poem, the thriller movie, Los Angeles, the freeway, all the way to Noam Chomsky in the final line, flow into each other without anything being prioritized.

As in deep boredom, everything is worth equally much and equally little. This poem is not a narrative. It can be viewed as a list of random and vaguely connected elements. It is perhaps the city's labyrinth that rises like a dream but perhaps not. The 'voice' that emerges from the collection's methodology is certainly disinterested; it babbles on about this and that without making a point. The collection is predominately in the present tense giving the sense of a continuous present where things flow in and out of view without making any impression. It is things as a whole that are shown to us in no particular thing is lifted into significance; they are passed over without any resistance. Something new is always there to take the place of whatever has just been passed over.

This poem, like the others, is forgotten almost the moment it is read. Riviere's 'impersonal methods of creation' show us something of the digitized subject described in Chapter 4. As we saw, the digital is the age where the subject of metaphysics is transformed into standing reserve, which stands by to be exploited. The digital subject becomes just a collection of arbitrary desires without what Dreyfus and Spinosa term 'long-term identities and commitments' (Dreyfus and Spinosa 1997: 162). The voice that speaks in Riviere's collection is without a long-term identity or particular concerns. It passes over content without resistance, just as the profoundly bored subject scrolls past whatever content is presented by the internet.

7.6 The essence of Google

While Riviere's collection is full of things, it would seem reasonable to claim that these things are enframed. Enframing means that things are challenged, that they cannot be shown in their essence or, rather, that they cease to have an essence. In addition, we can claim that the things presented in this collection are disclosed in the attunement of profound boredom. As we have seen, this is the fundamental mood that unconceals things in telling refusal. However, we know that great art is truth and truth, and, for Heidegger, this is linked to essence. From Heidegger's perspective, it would seem, at first sight, preposterous to claim that Riviere's collection can even be considered poetry.

However, the collection does seem to disclose something about technology and the enframement of things. How are we to account for this? First, it is important to note that as all the text in the collection comes from Google; that is, all the descriptions of things are simply fragments of internet content. While Google is not explicitly mentioned in the collection, it certainly pervades the entire collection. We can ask, is it Google, in its essence, that is brought to the light of unconcealment? But what is the essence of Google? As a search engine, Google is undoubtedly equipment. In relation to the peasant shoes, we are told equipment is, in essence, useful. Certainly, Google is also useful in an almost bewildering range of ways; it makes possible our lives as digital subjects. But it does not seem to be usefulness that is at play in these poems; in fact, quite the opposite. Riviere highlights the banality of much of Google's content. It would not seem that usefulness alone cannot capture the essence of Google. However, the poems do give us a sense of what it is like to use Google. The poetry's random nature reflects how hyperlinks embedded in the text allow the user to slip endlessly from page to page without ever landing at any destination. The poems are banal, random and concerned with celebrity and consumer products. As we have seen, things are floating unfixed by an overall narrative. They are presented to us in an almost dizzying sequence, each subsequent thing replacing the last, which is immediately forgotten. Google is revealed, then, as that which enframes. In this way, this collection shows us something of the essence of Google. Google is enframing in a way that is more fundamental than other examples of modern technology.

One clear way to understand how Google is the essence of technology is to consider Google Ads (formerly AdWords). Google Ads processes users' behavioural data by means of artificial intelligence to match advertisements with Google searches. Zuboff (2019) describes how what she terms a 'surplus' of behavioural data was initially a by-product of the technological processes involved in the operation of Google. In the beginning, Google used this data partially to improve the service. However, because Google wasn't making profits, its investors pressured it to develop a viable business plan. It did not take long to figure out that this surplus data could be used to target advertising to specific users. As is well documented, this targeting turned out to be very effective, generating huge profits for both Google and its advertisers. This success led Google to seek data from numerous other sources, generally through the employment of cookies, which considerably enhanced Google's store of UPI (User Profile Information). This increased UPI allowed exponentially greater specificity in targeting consumers with advertising, in effect transforming advertising from a guessing game to an almost sure thing. As Zuboff tells us, 'with Google's unique access to behavioural data, it would now be possible to know what a *particular* individual in a particular time and place was thinking, feeling, and doing' (Zuboff 2019: 78). The sheer quantity of data available alongside developments in artificial intelligence allowed Google to move from predicting an individual's behaviour to practically modifying or controlling their behaviour.

Zuboff theorizes this in terms of surveillance capitalism, but as we saw in Chapter 4, from a Heideggerian perspective, technology determines beings as standing reserve. It is this that allows Google the power to practically modify user behaviour. Once humanity becomes standing reserve, it stands by awaiting exploitation. The monstrousness of Google is that as you use it, it uses you. While we can see Google as merely another example of a digital technology, to do so is to miss out on the power of Heidegger's metaphysical understanding. Google is the essence of technology because it enframes both its content and its users. But though Google is the technology that arises to exploit humanity as standing reserve, the process by which humanity is enframed was well already underway before the specific technology used by Google was developed.

It is difficult to fully grasp this because technology, in all its senses, as devices, processes and as mode of unconcealment, is concealed from us. Most of us do not have the technological know-how to understand exactly how Google mines our data or how technology stalks us. But neither do we grasp the process by which we are being converted into standing reserve or how it is that we lose our own essence. When we use Google, we are being exploited but avoiding Google, even if this were still a possibility, would not save us. An account of Google as surveillance capitalism will not spare us either because it fails to acknowledge that humanity, as standing reserve, loses the ability to respond to that which enframes it. Even if Google's advertising strategy is 100 per cent effective because it can completely modify consumer behaviour, this is not what is most monstrous about technology because it already relies on the fact that humanity has become that which can be exploited in this way. The enframement of humanity is prior to the technology that exploits this enframement.

In Riviere's poems, we come to see this monstrousness of modern technology. Yet this monstrousness is not frightening or even disconcerting; it is simply matter-of-fact. Commentators, such as Flynn, who ask whether this collection simply reflects current tastes fail to see that this is entirely the wrong question. The collection doesn't reflect a choice that people make about how to see things. Instead, it shows us how things are and how we are, as the consumers of these things. Things are simply listed; they do not signify anything beyond themselves. We consider them briefly and then pass on to the next thing, neither bored nor engaged. This process continues without end. Heidegger tells us that this 'monstrousness' can be understood in terms of poetry; he cites poetry as an alternative to the monstrousness of enframing.

> In order that we may even remotely consider the monstrousness that reigns here, let us ponder for a moment the contrast that is spoken by the two titles: 'The Rhine,' as dammed up into the *power* works, and 'The Rhine,' as uttered by the *art*-work, in Hölderlin's hyme by that name. (Heidegger 1978:321)

The Rhine is enframed when it is viewed as a power work and forced to deliver its power, as electricity, over to storage. The Rhine, as a dammed-up power works, becomes thingless. Heidegger is clear that we cannot just alternate between these two understandings, as we do not control the unconcealment; rather, it holds sway over us. While it is human beings that have enframed the river, we cannot simply swap this for a more poetic mode of unconcealment. Similarly, we cannot simply revert to our pre-digital understanding of things and engage with them poetically because it is not just the river that has changed; we have also changed. We cannot simply dismiss Riviere's poetry, and write more traditional poetry, where things have meaning beyond themselves, understood as metaphorical meaning, because it is this very possibility that is driven out by technology. Enframing reveals things only as standing reserve. We may try to ignore this, but we are ultimately trapped.

Heidegger tells us that '[w]hat ever stands by in the sense of standing-reserve no longer stands over against us as an object' (Heidegger 1978: 322).

'The Question Concerning Technology' gives us the example of an airliner as a technology that presences in terms of standing by (*Bestand*). The airliner, on the taxi strip 'has standing only on the basis of the ordering of the orderable' (Heidegger 1978: 323). Like the airliner, Google is completely a product of the technological age. But unlike the river or the airliner, or most other examples of technological devices, we can argue that Google is enframing in its very essence. Google shares structural similarities with the mode of unconcealment that fosters it. For example, Heidegger tells us that enframing results in 'everything everywhere [being] ordered to stand by, to be immediately on hand, indeed to stand there just so that it may be on call for a further ordering' (Heidegger 1978: 322). The content of Google is always just a few taps or clicks away. Furthermore,

> [u]nlocking, transforming, storing, distributing, and switching about are ways of revealing. But the revealing never simply comes to an end. Neither does it run off into the indeterminate. The revealing reveals to itself to its own manifoldly interlocking paths, through regulating their course.

Again, this reflects how Google operates, through seemingly endless paths via hyperlink after hyperlink, never culminating in anything except another path. Google's content stands by, always ready for immediate access. It is presented to us as standing reserve, and thus, when you Google something, the results 'no longer stands over against us as an object'.

We must note, however, that Google is not a metaphor for enframing, any more than the earth from which the jug is formed is a metaphor for earth in Heidegger's use of the term. It is one of the strengths of Heidegger's account that by collapsing the sensuous/nonsensuous distinction, we can understand technology as an entire phenomenon, where devices are understood as being continuous with the way things are and the way we are. As we saw in Chapter 4, there is no significant, metaphysical distinction to be made between technology as a mode of unconcealment and our technological devices. Moreover, viewed in this way, we can see clearly how our devices feed into the way in which reality is understood within this historical epoch. Google is an expression of technology, but it is also technology expressing itself. It is only Heidegger's account of technology that allows us to understand Riviere's collection in this way and then to understand how Google shows up in this collection. Heidegger's ontologically broad use of the term technology does not distinguish between technology as a mode of unconcealment and the devices or processes that we normally associate with the term. Digital devices are continuous and inherently tied up with how digital things are. To draw a firm line between these two senses of technology is ultimately a slip into metaphysics.

7.7 How the sunglasses presence

If Riviere's poems succeed in capturing the essence of Google, they do so precisely by presenting things as standing reserve. We can see this by investigating the status of objects described within the poems. 'Sunglasses' is one of the words Riviere combined into the titles used to generate the poems. Therefore, eight poems in the collection contain the word 'sunglasses' in the title. For example:

american sunglasses

In the movie *The American*
(the 2010 film *The American*,
which sees George Clooney
as Jack, an assassin and gunsmith) George Clooney
(looking effortless in the Persol
3009) wears a pair of Havana-coloured Persol
2883 sunglasses.

While the content of this and the other sunglasses poems are random, the choice of title is not. By including 'sunglasses' as a title word, Riviere is using the image of sunglasses as a motif or as a theme in the collection. While traditional poetic exegesis may be tempted to view the sunglasses as a poetic metaphor by which the sunglasses stand in for or symbolize something like society's obsession with consumer products, such a reading does not seem correct in these poems. In fact, it is in Riviere's poetry that we get a glimpse of what Heidegger means when he says things become thingless. The sunglasses in the poems do not seem to stand in for something else, in the sense of metaphor, and yet neither do they 'thing' in terms of opening up the fourfold; in fact, they barely presence in the poems at all. As we saw in Chapter 3, Heidegger maintains that metaphor is the way by which aesthetics explains the poetic away so that it may be fitted into metaphysics.

While Heidegger criticizes such attempts, they are now no longer required to explain Riviere's treatment of the sunglasses. Now that the sunglasses are enframed, they are no longer capable of metaphoric excess; they do not thing. In fact, they barely come to presence at all, and this reflects the manner in which consumer goods come to presence in actuality. While I have seen the film *The American* mentioned in the first poem earlier, I had no memory of the sunglasses worn by George Clooney. I Googled them, and in doing so, I discovered how much it would cost me to buy a pair, and of course, I could have ordered a pair then and there if I had wanted to. Google allows me to turn each film I watch into a catalogue for meaningless consumer goods. The poems reference the sale of these glasses or their availability for sale; for example, 'FREE SHIPPING', is the last line in the poem *infinity sunglasses*. In the digital age, the enframing of things is linked directly to their instant availability as a product. In Heideggerian terms, rather than opening up the sunglasses in respect of what they signify or thing, the poems shut them down. They become mere stock or standing reserve. Enframing reveals the actual, in this case, sunglasses in the mode of ordering, that is as standing reserve. The sunglasses in the poems are revealed in this way, and the technological mode of unconcealment is also shown. The poems allow us to glimpse how Google enframes objects and presents them as standing reserve. It is only Heidegger's accounts of poetry and technology that allows us to understand the motif of the sunglasses in Riviere's poems.

However, the unconcealment of the glasses as standing reserve is only part of the story; a Heideggerian reading of Riviere's collection also allows us to grasp something of the enframed subject. As we have seen, Google is not the essence of technology simply because it presents things as standing reserve. Google simultaneously enframes its users. As we have seen, it does this in a very concrete sense by collecting behavioural data so that it can target them more effectively with content and advertisements. As we use Google, it harvests our behavioural data so that it can stand by to be ordered by someone else. As the source of this data, we also stand by as a resource awaiting this harvesting. But what sort of being can stand by to be used in this way? Although, as we have already seen, it is not the subject of modernist metaphysics, this subject could still metaphorically transpose one object for another. The 'subject' of *Kim Kardashian's Marriage* does not use metaphors in this way.

Moreover, as is often noted, lyric poetry dominates modern and contemporary poetry. The lyrical 'I' stands in a world of objects, some of which can stand in, metaphorically, for something else. Sometimes a great lyric can even manage to transcend the binaries of metaphysics. However, while *Kim Kardashian's Marriage* is composed of poems shaped like the short, neat lyrics, of modern poetry, there is no real narrator. Rather, there is only a shadow of the 'I' remaining. Though the fragments used by Riviere often include an 'I', this 'I' is an illusion. It is created by piecing together bits of data so that some sort of subject seems to emerge, but there is nothing deeper to this subject; it has no essence. It is the digital subject, a mere amalgam of pre-existing content. The I which emerges from Riviere's method is merely a collection of behavioural data: a Google-constructed I. Moreover, the capacity such a subject has to create or recognize a deeper meaning in things is now gone. In the case of *Kim Kardashian's Marriage*, we can see this clearly in terms of the non-metaphorical status of the poems; nothing stands in for anything else because the 'narrator' no longer possesses this ability. Sunglasses, God, vanilla ice cream and melodic death metal all present in the same way to this enframed subject, without the possibility of transcendence.

7.8 A free relationship

Given this, we can ask, does showing Google, as an essence of technological unconcealment, grant Riviere's poems the status of great art? To do so might seem a strange conclusion from a Heideggerian perspective. The mode of unconcealment at work does not seem to be *poiēsis*. If these poems unconceal truth, it is only the truth that we now interact with things in the profound boredom of the technological. Alternatively, we can ask whether these poems confront technology in order to lead to a free relationship with it. The sunglasses in Riviere's collection do not open up the fourfold; they do not thing; they cannot even stand in for anything else in terms of metaphoric transfer. If this is required for a free relationship, then this collection does not deliver this.

'Yet', we are told, 'it is not that the world is becoming entirely technical, which is really uncanny (*unheimlich*). Far more uncanny is our being unprepared for this transformation' (Heidegger 1966: 52). We are incapable of stopping the domination of the technical because it is not within our control. Thus, Heidegger's account allows us to understand the relentless pace of technological advancement and its increasing influence. But in order to develop a free relationship with technology, we need first to prepare ourselves for this transformation. We can find this new foundation in meditative thinking. Heidegger's notion of a free relation is, then, the possibility of an engagement with technology in the realm of meditative thinking. Heidegger links meditative thinking with autochthony, with being at home or being rooted. While the old at-homeness is lost in the new technology, Heidegger asks, 'may not a new ground and foundation be granted to man, a foundation and ground out of which man's nature and all his works can flourish in a new way even in the atomic age?' (Heidegger 1966: 53). Such a new ground must involve a way of being with technology, and Heidegger suggests a possible comportment towards technical devices.

> We can use technical devices, and yet with proper use also keep ourselves free of them, that we may let them go at any time. We can use technical devices as they ought to be used, and also let them alone as something that does not affect our inner and real core. We can affirm the unavoidable use of technical devices, and also deny them the right to dominate us, and so to warp and lay waste to our natures. (Heidegger 1966: 54)

This passage seems at odds with elements of his account of technology as unconcealment, and it may simply be that there is a contradiction in Heidegger's thinking in this respect. Perhaps the most obvious contradiction is the idea that a corrupted, technological subject can still respond to technology. As we saw in Chapter 4, it is fair to question whether the digital subject still has a 'real and inner core?' Dreyfus and Spinosa (1997: 161) tell us that the human being, as standing reserve, becomes a collection of desires, which are subject to manipulation and exploitation by various parties. Borgmann tells us that this new subject loses its 'long-term identities and commitments' (1993: 162). The idea that a post-modernist subject, enframed by technology, still has enough core to prevent technology from laying waste to its nature is one that is certainly questionable.

Moreover, if the ability to respond to technology still exists, will it continue when the generation raised on internet-enabled devices reaches maturity? Even in the time since Dreyfus and Spinosa wrote on the subject, we have seen some erosion of this possibility. Despite this, it is still fruitful to question what sort of response is offered by Riviere's collection. A key element of a free relationship involves dealing with technology consciously. At core, Heidegger is entreating us to deal with technological devices by both embracing them and letting them alone. 'I would call this comportment towards technology which expresses "yes" and at the same time "no" by an old word *releasement towards things* [*Gelassenheit*]' (Heidegger 1966: 54).

I have argued that we cannot simply look away from the technological and towards Borgmannian focal practices. Part of Heidegger's solution is to say 'yes' to technology. Riviere's collection does not look away from the technological to find non-technological focal practices, but rather it looks squarely at technology. While it may become locked within it, it does allow us to see the way in which objects are treated in the digital. This collection allows us to understand what it is we must say 'yes' to in order to develop a free relation to technology. We can agree, along with Heidegger, that things do not have the poetic significance they had in previous epochs. There are simply too many of them, and they are now too easily accessed. When everything is readily available, then noting is of particular significance. However, enframing is more than a result of abundance; this abundance of insignificant things is also a result of technology. To prepare a way to free relation with technology is to, at least in part, acknowledge this. We cannot return to our former engagement with things. To say yes to technology is maybe to accept that thing's status as the locus of human meaning has passed.

A part of this acceptance comes from keeping watch over the unconcealment. The unconcealment associated with enframing is not just a point of view or a way of looking at the world that can be easily changed. We are told that man 'merely responds to the call of unconcealment, even when he contradicts it' (Heidegger 1978: 324). What is required is

> essential reflection upon technology and decisive confrontation with it [this] must happen in a realm that is, on the one hand, akin to the essence of technology and, on the other, fundamentally different from it. . . . Such a realm is art.

When it is great, poetry is viewed by Heidegger as a way of transcending or breaking through metaphysics. In this way, the great poem operates at the level of metaphysics. Hölderlin's poetry is great because he writes poetry about poetry, and in this, he recognizes the power of poetry as the founding word. In 'Hölderlin and the Essence of Poetry', we are told, '[w]hat supports and dominates beings as a whole must come into the open. Being must be disclosed, so that beings may appear' (Heidegger 1971: 58). Riviere's collection can certainly be understood in terms of keeping watch over the unconcealment. By presenting internet content as poetry, Riviere brings us into a relationship with technology as a mode of unconcealment. Such a relationship can only take place within the realm of the poetic. It is in the realm of the poetic that we can see how technology discloses. However, this picture is still ambiguous because great poetry gives us the essence of things. The technological is that which blocks the unconcealment of essences-it prevents things from thinging. Thus, there is a tension when we consider Riviere's collection in terms of Heidegger's philosophy. On the one hand, it is only in the realm of poetry that we can see how technology drives out the essence of things, but on the other, how can poetry operate when the essence of things is thus driven out? It is perhaps in the face of this tension that we can understand Riviere's work in this collection.

7.9 Dwelling

Riviere highlights the unrootedness of the digital, and while, again, this may seem to contradict Heidegger's contention that the poetic is a dwelling, in fact, we can view it in terms of a preparation for a new dwelling within the technological. In 'Poetically Man Dwells', we are told that 'poetry is the original admission of dwelling' (Heidegger 1975: 225). While the point of this essay is ostensibly to tell us something about dwelling, it also tells us that the nature of poetry is a 'letting dwell'. Again, we find a point of tension between Riviere's poetry and the attempt to subject it to a Heideggerian analysis. Riviere's poetry is unrooted, even uncanny. Can such work let us dwell? However, in an age like this, it may be precisely the job of poetry to bring us home to bring us to dwell, and to do this, it must first bring us to dwell within the unhomely. Heidegger tells us that man can only dwell unpoetically because dwelling is, in its essence, poetic. (In the same way that the blind man is by nature endowed by sight, a piece of wood can never go blind.)

Furthermore, Heidegger tells us that if we dwell unpoetically, this is because of a 'curious excess of frantic measuring and calculating' (Heidegger 1971: 226). But again, we are told we can find our way 'home' to poetic dwelling, but only if we remain 'heedful of the poetic'. Riviere is indeed heedful of the poetic. Despite their banal content, the poems are constructed in terms of form and rhythm. These poetic elements bring a sort of beauty to this content. In this beauty, perhaps, we find a way to acclimate ourselves to the technological. Saying 'yes' in this sense does not mean to state that the technological is simply a positive development in human history; it doesn't mean that we simply embrace technological devices; rather, it means that we accept that it is already prior to us – that we cannot avoid it or escape it. Riviere's poetry acknowledges technology in all its apparent shallowness. Understanding this must, at least, be a part of the preparation of free relationship with it.

Just as *Kim Kardashians Marriage* can be fruitfully examined in terms of Heidegger's accounts of boredom and technology, we can come to understand something of Heidegger's account of the danger of both boredom and technology with recourse to this collection. The collection is comprised of internet fragments that refer to celebrity culture, consumer goods, pornography and other cultural elements. In this, it certainly discloses the boredom of the age, but perhaps it remains trapped within this boredom from start to finish. If, as Thiele suggests, boredom is a refusal of anxiety, then this collection may be trapped within a refusal of anxiety. In this, *Kim Kardashian's Marriage* may unconceal the mood of the age but does not point beyond it, and thus, it remains trapped within the metaphysics of technology. However, even in this entrapment, it does show us how powerfully how our use of technology shields us from the authenticating influence of anxiety. The collection points out the way in which technology, as a mode of unconcealment, brings beings into the open. Any poet who can disclose the truth of their age is certainly fulfilling the role of a poet. The collection does unconceal something essential about the nature of digital technology. What is shown is precisely that technology does not allow for the opening up of the fourfold, and thus the question of greatness is still ambiguous. However, all contemporary poetry which attempts to encounter technology faces this ambiguity. In order to develop a free relation to technology, as Heidegger suggests we do, it is impossible to escape this ambiguity because technology is ultimately in opposition to poetry. However, the situation is worse for poets who eschew the technological because they are trapped within a mode of unconcealment to which they are attempting to avoid. If Heidegger's account is to be taken seriously, we cannot wish technology away by simply avoiding it; technology is already too close to us for that. Thus, it can be argued that for poetry to be essential in the digital age, it must prepare a new ground within the technological.

7.10 Conclusion

In the earlier works, Heidegger critiqued metaphysics, which he argued tended to understand existence, or being, in terms of presence. Thus, in the pre-technological world, things were generally understood in terms of sensuous presencing. While things could 'thing' in the sense of opening up the fourfold, this was generally mischaracterized by philosophers and aestheticians in terms of metaphor. The thing was understood as a presence to which some subjective, metaphoric meaning could be attached subsequently. The meaning of something was understood in terms of a transference of subjective attributes to an object. However, even this brute objective presence is threatened in the digital age. Now things cannot thing; in fact, they can barely presence at all. Because of this, they are no longer able to symbolize or 'stand in' for something else. This obviously has significant implications for an analysis of contemporary poetry. In the *Principle of Reason,* Heidegger claims that only less than great poetry should be understood in terms of metaphor. It is clear that we now need to reconsider what poetic metaphor could mean in the age of Google. Riviere's collection is notable in that it shows how things are now, and how these things cannot be understood as metaphors.

8

Conclusion

It is not difficult to accuse this work of naivety. It is, perhaps, naïve in two interrelated ways. First, it characterizes the difficulties facing the world in terms of technology rather than in terms of socio-economic inequality or an impending ecological disaster. Surely, such a claim is naïve in a time of global pandemic, war, an unprecedented refugee crisis, increasing political polarization, the rise of the right across Europe, identity politics and civil unrest in the United States in terms of the Black Lives Matter Movement. While it is not naïve to suggest that technology plays a role in these situations, it is controversial to suggest that it is the root cause, and perhaps even more so to suggest that in order to address these difficulties, we need first to address technology. Second, this thesis concerns Heidegger's claim that poetry, or the poetic, is a way in which we can confront technology. Even if we agree that technology is inexorably tied up with the problems of our time, surely it is naïve to claim that poetry could play any role in ameliorating these problems.

This naivety is reminiscent of the innocence that Heidegger associates with the essence of poetry. He points us towards a line from a letter Hölderlin wrote to his mother, describing the act of writing poems as 'the most innocent of all occupations' (Heidegger 1971: 53) Poetry, Heidegger tells us, is viewed as little more than play. It remains within the realm of the imaginary. As we saw in Chapter 6, it is divorced from the sort of action that could affect real change in the world, and in this way, it is ultimately ineffectual or harmless. However, the distinction between action and inaction, as we generally understand it, is metaphysics. If we take Heidegger seriously, it is metaphysics which prevents us from recognizing the role of technology in how the world is for us. According to Heidegger, the poetic can confront this metaphysics. From within metaphysics, language is understood as a system of symbols, passively reflecting a pre-existing world. In this picture, what is important are the actual things in the world and how we interact with them; the words we assign to them are simply arbitrary sounds and symbols, which facilitate effective communication. From such a perspective, writing a poem is merely playing with language with no other aim than to please others. Because language already presents us with an unambiguous description of what is, the poem is just a way to present words in order to make them prettier. Such an account makes it difficult to account for the force and power of some poetry; it means that there is little choice but to view poetry as an innocent occupation. The poet is an innocent. She deludes herself if she thinks her occupation is important. Indeed, it is a delusion to think of poetry as an occupation; nowadays, it is simply a hobby.

But innocence here is not simply a misunderstanding of poetry's transformative power; it is also something inherent in the nature of poetry. In the next paragraph of his letter, Hölderlin writes that the innocent occupation is also one that he cannot give up without committing 'as great a sin, nay even greater, than sinning against one's own body' (Proietti 1999: 186). Poetry is inevitable to the poet; she sacrifices any other possibility, for example, the possibility of another profession or any other life, in order to write; if she does not, then she sacrifices her own life. But even in the face of this sacrifice, the poet is in danger; she remains 'inconsequential as compared to the work, almost like a passageway that destroys itself in the creative process for the work to emerge' (Heidegger 1978: 166). Both Hölderlin and Heidegger associate the innocence of poetry with risk or danger, the risk of saying something innocent. It is this innocence that is required to confront metaphysics, a metaphysics which now blinds us to the fact that all things are now unconcealed as technological things. Metaphysics obfuscates poetry's power, but poetry still retains the power to counter this. If we insist that language is simply a system of signs, we fail to understand its inherently active role in human affairs. Language points out states of affairs *as* they are to be understood, given the metaphysics of a time. If we learn anything from Heidegger, it is that throughout history, the way in which reality is disclosed by language changes. For Heidegger, it is poetic language that drives this metaphysical change.

But what does metaphysics actually mean here? The action/inaction dualism is only one of the binaries that Heidegger associates with and uses to characterize metaphysics. There is also the mighty subject/object dichotomy, the idea of things as formed matter, and of course, the division of language into the literal and figurative. But as we have seen, all these traits of metaphysics become eroded in the epoch of new technology. These dichotomies begin to break down; it becomes difficult, for example, to distinguish between the subject and the object or the literal and the figurative. It is a strength of Heidegger's account that his description of new technology resonates so clearly with the manifestations of digital technology that have occurred since his death.

While the dissolution of these metaphysical binaries in the digital could herald the end of metaphysics, it does not. The erosion of these metaphysical categories is not an overcoming of metaphysics but rather an intensification of it, which results in the enframing of both objects and subjects. In the digital, being is challenged and unconcealed only as standing reserve. We can illustrate this in terms of the literal/figurative divide with how it relates to poetic metaphor. As we saw in Chapter 3, the great poem is great precisely because it transcends the received metaphysics; that is, it cannot be understood in terms of some prior agreement as to what is sensuous. This transcending is not a one-off achievement, but rather poetry must always seek out a continually new appropriation. Less than great poetry, on the other hand, settles within a recognizable metaphysical framework. Its metaphors affirm the sensuous/nonsensuous divide. In short, a great poem overcomes the metaphysics affirmed by a lesser poem. The intensification of metaphysics, which we are associating with the digital, does not transcend the literal/figurative divide in the way a great poem does. For example, in Riviere's collection, the poems do not transcend metaphysics, but they do not disclose metaphorically either. In this way, Riviere's collection demonstrates how digital things lose the ability to stand in for other things. As an object becomes enframed, it loses the ability to be a symbol. Similarly, the subject/object dichotomy is also eroded in the digital. While Heidegger's account of *Dasein* in *Being and Time* is concerned with transcending Cartesian subjectivity, the erosion of subjectivity by technology is a negative development because it simply reframes both subjects and objects as standing reserve, that is, as that which cannot open the fourfold, or simply as that which is meaningless.

Despite this, Heidegger's account still includes the possibility of this enframed subject confronting technology. We must acknowledge, however, that there is some ambiguity with respect to this possibility in the digital age. If, as Heidegger tells us, subjectivity prevents us from understanding art, it is reasonable to ask whether there can be any possibility of art in an age where the subject, itself, becomes mere standing reserve. Taking an optimistic view, we can see that confronting technology means moving beyond a conception of reality as that which can be Googled and focusing, instead, on how Google discloses reality. While reality is viewed simply as that which we can Google, we cannot confront technology. We have seen how the post-internet poetry of Sam Riviere discloses something of how reality is now disclosed by Google and how this disclosure shuts down the possibility of meaning excess usually associated with poetry, whether we understand this in terms of the fourfold or in metaphoric terms. In Chapter 7, we saw how the objects that show up in *Kim Kardashian's Marriage* simply presence for a moment and then are replaced by some other object, which is in turn replaced with another.

By allowing a glimpse of how Google discloses reality as standing reserve, Riviere's poems allow us to see Google as the essence of technology. In this way, we can understand the full implications of Heidegger's ontologically broad use of the term 'technology'. Google is not a metaphor for how things are enframed by technology, but rather it is how things are enframed by technology. Heidegger's use of the term 'technology' is reminiscent, in some respects, of his non-metaphorical account of thinging or fourfold opening. To explain this, consider the jug Heidegger uses in order to illustrate things. In this discussion, the earth of the jug *is* earth. The fourfold captures elements of both what is considered literal and figurative from within a metaphysics. The fourfold does not emanate from the thing, implying that the thing is something prior to the fourfold. The thing *is* the fourfold opening. Just as in 'The Origin', the world and earth of a work are not isomorphic with the aesthetic categories of an art object and aesthetic qualities. In a similar way, technology is both the devices and the mode of unconcealment. As we have seen, the decision to grant some element of reality the status of sensuous or literal is metaphysics. Because of this, we can argue, in a Heideggerian way, that Google is the essence of technology and not a metaphor for how technology reduces things to standing reserve.

Google is not a thing in the 'mere' sense that Heidegger describes in 'The Origin'. It is not a rock, a book or a pair of shoes; it is, however, how all things are now enframed. Poetry is one of the things that Google enframes, which is partly why technology is so dangerous for Heidegger. We can Google a poem. Does this inevitably mean that poetry can only be another commodity on offer on the internet? Arguably, there is something different about the world of contemporary poetry. The internet at once democratizes poetry, bringing it to an exponentially bigger audience, and providing opportunities to poets whose voices would have once been ignored, but does it also devalue it? This is a thorny issue, one that is beyond this book's remit, but what is relevant here is how a poem is now something that can be instantly replaced with another and another. Like the endless stream of potential amours on Tinder, what happens to poetry when we can just swipe left, the minute something is unattractive to us or makes us feel uncomfortable? Doesn't poetry require that we dwell for a time? When everything is instantly available, nothing is significant and everything becomes boring. While we can see Riviere's poetry as an attempt to confront technology by showing us the unconcealment at play, this poetry is ultimately boring. However, this is, perhaps, the route we must take. We cannot turn back. To move forward, we must continue to confront technology. We must hit it head-on. This thesis argues that Riviere's poetry attempts to confront technology, but perhaps it only points us towards an awareness of the boredom of the digital age.

We learn from Heidegger that in order to confront technology, we need to, first of all, think the essence of technology, language and poetry. For example, if we move into the internet age without questioning what metaphor means now in terms of contemporary poetry, then we miss an opportunity to understand how technology discloses reality. Heidegger's account gives us a way in which to ask these questions and understand how language is used in contemporary poetry. This is true of poetry that explicitly deals with technology and poetry that does not. Poetry which eschews the technological and remains 'traditional' is still subject to technology. If what it means to use language has changed in the move from the old to the new technology, then appraising poetry in terms of traditional aesthetic categories is not just no longer relevant but rather it prevents us from recognizing the danger in which we now find ourselves. We cannot look away from technology. It is the poet's job to bring to an understanding of this danger and ultimately to transcend it. However, to do so, we must look with clear, perhaps naïve, eyes into the danger.

Notes

Chapter 1

1. After Quine, Contemporary analytic philosophers generally do not hold that that a proposition by itself, is an adequate vehicle for truth. For example in his influential essay *Five Milestones of Empiricism* (1981), Quine proposes a holist empiricism, which shifts the semantic focus from propositions to systems of sentences (1981: 67).
2. This represents a slip in to naturalism that is at odds with Lotze's general anti-naturalist view.
3. Although broadly speaking perception includes notions of materiality and extension.
4. Envisioning only has the possibility of fulfilment 'up to a certain level, since envisioning is never capable of giving the matter itself in its bodily givenness', Heidegger 1992: 44.

Chapter 2

1. It is worth noting here that 'the Gods' cannot be understood from within metaphysics. Later on in the essay, we are told that the appearance of the Gods is not a consequence of language but rather is simultaneous with it. The Gods in this picture are not metaphysical entities prior to language.

Chapter 4

1. *Poiēsis* was originally the mode of the being of nature which is reflected in human making-see Heidegger: 'On the essence and concept of phusis in Aristotle's Physics B, I', Heidegger, 1967.

Chapter 6

1 There is some debate on the relationship between Heidegger's treatment of things in Being and Time and the later account. See, for example, Mitchell (2015, p. 12), who argues that there is a fundamental difference to the way in which Heidegger approaches things in the later period. Specifically he claims, that *Being and Time* still objectifies the thing in terms of its status as equipment, which is subordinated to the will of Dasein. In this way Being and Time 'participates in the general ignorance of things endemic to the history of philosophy'.

2 I will discuss this this further in Chapter 7.

3 This approach is based on Bachelard's 'phenomenotechnics' and Simondon's 'order of granularity'.

4 I will define post-internet poetry in the next chapter.

5 In this case the software employed is mostly HTLM, which is not a real programming language but is used mostly to create links. This poem is from the 1990s and though the website has been updated, a poem made like this today would involve software with better functionality.

6 As we saw earlier Hui (2016) also focuses on the spectrum from code to phenomena, when giving an account of digital objects.

Chapter 7

1 The term 'Flarf' was coined by the poet Gary Sullivan, who also wrote and published the earliest Flarf poems. Its first practitioners, working in loose collaboration on an email listserv, used an approach that rejected conventional standards of quality and explored subject matter and tonality not typically considered appropriate for poetry.

Bibliography

Primary Texts: Heidegger

Heidegger, M. *Grundbegriffe der antiken Philosophie*, translated as Basic Concepts of Ancient Philosophy, translated by Richard Rojcewicz, (2007), Bloomington: Indiana University Press, 1926.
Heidegger, M. *On the Way to Language*, translated by Peter Herz, New York: HarperOne, 1959.
Heidegger, M. *Being and Time*, translated by J. Macquarrie and E. Robinson, Malden, MA: Blackwell Publishing, 1962.
Heidegger, M. *Discourse on Thinking*, translated by J. M. Anderson and H. E. Freund, New York: Harper and Row, 1966.
Heidegger, M. *Poetry, Language, Thought*, translated by A. Hofstadter, New York: Haper and Row, 1971.
Heidegger, M. *Early Greek Thinking*, translated by D. Krell and F. Capuzzi, New York: Harper and Row, 1975.
Heidegger, M. *Off the Beaten Track*, translated by A. Hofstadter, New York: HaperCollins, 1975.
Heidegger, M. *Basic Writings*, translated by D. F. Krell, London: Routledge, 1978.
Heidegger, M. *On the way to language* (1st Harper & Row pbk. ed.). San Francisco: Harper & Row, 1982.
Heidegger, M. *History of The Concept of Time: Prolegomena*, translated by T. Kisiel, Bloomington: Indiana University Press, 1985.
Heidegger, M. *Pathmarks*, edited by W. McNeill, Cambridge: Cambridge University Press, 1988.
Heidegger, M. *The Fundamental Concept of Metaphysics*, translated by W. McNeill and N. Walker, Bloomington and Indianapolis: Indiana University Press, 1995.
Heidegger, M. *The Principle of Reason*, translated by R. Lilly, Bloomington: Indiana University Press, 1996.
Heidegger, M. *Elucidations of Hölderlin's Poetry*, translated by K. Hoeller, New York: Humanity Books, 2000.
Heidegger, et al. *Off the Beaten Track*. Cambridge University Press, 2002.
Heidegger, M. *The Heidegger Reader*, edited by G. Figal and J. Veith, Bloomington: Indiana University Press, 2009.
Heidegger, M. *Contributions to Philosophy (Of the Event)*, translated by R. Rojcewicz and D. Vallega-Neu, Bloomington: Indiana University Press, 2012.
Heidegger, M. *Logic: The Question of Truth*, translated by T. Sheehan, Bloomington: Indiana University Press, 2016.

Other Primary Texts

Kennedy, B. and D. Wershler-Henry. *The Apostrophe Engine*, 2006. http://apostropheengine.ca/ (accessed 9 February 2020).

Riviere, S. *Kim Kardashian's Marriage*, London: Faber and Faber, 2015. Reproduced with Permission of Faber and Faber.

Squires. *Abstract Lyric and Other Poems*, 2012. https://read.amazon.co.uk/?asin =B00A2ZHV3W (accessed 12 August 2020).

Secondary Text: Heidegger

Babich, Babette. 'From Van Gogh's Museum to the Temple at Bassae: Heidegger's Truth of Art and Schapiro's Art History'. *Culture, Theory and Critique* 44, no. 2 (2003): 151–69.

Babich, Babette. 'On Günther Anders, Political Media Theory, and Nuclear Violence'. *Philosophy & Social Criticism* 44, no. 10 (2018): 1110–26.

Bernasconi, R. 'Poets as Prophets and as Painters: Heidegger's Turn to Language and the Hölderlinian Turn in Context'. In *Heidegger and Language*, edited by Jeffrey Powell, Daniel O Dahlstrom, Krzysztof Ziarek, Daniela Vallega-Neu, Richard Polt, William McNeill, John Sallis, Peter Hanly, Françoise Dastur, and Dennis J Schmidt, 146–162. Bloomington: Indiana University Press, 2013. Studies in Continental Thought.

Black, Max. 'Metaphor'. *Proceedings of the Aristotelian Society* 55 (1955): 273–94. http://www.jstor.org/stable/4544549.

Borgmann, Albert. *Crossing the Postmodern Divide*. Chicago: University of Chicago Press, 1993.

Botha, Catherine Frances. 'Heidegger, Technology and Ecology'. *South African Journal of Philosophy* 22, no. 2 (2003): 157–72.

Capobianco, R. *Engaging Heidegger*, Toronto: University of Toronto Press, 2010.

Casenave, G. 'Heidegger and Metaphor'. *Philosophy Today* 26, no. 2 (1982): 140–7.

Cazeaux, C. 'Metaphor and Heidegger and Kant'. *Review of Metaphysics* 49, no. 2 (1995): 341–64.

Dahlstrom, D. 'Heidegger's Method: Philosophical Concepts as Formal Indications'. *The Review of Metaphysics* 47, no. 4 (1994): 775–95.

Davies, B. *Heidegger and the Will: On the Way to Gelassenheit*, Evanston: Northwestern University Press, 2007.

Dahlstrom, Daniel O. *Heidegger's Concept of Truth*. Cambridge: Cambridge University Press, 2001.

Dreyfus, H. and C. Spinosa. 'Highway Bridges and Feasts: Heidegger and Borgmann on How to Affirm Technology'. *Man and World* 30 (1997): 159–77.

Dwan, D. 'Yeats, Heidegger and the Problem of Modern Subjectivism'. *Paragraph* 25, no. 1 (2002): 74–91.

Feenberg, A. *Questioning Technology*, New York: Routledge, 1999.

Forman, P. 'The Primacy of the Science in Modernity, of Technology in Postmodernity, and of Ideology in the History of Technology'. *History and Technology* 23 (2007): 1–152.
Gosetti-Ferencei, J. A. *Heidegger, Hölderlin, and the Subject of Poetic Language: Towards a New Poetics of Dasein*, New York: Fordham University Press, 2004.
Greisch, J. *La Parole hereuse: Martin Heidegger entre les choses et les mots*, Paris: Beachesne, 1987.
Hui, Yuk. *On the Existence of Digital Objects*. Minneapolis: University of Minnesota Press, 2016.
Ihde, D. *Heidegger's Technologies. Phenomenological Perspectives*, New York: Fordham University Press, 2010.
Irwin, Ruth. *Heidegger, Politics and Climate Change*. London: Bloomsbury Publishing Plc, 2011.
Ma, L. and J. van Brakel. 'Heidegger's Thinking on the "Same" of Science and Technology'. *Continental Philosophy Review* 47, no. 1 (2014): 19–43.
Mitchell, A. J. *The Fourfold: Reading the Late Heidegger*, Evanston: Northwestern University Press, 2015.
Moore, I. A. 'Gelassenheit, the Middle Voice, and the Unity of Heidegger's Thought'. In *Perspektiven mit Heidegger*, edited by G. Thonhauser, 25–39. München: Verlag Karl Alber Freiburg, 2017.
Nowell Smith, D. *Sounding/Silence: Martin Heidegger at the Limits of Poetics*, New York: Fordham University Press, 2013.
O'Brien, M. 'Death, Politics, and Heidegger's Bremen Remarks'. *The Southern Journal of Philosophy* 60, no. 2 (2022): 249–76.
Parmar, S. 'Is Contemporary Poetry Really in "A Rotten State" - Or Just a New One?'. *Guardian*, 22 November 2018. https://www.theguardian.com/books/2018/nov/22/is-contemporary-poetry-really-in-a-rotten-state-or-just-a-new-one (accessed 12 August 2020).
Poetry Foundation. 2020. https://www.poetryfoundation.org/foundation/press/153832/a-message-to-our-community-contributors (accessed 12 August 2020).
Polt, R. *The Emergence of Being: On Heidegger's Contributions to Philosophy*, Ithaca: Cornell University Press, 2006.
Proietti, M. L. 'Figures of Destiny in Martin Heidegger & Friedrich Hölderlin'. *Differentia: Review of Italian Thought* 8 (1999): Article 15.
Rae, G. 'Being and Technology: Heidegger on the Overcoming of Metaphysics'. *Journal of the British Society of Phenomenology* 43, no. 3 (2012): 305–25.
Richardson, W. J. *Heidegger: Through Phenomenology to Thought*, 2nd edn, The Hague: Martinus Nijhoff, 1967.
Riis, S. 'Towards the Origin of Modern Technology: Reconfiguring Martin Heidegger's Thinking'. *Continental Philosophical Review* 44 (2011): 103–17.
Rosół, Piotr. 'Being Good, Moral and Rational in a Context of Climate Change'. *Ethics in Progress* 7, no. 1 (2016): 21–31.
Schrijvers, J. 'A. Mitchell, P. Trawny, Heidegger's Black Notebooks'. *Phenomenological Reviews* 4, no. 1 (2018): 4. Web.

Sheehan, T. 'What, After All, was Heidegger About?' *Continental Philosophy Review* 47, no. 3–4 (2014): 249–74.
Shoptaw, J. 'Why Ecopoetry?'. *Poetry Magazine*, January 2016. https://www.poetryfoundation.org/poetrymagazine/articles/70299/why-ecopoetry.
Smith, D. N. *Sounding/Silence: Martin Heidegger at the Limits of Poetics*, New York: Fordham University Press, 2013.
Stellardi, G. *Heidegger and Derrida on Philosophy and Metaphor: Imperfect Thought*, Amherst: Humanity Books, 2000.
Thiele, L. P. 'Postmodernity and the Routinization of Novelty: Heidegger on Boredom and Technology'. *Polity* 29, no. 4 (1997): 489–517.
Thomson, I. 'Rorty, Heidegger, and the Danger and Promise of the Technological Archive'. 2010. http://escholarship.org/uc/item/4b09r4st (accessed 12 August 2020).
Thomson, Iain D. *Heidegger, Art, and Postmodernity*. Cambridge: Cambridge University Press, 2011.
Tugendhat, E. 'Heidegger's Idea of Truth'. In *Critical Heidegger*, edited by C. McCann, 227–240. London: Routledge, 1994.
Verbeek, P. *What Things Do: Philosophical Reflections on Technology, Agency and Design*, University Park: Pennsylvania State University Press, 2005.
White, D. A. 'Heidegger on Sameness and Difference'. *The Southwestern Journal of Philosophy* 11, no. 3 (1980): 107–25.
Wrathall, M. *Heidegger and Unconcealment*, Cambridge. Cambridge University Press, 2011.
Young, J. *Heidegger's Philosophy of Art*, Cambridge. Cambridge University Press, 2001.

Other Sources

Berry, D. *The Philosophy of Software: Code and Mediation in The Digital Age*, Basingstoke: Palgrave Macmillan, 2011.
Berry, E., A. Carson, and S. Collins. *Modern Poets 1: If I'm Scared, We Can't Win*, United Kingdom: Penguin, 2016.
Black, M. *Models and Metaphors*, Ithaca: Cornell University Press, 2019.
Borgmann, A. *Crossing the Postmodern Divide*, Chicago: University of Chicago Press, 1992.
Burke, H. *I Love Roses When They Are Past Their Best*, London: Test Centre, 2015.
Burnett, R. and P. D. Marshall. *Web Theory: An Introduction*, London: Routledge, 2003.
Capurro, R. 'Towards an Ontological Foundations of Information Ethics', *Ethics and Information Technology* 8 (2006): 175–86.
Cartwright, N. *The Dappled World: A Study of the Boundaries of Science*, Cambridge: Cambridge University Press, 1999.
Cazeaux, C. *Metaphor and Continental Philosophy: From Kant to Derrida*, London: Routledge, 2007.
Colburn, T. *Philosophy and Computer Science*, New York: Routledge, 2015.
de la Cruz Paragas, F. and T. T. Lin. 'Organizing and Reframing Technological Determinism'. *New Media & Society* 18, no. 8 (2016): 1528–46.

Dreyfus, H. *On the Internet*, New York: Routledge, 2001.
Evans, L. 'A Phenomenological Analysis of Social Networking'. In *Humanity in Cybernetic Environments, Critical Issues*, edited by Daniel Riha, 219–26, Oxford: Inter-Disciplinary Press, 2010.
Flores, Leonardo. 'Digital Poetry'. In *The Johns Hopkins Guide to Digital Media*, edited by Marie-Laure Ryan, Lori Emerson, and Benjamin J. Robertson, 155–161. Baltimore: JHU Press, 2014.
Flynn, L. 'Thanks for Sharing'. 2016. eontiaflynn.com/thanks-for-sharing-post-internet-p oetry/ (accessed 12 August 2020).
Frege. *Logical Investigations*, edited by P. T. Geach, Oxford: Blackwell, 1977.
Funkhouser, H. T. *New Directions in Digital Poetry*, New York: Continuum, 2012.
Gifford, Terry. *Green Voices: Understanding Contemporary Nature Poetry*. Manchester: Manchester University Press, 1994.
von Goethe, J. W. *Goethe's Theory of Colours*, (1840) translated by Eastlake, R. A. Project Gutenberg.
Gruber, T. 'Toward Principles for the Design of Ontologies Used for Knowledge'. *International Journal of Human-Computer Studies* 43, no. 5–6 (1995): 907–28.
Hirshfield, J. *Ledger*, Bloodaxe Books, 2020. Reproduced with permission of Bloodaxe Books.
Hölderlin, F. *Gedichte*, Stuttgart: Tübingen, 1826.
Hughes, T. *Crow: From the Life and Songs of Crow*, London: Faber and Faber, 1972 Reproduced with permission of Faber and Faber.
Husserl, E. *The Idea of Phenomenology*, The Hague: Nijhoff, 1964.
Introna, L. 'On Cyberspace and Being: Identity, Self and Hyperreality'. *Philosophy in the Contemporary World* 4 (1997): 1–10. doi:10.5840/pcw199741/22.
Jones, R. S. *Physics as Metaphor*, University of Minnesota Press; Reissue edition, 1990.
Keane, N. 'The Silence of the Origin: Philosophy in Transition and the Essence of Thinking'. *Research in Phenomenology* 43, no. 1 (2013): 27–48.
Keating, K. *Contemporary Irish Poetry and the Canon Critical Limitations and Textual Liberations*, Cham: Palgrave MacMillan, 2017.
Krell, D. F. 'A Thought in Full Self-Possession: On Charles Scott's *The Language of Difference* and *The Question of Ethics*'. *Research in Phenomenology* 21 (1991), Periodicals Archive Online: 142.
Kuhn, T. S. *The Structure of Scientific Revolutions*, 2nd edn, edited by Enl. Chicago: U of Chicago, Print. International Encyclopedia of Unified Science, 1970.
Lewin, D. 'The Middle Voice in Eckhart and Modern Continental Philosophy'. *Medieval Mystical Theology* 20 (2012). doi:10.1558/mmt.v20.28.
MacNiece, L. *Collected Poems*, Faber and Faber, 2016. Reproduced with permission of David Higham Associates.
McCloskey, D. N. *The Rhetoric of Economics*, Madison: University of Wisconsin Press, 1985.
McGukian, M. *Selected Poems, 1978–1994*, County Meath: Gallery Press, 2013.
McNish, H. C. https://holliepoetry.com/2015/10/05/cocoon/ (accessed 18 June 2020). Reproduced with permission of Hollie McNish and Lewinsohn Literary Agency.
Millar DuMars, S. *Naked: New and Selected Poems*, Ireland: Salmon Poetry, 2019. Reproduced with permission of Salmon Poetry.

Mirowski, P. *More Heat than Light*, Cambridge: Cambridge University Press, 1989.
Mitchell, A. J. and P. Trawny. *Heidegger's Black Notebooks*, New York: Columbia University Press, 2017.
Morten, T. *Ecology Without Nature: First*, Cambridge, MA: Harvard University Press, 2009.
O'Reilly, T. *What is Web 2.0: Design Patterns and Business Models for the Next Generation of Software*, 2019. https://www.oreilly.com/pub/a/web2/archive/what-is-web-20.html (accessed 12 August 2020).
Papineau, D. *The Philosophy of Science*, Oxford: Oxford University Press, 1996.
Quine, W. V. O. *Theories and Things*, Cambridge, MA: Harvard University Press, 1981.
Ricoeur, P. *The Rule of Metaphor: Multi-disciplinary Studies in the Creation of Meaning in Language,* translated by Robert Czerny with Kathleen McLauglin and John Costello, Toronto: University of Toronto Press, 1977.
Roberson, R. 'The Poetry World is Polarised. I'm in the Middle, Vaguely Appalled'. 2018. https://www.theguardian.com/books/2018/sep/28/robin-robertson-never-give-books-as-presents (accessed 12 August 2020).
Salzberger, L. S. *Holderlin*, Cambridge: Bowes & Bowes, 1952.
Scollo, Daniele. 'Things that exist: The world is horizontal. Günter Anders' thought and contemporary world'. *Montesquieu.it : Biblioteca Elettronica Su Montesquieu E Dintorni, Montesquieu.it : biblioteca elettronica su Montesquieu e dintorni*, 9, no. 1 (2017).
Scott, C. E. 'The Middle Voice of Metaphysics'. *The Review of Metaphysics* 42, no. 4 (1989): 743–64.
Seiça, Á. 'Digital Poetry and Critical Discourse: A Network of Self-References?' *Materialidades da Literatura* 4, no. 1 (2016): 95–123.
Sharpiro, M. 'The Still Life as a Personal Object in Theory and Philosophy of Art: Styles, Artists, and Society'. Selected Papers. New York: George Brazillier, 1994.
Shoptaw, J. *Near-Earth Object*, 1st edn, Atlanta: Unbound Edition Press, 2023. Reproduced with permission of Unbound Editions Press.
Soames, S. *Philosophy of Language*, Princeton: Princeton University Press, 2010.
de Sousa, G. J. '"Peter Larkin: Poetry, Phenomenology, and Ecology", University of Warwick, 26th of April 2017'. *Journal of British and Irish Innovative Poetry* 12, no. 1 (2019). doi:10.16995/bip.1340.
Stahl, F. A. 'Physics as Metaphor and Vice Versa'. *Leonardo* 20, no. 1 (1987): 57–64.
Stevens, W. *The Collected Poems of Wallace Stevens*, New York: Alfred A, Knopf, 1990.
Tomkins, C. *Duchamp*, New York: H. Holt, 1996.
Turner, R. and A. Eden. *Towards a Programming Language Ontology*, 2007. https://www.researchgate.net/publication/242381616_Towards_a_Programming_Language_Ontology.
Watts, R. 'The Cult of the Noble Amateur'. *PN Review* 44, no. 3 (2018): 239.
WHO. *Guidelines on Physical Activity, Sedentary Behaviour and Sleep for Children Under Five Years of Age*, Geneva: World Health Organization, 2019.
Wittgenstein, L. et al. *Tractatus logico-philosophicus*, Milano: Fratelli Bocca, 1954.
Wittgenstein, L. *Philosophical Investigations*, 3rd edn, Oxford: Blackwell, 1967.
Young, K. S. 'The Evolution of Internet Addiction'. *Additive Behaviours* 64 (2017): 229–30.
Zuboff, Shoshana. *The Age of Surveillance Capitalism: The Fight for a Human Future at the New Frontier of Power*, 1st ed. New York: PublicAffairs, 2019.

Index

Adorno   109
AdWords   194
aesthetics   36, 39, 80, 100, 151, 152, 154, 180, 199, 204, 210
Alethia   2, 36, 50, 96, 140, 156
analytic philosophy   46, 65, 67, 75, 100
anxiety   5, 127, 184–6, 190, 192, 204, 205
apostrophe engine   9, 168–70
appropriation   35, 55–7, 78, 79, 85, 87, 92, 209
Aristotle   37, 49, 66, 107
autochthony   201

Babbett, Babich   61, 99, 109
Bauch, Bruno   16
Baudrillard, Jean   109
Being and Time   14, 25–7, 35, 37, 40, 47, 51, 60, 104, 119, 127, 154, 174, 184, 209
Berry, D.   170
beyng   98
Black, Max   65, 66, 74
Black Lives Matter   2, 207
boredom   5, 183–94, 200, 204, 211
Borgmann, Albert   3, 4, 95, 107, 108, 111, 145, 149, 202
Botha, Catherine Frances   8, 125
Burke, Harry   182

calculative thinking   113, 114, 116
Capurro, R.   106, 107
Carnap   99
Carson, Ann   160
Cartesian metaphysics   138
Cartwright, Nancy   102

Casenave, G.   73
catachresis   66
categorial intuition   16, 18, 22, 31, 152
Cazeaux, C.   79
ceteris paribus   13, 102
Church Alonzo   171
climate change   124–6, 133
Clooney, George   199
code   164, 170
code poetry   162
Colburn, T.   171
comparison view of metaphor   65, 66
computer programming languages (CPL)   170, 172, 173
computer science   172
conceptual art   161
concrete poetry   161
confrontation   4, 8, 10, 111, 112, 116, 145, 163, 170, 177, 203
Contributions to Philosophy   62, 98, 127
correspondence theory   2, 3, 5, 23, 26, 29, 30, 34, 39
createdness   41–3
crisis   2

Dada   161
Dahlstrom, Dan   14–17, 36, 60, 61
Dasein   26–8, 30, 31, 33, 34, 40, 41, 135, 184, 185, 190, 191, 209
Das Man   30, 35
Derrida   73
Descartes   7, 11, 12, 19
de Sousa, G. J.   123
destining   108, 115

die Kehre 47
displacement 42
divinities 4, 147–9, 174
dot-com bubble 106
Dreyfus, H. 3, 4, 99, 107, 110, 111, 141, 145–9, 193, 201, 202
Duchamp, Marcel 182
dwelling 101, 114, 125, 156, 157, 203, 204

ecology 8, 123–5
Eden, A. 173
electoral manipulations 109
enframing 4, 94, 97, 104, 108, 109, 115, 170, 193, 194, 196, 197, 199, 202
environmentalism 8, 123, 133, 136
epoch 1, 7, 9, 90, 93, 94, 96–100, 106, 115, 117, 120, 127, 129, 138, 148, 152, 155, 156, 197, 209
equipmental 37, 144, 154, 174
essence 10, 36–8, 40, 41, 95, 96, 108, 115, 116, 121, 144, 156, 157, 167, 174, 175, 179, 190, 193, 194, 198, 203, 204
Evans, Leighton 109
existentiale 27, 33
experiment 13, 103, 175

Facebook 108, 160, 161
Feenberg, A. 108
film poetry 161
flarf poetry 182
Flores, Leonardo 162
Flynn, Leontia 183, 196
focal practices/focal event 4, 111, 145, 146, 148, 149, 202
formal indications 60–2
Forman, P. 101
Forward Prize 182
fourfold 4, 9, 105, 114, 123, 134, 135, 139–41, 145, 147–51, 156, 174, 175, 199, 201, 205, 210
free relation 4, 8, 9, 94–6, 111–13, 120, 145, 146, 150, 177, 179, 200–2, 204, 205
Frege, Gottlob 15, 171
Funkhouser, H. T. 161, 162, 167, 170

gelassenheit 8, 95, 111–13, 120, 121, 145, 148, 202
generative poetry 162
gestell 94
Gifford, Terry 130, 131
Google 10, 133, 139, 181, 183, 193–5, 197–200, 206, 210, 211
Gottfried, Benn 71
Greisch, J. 73
Gruber, Tom 172
Gunter, Anders 95, 97, 109

Hausman 79
Heaney, Seamus 123, 166
heimlich/unheimlich 184, 185, 201
Hirshfield, Jane 9, 124, 139–41
historiography 98
Hölderlin, F. 6, 8, 24, 57–9, 71, 72, 92, 103, 105, 114, 115, 127–9, 157, 196, 203, 207, 208
Horkheimer 109
Hughes, Ted 88, 130
Hui, Yuk 163, 164
Hume, David 22
Husserl, Edmund 5, 14–16, 18, 22, 31, 32, 43, 123
hyperlink poem 167, 168
hyperreality 107, 108
hypertext poetry 162

ideal language 45, 171, 172
idle talk 28, 51
Ihde, Don 3, 100, 106
intentionality 5, 18, 20, 21, 43
interactive poetry 162
Irwin, Ruth 124

Jones, R. S. 74
Joyce, James 166

Kant, Immanuel 13, 79
Kavanagh, Patrick 166
Keating, Kenneth 165, 166
Kennedy, Bill 168
kinetic poetry 162

Kuar, Rupi   80
Kuhn, Thomas   77, 78

language   Passim
Larkin, Peter   123
Leibniz, Gottfried Willhelm   67, 68
Lewin, D.   119
LGBTQ+   129
linguistics   45
literal/figurative divide   4, 6, 65–7, 69, 73, 74, 85, 133, 134, 149, 151, 179, 180, 209
Llewellyn-Williams, Hilary   131
logic   13–15, 17
Logical Atomism/Logical Positivism   11, 45, 46, 65, 77, 171, 172
logical Prejudice   13–15, 25, 172
Lotze   15–18, 36
lyric   160, 166, 200

Ma, L.   100, 101, 106
McCloskey, Deirdre   74
McGukian, Maedbh   182
MacNeice Louis   86–8
MacNeill and Walker   189
McNish, Hollie   81, 82, 84–7, 133
Mathematics   24, 61, 102, 172
matter and form   20, 37, 153, 154
metaphysics   Passim
middle voice   8, 95, 116–20
Millar, DuMars Susan   82–4, 86, 87
Mirowski, P.   74
Mitchell, A. J.   105, 128, 135, 147, 157
Moore, I. A.   119
Morten, Timothy   139
multimedia poetry   162

National Socialism   35, 128
natural languages   46, 65, 171, 173
Newton   33
Nowell Smith, D.   49, 73, 75, 76, 83

O'Brien, M.   128
O'Reilly, T.   106
objectivity   13, 36, 79, 135, 148

ontic   102
ontological difference   17, 172
ontology   18, 143, 170, 172
Origin of the Work of Art (the)   36, 37, 39, 41, 42, 47, 57, 90, 93, 99, 100, 103, 126, 133, 138, 144, 151, 156, 157, 197, 210, 211
owning   54, 55, 87

Padrutt   124
Papineau, D.   12
Parmar, S.   2
Parmenides   27
Paterson, Don   81
philosophy of Science   11, 12, 74, 77, 102
physics   74, 97, 101, 102, 106, 144, 159, 175
Plato   16, 17, 35, 99
poetic greatness   71, 72, 76, 126
Poetry Foundation   2, 161
poiēsis   7, 96, 99, 104, 115, 138, 176, 200
post-internet poetry   10, 168, 179, 182, 210
Postman   109
preservers/preservation   3, 39, 42, 43, 76, 138
primary being of truth   5, 14, 15, 36
primordial   5, 27–9, 31, 43
Principal of Reason   67, 68, 76, 150, 206
Proietti, M. L.   208
propositions   12–15, 18, 24, 29, 35, 43, 45, 46, 63, 70, 152

Question concerning technology   114, 115, 138, 144
Quine, W. V. O   173

Rae, G.   97, 101
ready-to-hand   37, 48, 62, 71, 72, 86, 140, 154
relativism   3, 34, 35, 78
rhyme   159
Richardson, W. L.   60
Ricoeur, P.   73
Riis, S.   101

Riviere, Sam   5, 10, 181–4, 192–4, 196, 198–204, 206, 209–11
Roberson, Robin   2, 90
Rorty, Richard   97
Rosół, Piotr   125
Russell, Bertrand   15, 46, 172

same (*das Selbe*)   23, 27, 48–50, 101
saving power   8, 114–16, 143
Saying   50–7, 76, 140, 180
scientific methodology   11, 13, 46, 61
scientific model   6, 66, 74, 78, 134
scientific realism   12, 133, 134
Scott, C. E.   95, 117–20
Seiça, A.   161, 165
semblance   28, 51, 87
semiotics   50
Shapiro   37
Sheehan, Tom   60
Shoptaw, John   88, 90, 131–4, 136, 137, 139
Silesius, Angelus   68
Simondon   164
Soames, S.   45
social media   81, 106, 108, 109, 130, 160, 182
software   9, 106, 144, 163, 164, 168, 170, 171
spielraum   40, 41, 167, 176
Spinosa, C.   4, 99, 110, 111, 141, 145–9, 193, 202
spoken word   81, 82, 160
Spotify   146
Squires, Geoffrey   9, 165–8
Stahl, F. A.   74
Stellardi, G.   73
Stevens, Wallace   91
strife   39–42, 151, 155–7, 166, 169, 170, 174, 181
Stumpf, Carl   15
subjectivity   4, 79, 105, 110, 111, 116, 119, 133, 135–7, 141, 166, 209, 210
substitution view of metaphor   65
symbol   152, 180

technē   96
technological determinism   94, 97
technology   Passim
Tempest, Kate   80
temporality   40, 107
Thiele. L. P.   5, 181, 185, 186, 204
Thompson, Iain   99
Thunberg, Gretta   125
Tomkins, C.   182
Trawney, Peter   128
truth   passim
Tugendhat, Earnst   3, 25, 26, 31, 33–5
Turing, Alan   171
Turner, R.   173

unconcealment   29, 51, 59, 79, 94, 104, 112, 113, 115, 116, 138, 156, 157, 173, 175, 176, 179, 196, 199, 200, 202, 203, 205
user profile information   194

validity   23, 25, 171
van Brakel, J.   100, 101, 106
van Gogh   37, 38, 99, 103, 140, 152, 154, 174, 180
Verant, Jean-Pierre   119
Verbeek, P.   108
versagen   189, 190
Vienna Circle   45
visual poetry   162
von Goethe, J. W.   55, 69

Watts, Rebecca   80, 81, 84, 86
Web 2.0   3, 106–8, 118
Wershler-Henry, Darren   168
White, D. A.   48
Whitehead   15
Wild Atlantic Way   123
Wittgenstein, L.   15, 45
Wrathall, M.   4, 29, 98, 100, 102, 147, 149

Young, J.   36, 37

Zuboff, Shoshana   194, 195

www.ingramcontent.com/pod-product-compliance
Lightning Source LLC
Chambersburg PA
CBHW071834300426
44116CB00009B/1539